The American Political Landscape

The American Political Landscape

Byron E. Shafer and Richard H. Spady

 Harvard University Press

Cambridge, Massachusetts
London, England
2014

Library of Congress Cataloging-in-Publication Data

Shafer, Byron E.
  The American political landscape / Byron E. Shafer and Richard H. Spady.
    pages cm
  Includes bibliographical references and index.
    ISBN 978-0-674-04559-0 (hardcover : alk. paper)
    1. Politics, Practical—United States.   2. Political campaigns—United States.
3. Elections—United States.   4. United States—Politics and government—1989–
I. Spady, Richard H., 1952–   II. Title.
  JK1726.S53 2014
    324.0973—dc23   2013020186

Contents

Preface

Social scientists have measures. Campaign strategists have lore. The best measures have the indisputable virtues of being precise, objective, and portable—from place to place and election to election. Yet they frequently achieve these virtues by isolating critical elements of politics from each other, thereby losing the context that normally determines winners and losers while highlighting alleged laws of behavior that, if true, are strategically immutable. By contrast, the best lore has the indisputable virtues of being concrete, experiential, and rooted—in real places and real times. Yet it frequently achieves these virtues by being imprecise, contentious, and untestable. It is as if the two groups were two nations, formed by dividing a once-common homeland and thereafter scrupulously ignoring each other, while continuing to claim sovereignty over all.

This book aspires to speak to both nations, by revealing what is in effect the strategic landscape for electoral politics in the United States and by tracing its evolution over the last quarter-century. A focus on this landscape is our way of bringing back together the grand elements of electoral politics: social backgrounds, political values, and voting behavior. These are the elements that give the political landscape its theoretical contours. Those contours are what campaign strategists concretely address. For the social scientist, this approach must involve a new way of handling public opinion data and a new way of displaying the result. Without a different approach, there can be only the same old elaboration. For the campaign strategist, this approach converts what are otherwise sophisticated and demanding measures into a simple mapping format, one that highlights strategic choices but requires little more technical skill than conventional map-reading. Every political practitioner does this. It is just that some know that they do, while others practice in blissful ignorance of their own craft.

More concretely, the purpose of this book is to describe how different social characteristics are associated with different political attitudes; how these attitudes are themselves organized; and how this organization, persistent as it is, can nonetheless permit different ultimate partisan outcomes. In some ways, the initial stimulus for this book was another, *The Two Majorities*, written by Byron Shafer and William J. M. Claggett and published in 1995. That book argued for two grand clusters of issues—an economic/welfare cluster and a cultural/national cluster—which gather much of the substance of political conflict and on which the American public had persistent majorities.

One of the incidental virtues of the current project is to call into question the manner and the degree to which this clustering can still be said to be true. Regardless, the years immediately following publication found Byron and Richard together at Nuffield College, Oxford. By an accidental miracle that is supposed to be a conscious effect of the design of our academic institutions, Richard began reading Byron's books and attending his seminars on American politics. Apparent adulation, however, was inevitably accompanied by scholarly critique. "I can do it better," Richard modestly proclaimed. "Okay, wise guy," said Byron, "show me." The result is the book before you.

The jumping-off point was two ostensible contradictions in *The Two Majorities*. First, what can it mean for "most people" to be liberal on economics or conservative on culture? Does the median not cut the population precisely in half, with those lying to one side being conservative and those on the other liberal? This could remain a hollow—a merely numerical—objection, but for a second contradiction. Should the political parties not reliably feel a moderating pressure to move to the center of the political spectrum, so as to cut the population in half (or half plus one) by appropriately framing the issues? And would that framing not give us a world in which the median voter was indeed a definitional moderate?

Questions like these give rise to the methodological premises of the current volume. People have underlying dispositions on two great issue dimensions. These dispositions can in principle be rank-ordered across the whole of society for each dimension, such that every position on this spectrum can be given a percentile number. An underlying position then disposes an individual to assent or dissent from specific items on opinion surveys. Beyond that, all such respondents at each valuational position have social characteristics—a social class, a race or ethnicity, a religious background, and so on—that both shape their political values and make a direct further contribution to their partisan choices.

From there, it is a short hop through some rules of elementary probability theory to describe how middle-income married Catholic men who are culturally moderate but economically liberal tend to vote, compared to upper-income unmarried Protestant women who hold the same views. In the process, it is also possible to determine whether the views of the two groups are largely similar or dissimilar. The problem, of course, is the force of the qualifier "in principle." In that light, we strive to accomplish three goals:

- To develop and apply a methodology that is adequate for these problems but that can be graphically captured in ideological maps of the political landscape.
- To explain this methodology with a precision sufficient for the specialist but without the technicalities that would quickly drive away the more general reader.
- To apply this approach across years and across survey designs in a fashion that nevertheless responds to the demands and vagaries of individual surveys.

This decision to convey the main components of our analysis in graphical forms that are consistent from year to year and from subject to subject has allowed us to display concisely a sweeping argument about social and political forces. On the other hand, there remains a wealth of technical analysis and an array of associated decisions arising from statistical theory and practice that are part and parcel of these methods. There are, for example, slightly different smoothing adjustments when the sample size is 950 rather than 4,000. We have chosen not to lead with those details. Rather, we have favored simplicity in model formulation, consistency across survey years, and a slight degree of undersmoothing. While various technical options do occasionally have a discernible visual effect (when, for example, curves or contours are a little more wiggly than could be achieved with a heavier hand), these do not really affect the main lineaments of the story.

In other words and in the end, all such technical niceties by their very nature cannot make a truly *substantive* difference. Our narrative about the evolution of the American polity is hemmed in by the facts, in the same way that the models that help produce this narrative are inherently restricted in their range. Theorists and practitioners, each in their own way, must ultimately confront the same survey evidence. The simple device of arraying respondent positions by percentile scores within each survey can constrain both. All models—not to mention all prejudices—are not equal. Accordingly, Chapter 1 begins at the end, with a quick picture of the payoff on both sides of the aisle for proceeding in this way.

Along the way, we have had some exceptional assistance. Amber Wichowsky, now in the department of political science at Marquette University, provided research assistance as we got back to work in a serious way. Pär Jason Engle, completing his doctorate in the department of political science at the University of Wisconsin, inherited the major tasks of data presentation. Jason began as an assistant and ended as a collaborator; his innovative responses to the associated problems are scattered throughout this book. Late in the day, Alexander Tahk gave the entire setup a crucial—and demanding—review. We needed a comprehensive reading by an outside expert, and Alex provided it.

We also had several opportunities to present pieces of the project at the annual meetings of the American Political Science Association, as well as several opportunities to present pieces at the American Politics Workshop at the University of Wisconsin. Presentations focused on methods were given at the Econometric Society, the European University Institute, Oxford University, and Johns Hopkins. We benefited especially from discussion and criticism among participants in the "Measurement Matters" conference at the Centre for Microdata Methods and Practice (cemmap), held to mark its transition to an ESRC research center. Discussions over the years with the members and visitors of cemmap, and especially its director, Andrew Chesher, have proved invaluable.

All of the computations and graphics for this book were carried out using the statistical computing environment R, so that we are hugely indebted to the R Development Core Team and the R community. Users of R will know that efforts large and small by all its contributors can have profound effects. We were particularly helped by the contribution of M. H. Praeger of the National Oceanographic and Atmospheric Association, whose four-dimensional contour-plotting function is the basis of the contour plots that are found in Chapters 6 through 8. We really cannot say that had we not seen it, we would have invented it ourselves.

Along the way, Michael Aronson, social science editor at Harvard University Press, was willing to give serious consideration to a project that was long on conceptualization but short on fully realized text. We hope that the ultimate product justifies his faith. Edward Wade, at Westchester Publishing Services, managed production of a complex manuscript with many moving pieces. Susan Campbell rose to the challenge of what was likewise a demanding copyedit. We appreciate their efforts.

The strongest wills cannot elicit non-existent forces from nothingness, and the shocks of experience constantly dissipate these facile illusions. Besides, even though through some incomprehensible miracle a pedagogical system were constituted in opposition to the social system, this very antagonism would rob it of all effect.

—Emile Durkheim, *Suicide: A Study in Sociology*

Man is double. There are two beings in him: an individual being which has its foundation in the organism and the circle of whose activities is therefore strictly limited, and a social being which represents the highest reality in the intellectual and moral order that we can know by observation—I mean society. This duality of our nature has as its consequence in the practical order, the irreducibility of a moral ideal to a utilitarian motive, and in the order of thought, the irreducibility of reason to individual experience. In so far as he belongs to society, the individual transcends himself, both when he thinks and when he acts.

—Emile Durkheim, *The Elementary Forms of the Religious Life*

The American
Political Landscape

1

The Strategic
Landscape How to Find It,
How to Read It, What It Reveals

To begin at the end: when a fresh methodological approach is applied to the evolution of American politics over the past quarter-century by way of continuing and consistent survey items, it becomes evident that:

- There was an old order to American politics in which the political landscape was organized principally by economic values, though by the time these data tap into this order in the 1980s, cultural values had begun to show substantial nascent influence as well. In that world, there was one political party, the Republicans, that was united by economic conservatism but remained heterogeneous on culture, while there was another political party, the Democrats, that, with noteworthy exceptions, was united by cultural liberalism but remained heterogeneous on economics.
- A quarter-century later, there is a new order to American politics in which the political landscape is organized simultaneously by both economic and cultural values. In this world, economics has actually gained aligning power, but culture has gained more rapidly, to the point where the landscape is now organized symmetrically across the

full range of both ideological continuums. The modal Republican is thus a joint economic and cultural conservative, just as the modal Democrat is now a joint economic and cultural liberal.

- This is, by extension, a world in which political values play a greater role in aligning the vote than they once did. Yet evolution toward this world has been uneven and mottled in both a minor and a major way. In the minor way, the two elections of the 1990s in which Ross Perot was an independent candidate prove to be the transitional period, though not in the manner usually adduced. For Perot did not so much elicit, or even crystallize, this transition as he provided a parking place for voters who were breaking loose from the old order and seeking their proper place in the new.

- In the larger mottling influence, one that is still very much with us, different social groups responded to national change—and shaped it—in distinctive ways. Few remained impervious to national trends, though there were groups whose members resisted and even groups whose members actually moved away. Most, however, integrated national trends with the social backgrounds and political values that characterized the group, beginning and ending at different places on the ideological landscape and sometimes changing intergroup relationships as well.

- Implicitly, as a result, some established ways of thinking about American politics—ways that are theoretically revered by social scientists and compulsively applied by campaign strategists—suffered a serious loss of plausibility. The methodological and conceptual innovations used here are in this sense an effort to create a framework that might substitute for these approaches, while bringing theorists and practitioners, kicking and screaming, at least somewhat closer together.

The Search for a Political Landscape

This project necessarily begins with a methodologically distinctive approach. Most critically, this revised methodology does not make the unnecessary—even arbitrary—assumptions that most research on public preferences and voting behavior reflexively does, and indeed must. Instead, two great attitudinal domains, involving public preferences in the realms of economics and culture, are allowed to produce vote distributions stochastically. Individuals are still conceived as having an intrinsically unobservable position in this two-dimensional attitude space. Yet the latter can nevertheless be expressed formally in percentiles relative to the general population, and because the statistical laws that determine relations between attitude position and item response can be estimated from observable data, it is possible to compute a probability distribution of those attitudes for every individual.

So, rather than simply assigning scores plus an error term to these individuals, this approach works from attitudinal distributions that are then cumulated, for a particular group or for the nation as a whole, to yield a political landscape. Even at the purely methodological level, this approach works to unite social scientists and campaign strategists.[1] The former insist on seeing statistical normality everywhere. The latter just try to adapt to whatever they find on the ground. A map of the ideological terrain escapes the imposed preferences of the former while forcing systematic description on the latter. This is done not merely in the absence of conventional assumptions but in a way that credibly demonstrates how concepts that are not directly observable—the latent values—can explain an outcome that everyone recognizes, namely the vote.

The project likewise begins with two conceptually distinctive approaches. In the first, it treats voting behavior not as a bivariate outcome, Democratic or Republican, but always as a tripartite result—Democratic voting, Republican voting, or Non voting—and sometimes, when there is a credible third candidate, as a quadripartite result. This means that the same things do not have to be going on, as simple reciprocals, among Democratic and Republican voters. Analytic results are not simply imposed through this assumption, as they so often are in conventional vote analysis. In consequence, the social coalitions dominating the Republican and Democratic parties are not only free to live in different places on the ideological landscape; they can even be constructed from different policy realms, mixed differentially.

In the second conceptually distinctive approach, this way of proceeding pays much-expanded attention to the *distribution* of political values among partisan voters—to their actual density within the voting public; that is, to how many people actually stand where—rather than just to *relationships*

to this vote. It is a commonplace in teaching political analysis to emphasize that the nature of an underlying distribution can be more important,
depending on the question, than any statistical relationship within that
distribution. Yet most research (and here, not excepting research on voting behavior) then pays little further attention to this possibility.

A focus on campaign strategy, however, brings actual distributions
insistently to the fore, sometimes to theoretically provocative effect. For
example, voting relationships, much loved by social scientists, are commonly interpreted to counsel a move toward the ideological center. Yet
density maps frequently suggest that this is foolish and sometimes even
counsel a move away. As often as not, it is these distributions that shape
the strategic thinking of real campaigns, so that this becomes yet another
incarnation of the enduring differences between social scientists and campaign strategists.

In any case, the end result is a picture of the strategic environment for
electoral politics in the United States over the last twenty-five years. This
is a picture of American ideological terrain unlike standard two-dimensional
(not to mention one-dimensional!) portraits. It is a picture that brings into
focus the strategic choices facing *both* major political parties, in a world
that is nevertheless constantly evolving. As above, there is a fully national
aspect to this picture, where what was once overwhelmingly a politics of
economic preferences has evolved into a politics in which both economics
and culture are normally in play, across the full ideological spectrum and
in a more or less symmetric fashion.

Nevertheless, there are multiple and various group aspects to this national story as well, since social groups do not simply recapitulate national
trends within their individual memberships. At a minimum, a composite
national picture leaves room for (and effectively requires) multiple responses,
as diverse groups respond to national developments in ways that reflect
the social backgrounds and political values of group members, rather than
of some abstract national median. Beyond that, social groups differ in the
extent to which group membership itself—social identity—has the power
to shape the role of political values. At the extremes, some groups have lost
this shaping power, while others have remained more or less impervious
to external developments. And most, of course, are a mix of group-based
and nationwide influences.

A different way to summarize what has happened to the American political landscape over the last twenty-five years is occasioned by a shift of focus from voting relationships to density maps, both within social groups and for the nation as a whole. Two developments stand out. In the first, Republican and Democratic voting blocs within most social groups have actually pulled farther apart in ideological terms. From one side, this separation was a development fueled especially by the national rise of cultural values as a voting influence. From the other side, this separation has been exaggerated in a partially autonomous fashion by the political parties themselves, most especially by changes inside the Republican Party.

In the second, closely related, development, the dominant coalitions inside these parties have in turn converted the older pattern under which these coalitions were previously constructed—with Republicans anchored by economic preferences and Democrats anchored by cultural preferences—into the modern pattern of joint ideological polarization. Now, the Republican coalition is anchored by individuals who are both economic and cultural conservatives, just as the Democratic coalition is anchored by individuals who are both economic and cultural liberals. The Democratic coalition does, however, contain a secondary concentration of supporters that has no counterpart on the Republican side and that presents special advantages and special challenges for strategic management.

Along the way, a popular theoretical approach to parties and coalitions—one that emphasizes median voters and partisan convergence—fares very badly. The real world has been insistently unkind to this otherwise-elegant framework, and we have no desire to kick any theory that is already down. Yet a focus on voting relationships to economic or cultural values individually, on voting relationships to economic *and* cultural values jointly, but most especially on the density maps associated with both relationships, does, in passing, offer two reasons for this less-than-sterling empirical performance.

The first merely emphasizes countervailing influences. When mapped onto an ideological landscape for electoral politics, Republican and Democratic voting blocs are disproportionately headquartered in terrain that is more or less inherently hostile to moves toward the ideological center. And those living there tend to be advantaged in expressing their hostility. A second countervailing effect is more abstractly provocative. Stratified by political values, by group memberships, and by partisan voting blocs, the American political landscape can be—it is not always, but it always can be—effectively empty at the center. Regardless, it is more often voters at the ideological extremes, not voters in the middle, who can be convinced to abandon their usual partisan choice, albeit normally in favor of some third alternative rather than of the other major party.

At a less grand level, there are numerous smaller but still-consequential aspects of the American political landscape that heave into view in the process of using these methodological approaches to uncover those larger stories. Thus there are social groups where group identity is nearly everything and political values nearly nothing. Black Americans are the outstanding example. Conversely, there are social groups where political values are nearly everything and group identity nearly nothing. Men and women do differ in their partisan propensities, yet men and women holding identical values vote in effectively identical ways. There are groups that have not surrendered the clear dominance of economic values in their voting behavior—high school dropouts are the best example—just as there are groups that have enshrined cultural values to the near-exclusion of economics—of which postgraduates are the archetypal case.

The presence of identical items across a quarter-century—this is a great virtue of the Pew Values surveys, which contribute the central measures here—allows the further pursuit of change in these relationships. Hispanic Americans provide the greatest single instance, in which a social group that was largely impervious to the national link between political values and voting behavior moved into (its own version of) full conformity with national relationships, even as these latter were themselves changing impressively. Yet other principles of social division have also reordered their group-related behavior in major ways: the augmented Republicanism of the Evangelical Protestants, at every point from the far right to the far left; the augmented Democracy of the non-Christians, likewise at every point; and the collapse of old differences between Catholics and Mainstream Protestants in the ideological middle; all these provide obvious and insistent examples. Finally, some social groups remain remarkable for the opposite reason. Thus social class as measured by family income has managed to foster strong relationships to political values while keeping intragroup relationships remarkably invariant.

The Organization of the Book

In order to unpack this comprehensive story, Chapter 2 sets up the analysis, introducing the theory and the method by which opinion data will be handled throughout. Chapter 3 isolates the contribution of various demographic categories—social class, race and ethnicity, religious background, and domestic roles—to the economic and cultural values associated with them. Chapter 4 introduces the social groups that provide a structure to these political values, in ways that can potentially be linked to voting behavior. Chapter 5 then returns to method, setting up the analytic devices by which these links can be teased out and displayed.

Chapter 6 applies these devices to the year with the earliest and richest relevant data, in order to elaborate a benchmark survey of national and group relationships among social backgrounds, political values, and voting behavior. Chapter 7 traces the evolution of the national picture from 1984 through 2008, concentrating on the opening and closing surveys in this series but stopping along the way to capture important intervening developments. Chapter 8 traces the group-based side of this same evolution, seeking the role of social groups in placing individual members within national trends. And the Conclusion returns to the grand strategic questions—even dilemmas—that maps of this ideological landscape inescapably pose.

We have tried to make these elements fit together seamlessly. To that end, theoretical concepts that would already have been recognizable at the turn of the twentieth century—social backgrounds, political values, and voting behavior—have been reinterpreted through methodological approaches that are only just coming into fashion at the turn of the twenty-first. The idea is to keep two things at the forefront of the analysis: (1) who people are—that is, their social backgrounds, presumably as these reflect common experiences and encourage common interests; and (2) what people want—that is, their political values, as these are captured by two great underlying dimensions of public policy and reflected in the policy conflicts that come to define the substance of politics. Together, social backgrounds and political values create the ideological landscape upon which voting behavior occurs and through which the resulting voter distributions come to constrain electoral strategies.

Despite all that and at the risk of underlining the obvious, a reader who cares greatly about the specifics of political conflict and little about the devices that went into measuring it could invest heavily in Chapters 3, 4, 6, 7, and 8, and only just enough in Chapters 2 and 5 to make the others comprehensible. Conversely, a reader who wants to consider the appropriateness of these methods and approaches for their potential use in other realms could attend carefully to Chapters 2 and 5, using the other chapters principally as exemplification. A reader centrally interested in what may be the greatest dynamic in all of social science—the interaction between social structure and substantive values—could attend disproportionately to Chapters 2, 3, and 4, while going light on those that follow. On the other hand, a reader who craves the meat of political analysis could skim quickly to Chapters 6, 7, and 8 and, once there, browse slowly through them. We hope to convince readers that each chapter leads logically to the next, though we readily acknowledge—almost celebrate—the different interests that different readers might bring to this comprehensive story.

2

Mapping the Political Landscape The Nexus of Demographics and Preferences

Investigating the effects of public opinion on voting behavior involves the difficult problem of describing and measuring political values that are simultaneously generalized and latent. On the one hand, we conceptualize these values as being broad-based in their impact, such that they would affect both specific policy preferences and concrete political behavior. On the other hand, we accept that they are nevertheless not directly observable. The only available strategy is thus to turn to defensible indicators of these generalized but latent variables. In this, we shall take the familiar and conventional view that values are reflected in responses signifying the intensity of agreement or disagreement to items such as "The government should take care of those who are unable to take care of themselves" or "Women should resume their traditional role in society."

As part and parcel of this approach, we take the additional view that the valuational positions of individuals can in principle be ranked relative to other individuals, but cannot meaningfully be assigned a cardinal measure. The force of *in principle* is that we cannot know the attitude of any particular individual, but only his or her responses to a set of items—indicators—while we can and do know that it would be unrealistic to assume that two individuals who give the same responses to a relatively small number of items have exactly the same values. What we can hope to do in such a situation is to characterize the likely valuational position of any particular respondent, and to glean from hundreds or thousands of such characterizations, first, the regularities that exist among the values of significant social groups, and second, the effect that these values have on political behavior.

The second of these tasks is especially and additionally difficult, since it implies inferences of causation between political values on one side, which in no particular individual can be observed exactly, and voting behavior on the other, which is self-reported. Because individuals vary widely in non-valuational characteristics that might also be thought to affect political behavior, most especially by way of their social backgrounds, an actual inference of causation would be difficult even if values were to be completely and precisely observed. That they can be observed only with error and uncertainty makes the task even more difficult.

Experienced analysts may view these considerations as little more than the usual difficulties of any research involving public opinion. They are restated here because, with these concerns in mind, we have been guided by five further considerations that largely dictate our methodological approach:

- The statistical methods that are employed should be precisely matched to the conceptual scheme that is presumed to generate item responses.
- The items selected should remain constant over time and across public opinion surveys. Much ambiguity—and associated argument—is avoided by not having to assert (much less prove) that different items nevertheless represent the same thing.
- Conversely, we accept and explicitly address the error and imprecision that arise from these more-limited measurements, rather than expanding errors and imprecision by way of items that lack thematic homogeneity.
- Rather than treat all available information as part of the same setup, we carefully separate the explanatory variables (in this case, political values and social backgrounds) from the behavior to be explained (in this case, presidential voting).

- In particular, although voting behavior can itself be informative about the likely attitudinal position of a respondent, we will not use this information to define the valuational scales initially nor to characterize the subsequent link between social backgrounds and political values.

With that as prologue, Chapter 2 introduces the specific theory used herein to guide the search for political values. It introduces the two key measures, of economic and cultural values, that result. It covers the specifics of estimating values for these two measures in some detail. It introduces graphical representations of these estimates, in the form of figures that are essential to everything that follows. And it exemplifies these through two putative social categories, Soccer Moms and NASCAR Dads, once beloved of campaign strategists but always scorned by social scientists. The substantive analyses of Chapters 3 and 4 will shift to the social backgrounds more typically favored by social scientists, namely *demographic categories* and then *social groups*, delineated by class, race and ethnicity, religion, and gender. Yet our constant theme—of measurement advances that nevertheless bring social scientists closer to the applied approach of campaign strategists—is nicely reinforced by introducing these methodological advances here through the more-journalistic categories of Soccer Moms and NASCAR Dads.

An Item Response Theory

Item response theory (IRT) is a class of psychometric models used to describe the relationship between individual responses to survey questions and underlying (latent) mental attributes.[1] In an academic test with multiple choices, such as the ubiquitous ACT or SAT item response theory typically relates the probability of a correct answer to the skill or knowledge of the respondent, in the process revealing the substantive difficulty and discriminatory power of the questions. In the context of personality assessment, instead, item response theory analogously relates choices among statements concerning sentiment or proclivity to an underlying disposition. In the context of political values, finally, an attitude such as "economic liberalism" influences the strength of assent or dissent to statements such as "The government should do more to help the needy, even if it means running bigger deficits," just as an attitude such as "cultural conservatism" influences the strength of assent or dissent to statements such as "Public school boards should be allowed to fire homosexual teachers."

In each of these cases, there is a formal statistical theory of how the probability of a response is related to latent and observed characteristics. The genesis of the responses and the purpose of the analysis thereafter dictate the focus of any particular class of models that fit within this broad theory. In classical test theory, as with academic testing situations in which many items will be answered and for which item generation is relatively easy, the number of correct, incorrect, and unanswered items may be the only inputs to a single score. In IRT applications, by contrast, a series of items of increasing difficulty but similar content can be defined and administered until consistent successive failure or non-assent is observed in a more empirically rigorous fashion.

Measuring latent ability through test scores, however, differs in important ways from the situation of political attitudes, with the result that measurement models appropriate to rating *ability* become less appropriate to eliciting *values*, at least in any straightforwardly mechanical transfer.[2] In particular, this is because the political context is characterized by (1) ordered responses within a particular item but (2) a lack of ordering *across* items; that is, by no inherent inter-item ordering. "No inter-item ordering" means simply that there is no logical requirement that assent to one item implies assent to another. Even in the abstract, a policy preference for, say, pursuing peace through diplomacy need have no logical implications for a preference for removing dangerous content from school libraries. Likewise, behaviorally, one does not have to give up a preference for peace through diplomacy just because one supports minimizing danger in schools, even though those who favor banning dangerous texts do tend empirically to prefer peace through strength rather than through diplomacy.

Psychometric methods more appropriate for this political context do exist, and these are indeed the ones that have been routinely employed within political science or political sociology. Yet these adoptive methods come with their own major and inherent drawbacks. Most fundamentally, they regularly make special assumptions about the relationship between latent attitudes and item responses, generally by considering only restrictive classes of probability models for the ordered responses from each item. They often assume Gaussian or logistic errors and impose specific functional forms for the response curves. Our goal instead is to proceed with methods that are equally appropriate to the political context, but that escape these associated (and unnecessary) assumptions. This explains our intent, above and below, to return to first principles and to progress from them. Accordingly, we start from a few elementary concepts and associated assumptions, which either elaborate on or follow from the preceding. These include the propositions that:

1. Values cannot meaningfully be given a cardinal measure, unlike, for example, weights or lengths. We can, however, rank or order respondents by how much of a given value they have.

2. These rankings can correspond to the orthodox ideological notions of "liberal" and "conservative." Mathematically, we adopt the convention that liberal attitudes will receive the higher numbers, so that we can, in principle, order the population by number from most liberal to most conservative.

3. Yet when we say that two people have the same values—the same number—on a particular scale, we mean that their responses on items that depend solely on that scale have the same probability distribution. It is in this sense that two people can be equally liberal or equally conservative.

4. By extension, when we say that one point on the scale is more liberal than another, we mean that people with the more-liberal attitudes give more-liberal answers on average than those who are at some less-liberal point. In other words, the responses of the first population first-order-stochastically-dominate the responses of the second, a feature that is discussed further below.

5. This formulaic application of point #4 remains true for any monotonic transformation of "a." Consequently, we can normalize a to any distribution we like for any well-defined reference population we care to choose. This final proposition retains its methodological importance in everything that follows.

Apart from drawing some further implications concerning point #4 above, these assumptions seem both necessary and sufficient to a simple but complete response theory for a single item. To fix ideas concerning point #4 further, suppose we have the item "Congress should pass laws making abortions more difficult to obtain," with the most liberal response being "strongly disagree" and the other possible responses being "disagree," "agree," and "strongly agree." The relationship between some latent attitude and the probability of each of four responses could then be represented as in Figure 2.1, where the lines represent probabilities of giving a response that is at least as conservative as the response to which they correspond. Thus the lowest (black) line is the probability of responding "1," the second (red) line the probability of responding "2" *or* "1," and the third (green) line of responding "3," "2," or "1." Stochastic dominance requires that all lines slope (weakly) downward; definitions of probability theory require that they do not cross.

The figure as drawn illustrates the computation of probability distributions and corresponding probabilities at $a = -1$. This and computations for other values of a are then illustrated in the following two tables. Table 2.1 converts Figure 2.1 into tabular format. To get the response probabilities in each category, we then take differences between the columns of Table 2.1 to obtain Table 2.2. In short, these *item characteristic curves*—a "box model" such as that shown in Figure 2.1—give a complete representation of the item response model when the item is determined by a single attitude.

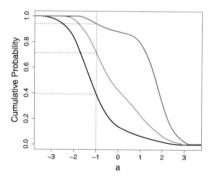

Figure 2.1   Box Model for Abortion Preferences

Key: Black = "$r = 1$", Red = "$r = 2$ or less", and Green = "$r = 3$ or less."

Table 2.1 Distribution of Response Probabilities for Abortion Preferences

Response:	1	2 or less	3 or less	4 or less
−1	0.391	0.720	0.945	1
0	0.144	0.425	0.878	1
1	0.059	0.230	0.796	1

Table 2.2 Response Probabilities by Category for Abortion Preferences

Response:	1	2	3	4
Attitude				
−1	0.391	0.329	0.225	0.055
0	0.144	0.281	0.453	0.122
1	0.059	0.171	0.566	0.204

Table 2.3 Distribution of Response Probabilities for Preferences on Abortion plus Military Action

Abortion→	1	2	3	4	Total
Military↓					
1	0.1125	0.0597	0.0671	0.0385	0.2778
2	0.0360	0.0267	0.0435	0.0165	0.1227
3	0.0364	0.0308	0.0491	0.0158	0.1321
4	0.1302	0.0991	0.1510	0.0870	0.4674
Total	0.3151	0.2163	0.3108	0.1579	

When there are multiple items, each possible combination of item responses then constitutes a "cell," such as those in Table 2.3. The probabilities in this particular case are from a sample of 3,829 responses. They can be exactly reproduced by two box models of the type exemplified by Figure 2.1, one for each item, with the probability of the joint response $\{i,j\}$ conditional upon attitude a being the probability of $p(r_1=i|a)^*p(r_2=j|a)$—which is to say that after conditioning on the scalar attitude a, the two responses are independent. In such a case, we will say that the item responses have a monotonic scale representation. When multiple items are determined by a single valuational scale, the probability of a particular response pattern (or cell) conditional upon a is simply the product of the constituent item probabilities.

By saying that a collection of m items have a "monotonic scale representation," then, we assume:

$$p(r_1, r_2, \ldots, r_m \mid a) = p_1(r_1 \mid a) p_2(r_2 \mid a) \ldots p_m(r_m \mid a) \tag{1}$$

Consequently, the probability of the response $r_1, r_2, \ldots, r_m$ is given by:

$$p(r_1, r_2, \ldots, r_m) = \int p_1(r_1 \mid a) p_2(r_2 \mid a) \ldots p_m(r_m \mid a) f(a) da \tag{2}$$

If the "true" or "population" cell probabilities generated by a set of item responses can be exactly reproduced for a given choice of $f(a)$ by suitable choice of the functions $p(r_1 \mid a)$, then a strictly monotonic transformation of a yields $f(a)$ and new functions $p(r_i \mid a)$ that also exactly reproduce the population cell probabilities.

A difficulty with this strategy is to enforce the monotonically declining/no-crossing properties of the desired item characteristic curves. Estimation will be much easier if these properties can be enforced by parameterization within a sieve family. We address this problem through the following steps:[3]

(1) Transform a to take values on $[0, 1]$. Call the transformed variate u.
(2) A distribution function $G(u)$ on $[0, 1]$ will be monotonic increasing, and the hazard function $1 - G(u)$ will be monotonically decreasing. So the problem is to find distribution functions $G_1(u), \ldots, G_{k-1}(u)$ such that for each item with k responses $G_{k-1}(u) \le G_{k-2}(u) \le \ldots \le G_1(u)$.
(3) If for example $G_2(u) \le G_1(u)$ then $G_2(u) = h(u) G_1(u)$ for some $h(u)$ with $1 \ge h(u) \ge 0$. It is convenient (though with some loss of generality) to require $h(u)$ to be a distribution function and from a collection of such distribution functions $F_1(u), F_2(u), \ldots, F_{k-1}(u)$ form the sequence:

$$G_1(u) = F_1(u)$$

$$G_2(u) = G_1(u) \, F_2(u)$$

$$\vdots$$

$$G_{k-1}(u) = G_{k-2}(u) \, F_{k-1}(u)$$

(4) We specify $F_1(u)$, $F_2(u)$, ..., $F_{k-1}(u)$ to be integrals of regular exponential family densities on the unit interval formed by modeling log densities with a polynomial basis, as in Barron and Sheu (1991):

$$F_i(u) = \int_0^u \frac{e^{t_1 x + t_2 x^2 + \ldots t_m x^m}}{M(t)}\, dx = \int_0^u f_i(x)\, dx$$

$$M(t) = \int_0^1 e^{t_1 x + t_2 x^2 + \ldots t_m x^m}\, dx$$

(5) With $G_{k-1}(u) \leq G_{k-2}(u) \leq \ldots \leq G_1(u)$ now defined, use $1 - G_j(u)$ as $prob(r=j|u)$: Transform u back to a, i.e. compute $prob(r=j|a)$, where a is the attitude measured on a $[-\infty, \infty]$ scale, as e.g. $prob(r \leq j|a) = prob(\{r \leq j\}|\{u = \Phi(a)\}) = 1 - G_j(\Phi(a))$, where $\Phi(\cdot)$ is the standard normal distribution function. (The use of $\Phi(\cdot)$ is not essential: any similar monotonic function from $[-\infty, \infty] -> [0, 1]$ will do, since in principle the $F_i(\,)$'s are flexible.)

After that, the choice of $f(a)$ is largely a matter of convenience, allowing the analysis to be more flexibly response-driven.

Note that this is an embodiment of our attempt to avoid making special (and restrictive) assumptions about the relationship between latent attitudes and item responses. By contrast, the most common applications of these box models to political analysis force all item characteristic curves to have the same form. There must be some opinion items for which this imposition would not distort the analysis. Yet our example of abortion attitudes at Figure 2.1 is clearly not one of these, and such a forced parallelism would likewise be inappropriate for nine of the ten items that we use for our cultural and economic scales (with relevant box models at Figures 2.2 and 2.3 respectively). Speaking graphically but colloquially, the "wiggles" apparent in the item characteristic curves at Figure 2.1 (or Figures 2.2 and 2.3) contrast with the more familiar restrictive form for such box models, and thus allow for the rich (thick) description that we hope to achieve by proceeding in this alternative way.[4]

Item Selection

In the following section there are two scales, one aimed at representing economic values and the other cultural values. This is a familiar but not uncontested way to conceptualize the structure of the latent attitudes relevant to policy preferences within the American public. There is a vast and rich literature that, while individual authors may prefer their own nomenclature, does carve the attitudinal world in precisely this fashion.[5] There is likewise a substantial contrary literature that prefers attempting to scale all individuals, or all items, on some single underlying dimension. We find the former approach more persuasive even in the abstract.

For us, the notion that all respondents can be arrayed by increments or decrements on some single characteristic, sufficient to explain critical behaviors, strains credulity. Yet the more important points here are empirical. Assuming unidimensionality in the setup makes multidimensionality difficult to retrieve, while assuming multidimensionality allows the analysis to collapse to some single underlying dimension, as and when the two posited dimensions prove roughly similar. In the analysis that follows, there are in fact isolated social subgroups that come close to varying along one dimension but not the other. Yet this is never true of the nation as a whole, just as it is never true of most subgroups within this nation.

In any case, we are looking for the broadest possible set of items that can plausibly be related to one or the other of two underlying political values. Note that these two values do not need to be statistically independent, though each must, by itself, be able to explain the observed cell frequencies of multidimensional—m-way—extensions of Table 2.3. Our data consist of the Pew Research Center surveys for the years 1987–2009, covering the presidential elections of 1984–2008, inclusive. While these surveys vary from year to year in their overall content, they do make it possible to avoid items idiosyncratic to a particular year. Scales in one or another year may still lack one or another item from the original survey in 1987, with its focus on the 1984 election, but item form is consistent throughout and scale content is largely uniform.

In selecting items for the economics scale, we conceive of economic values as referring to the preferred distribution of goods in society. This is in some sense a "materialist" continuum, and we expect the referents to involve preferences both for an acceptable minimum and for the proper degree of equalization of material conditions. For the economics scale within those standards—distributions of goods as the substantive core, for items that can be extracted from all relevant surveys—we have chosen:

1. The government should guarantee everyone enough to eat and a place to sleep.
2. The government should take care of those who can't take care of themselves.
3. The government should do more to help the needy, even if it means running bigger deficits.
4. More should be done to improve the position of black people in this country, even if it means giving them preferences.
5. The government should assure equal opportunity for everyone.

In the same way, in selecting items for the culture scale, we conceive of cultural values as referring to the preferred distribution of social norms. This is in some sense a "behavioral" continuum, and while we expect most referents to involve the conduct of everyday life—What kind of a society would you prefer to have?—we do include projection of American values in the outside world as well. For the cultural scale within these standards— norms of behavior as the substantive core, for items that can be extracted from all relevant surveys—we have chosen:

1. Women should resume their traditional role in society.
2. Peace is best assured through diplomacy/military strength.
3. Police should be allowed to search known drug dealers without a warrant.[6]
4. Dangerous books should be banned from public school libraries.
5. Public school boards should be allowed to fire homosexual teachers.

Isolation of these items is inevitably a compromise. In some years, for example, there is an abortion item, a topic classically connected to cultural conflict in the United States. Yet this item is missing in many years, while the wording is inconsistent even when the topic appears. In other years, we possess as few as three of the five items from one or the other scale.

The good news here is twofold. First and most important, attrition of items makes surprisingly little difference to the results: it is possible to run analyses for richer years using only these reduced items, and this does not alter the main substantive conclusions that follow. Second, we do have all the relevant items of the Pew Values surveys for the first and last presidential elections—those of 1984 and 2008—the two that play the largest single roles in substantive interpretation.[7] Respondents are asked whether they strongly disagree, disagree, agree, or strongly agree with each item statement, and responses are coded "1" to "4."[8]

In discussing results, we accept conventional usage for the terms "liberal" and "conservative" in these realms, though that usage does not sit entirely comfortably with an analysis that does not force consistent liberalism or conservatism on respondents across both dimensions. Nevertheless, in common with popular commentators, we shall describe economic liberals as those who favor governmental intervention in the commercial marketplace to guarantee minimum conditions or foster greater equality, and economic conservatives as those opposing such market interventions. The more classically correct way to describe these two groups would involve the terminology of "left" for the former and "right" for the latter. In the same way, we shall describe cultural conservatives as those who favor governmental intervention in society to reinforce common values, and cultural liberals as those opposing such normative interventions. The more classically correct way to describe these two groups would involve the terminology of "traditionalists" for the former and "progressives" for the latter.

With the proposal of two sets of items that solely reflect values on their respective scales, it is useful to be explicit not only about the construction of scales but also about the relationship between them. We take the view that *if* the population cell probabilities for all response patterns for a given set of items are exactly reproduced by a model characterized by (1) *monotonicity of response* (in the sense of stochastic dominance) and (2) *conditional independence of response*, then that model is a complete representation of the stochastic structure of the item response set, and the corresponding scale interpretation cannot be contradicted by any evidence drawn solely from cell counts. The two requirements of monotonicity and conditional independence seem to be the minimal assumptions that embody the notion of complete explanation via scale interpretation. Beyond that, there seems to be no reason why a particular item must necessarily depend on a single valuational continuum. We will, for example, hold that voting behavior depends on both of the values we have defined, though a coherent generalization of scale representation to the multi-scale case does still seem to require both monotonicity and conditional independence.

Methods of Estimation

In combination with the item response model, our basic strategy is to approach the estimation of item characteristic curves such as those in Figure 2.1 by flexibly specifying each category curve, subject only to the basic constraint that they remain monotonically decreasing and do not cross. This looks forward to a strategy of sieve ML (maximum likelihood) estimation. In this, item response models will be estimated by a suitable sieve.[9] In this section, we introduce the function of $f(a|W)$, which can similarly be estimated by a sieve; the resulting likelihood function can then be estimated by maximum likelihood , using numerical quadrature for the integration.

As previously, equation (2) gives the cell probability of responses $r_1, r_2, \ldots, r_m$ as a function of the m item-response box models $p_1 (r_1|a)$, $p_2 (r_2|a), \ldots, p_m (r_m|a)$ and the density $f(a)$ on the attitude a:

$$p(r_1, r_2, \ldots, r_m) = \int p_1(r_1|a)p_2(r_2|a) \ldots p_m(r_m|a)f(a)da \qquad (2)$$

In other words, a particular response pattern such as {2,2,4,3,1} has a probability that is given by the probability of answering with a "2" on item #1 given a particular value of a, times the probability of answering "2" on item #2 given that same a value, and so on, then averaging this over the relative probabilities of different values of a.

We have said that as long as no inessential or arbitrary assumptions are made about each of the box models, one can choose to standardize a in any useful way, by choosing to measure it in such a way as to impose a specific probability distribution of a for either the whole population or some well-defined subpopulation. The estimation of equation (3) can be carried out by the method of maximum likelihood, using only the response pattern of each respondent, provided there is a suitable specification of each of the m

box models. Given the box model specification, the data can be reduced to a frequency count in each potential cell.

In addition to each person's responses, we have observations of each person's demographic characteristics, including income and education, race and ethnicity, denomination and religiosity, plus sex, parenthood, and age. These variables are thought to affect a person's values naturally. Using W to denote a generic vector of such characteristics and W_i to denote the specific values for respondent i, one very effective way to incorporate the effect of such variables is to write:

$$p(r_1, r_2, \ldots, r_m \mid W=W_i) = \int p_1(r_1 \mid a, W_i)\, p_2(r_2 \mid a, W_i) \ldots$$
$$p_m(r_m \mid a, W_i)\, f(a \mid W_i)\, da \tag{3}$$
$$= \int p_1(r_1 \mid a)\, p_2(r_2 \mid a) \ldots p_m(r_m \mid a)\, f(a \mid W_i)\, da \tag{4}$$

Equation (3) is a tautology. The suppression of the W_i argument in the box models of equation (4) is a substantive assumption. It says, in accord with the concept of a "value" above, that the probability distribution of the responses of two people with the same values is the same, regardless of their other characteristics. One way of looking at this is to say that we are defining a value; we are stating what a value is. Yet we are additionally saying that this characterizes the relation between survey responses and political values for every item under consideration.

What does differ based on demographic characteristics—social backgrounds—in equation (2) is the *distribution* of values. If we can indeed normalize a to have any distribution we prefer for any well-defined reference population we care to choose, then, if we take the population of White non-Evangelical Protestant men who are middle-aged, middle-income, and so forth, we can decide that their attitude on a particular scale has the standard normal or Gaussian distribution. Using W_0 to denote the value of W for our standard (sub)population, we can express our standardization as $(a \mid W=W_0) \sim N(0,1)$. Once we have chosen W_0 and this particular standardization, everyone in the population has a value on the scale—since two people with the same probability distribution for their responses on the relevant items have the same value—though we can no longer say that any population other than the reference population has a normal distribution (or any other distribution for that matter), except by making an assumption.

We now make just such an assumption, and exploit it to estimate the distribution of the attitudes conditional upon demographic characteristics. We will assume that a is normally distributed conditional on W, with mean given by $E(a|W) = W\beta$. W is measured so that $W_0 = 0$, as required by the standardization $(a|W=W_0) \sim N(0, 1)$: Additionally we assume either that $\sigma(a|W) = 1$ or $\sigma(a|W) = W\gamma$. Both the assumption that a is conditionally normal given W and that its log conditional standard deviation is either 0 or a linear function of W are assumptions of convenience, but there is not much evidence against either assumption once the standardization as $(a|W=W_0) \sim N(0, 1)$ is made.

One implication of these model assumptions is that even though a is unobservable, we can estimate its "regression" against W. We will consider the interpretation of this regression below. An interpretation of the role of W is that it serves as an *instrument* for a: these variables affect a but do not affect r either directly or conditional upon a. A further elaboration of this view is that nature subjects different people to different Ws, which in turn affect their a. We use equation (3) as the basis of our estimation method. That equation shows how to calculate the probability that a person gives a particular response given his or her social background plus the unknown parameters that are the target of estimation.

These unknown parameters, in turn, fall into two classes: (1) those that describe the *item characteristic curves* (those box models that relate values to responses) and (2) the *conditional distribution of the value* given social characteristics. The unknown parameters are chosen so that the model's estimate of the probability of observing what in fact happened is maximized—the method of maximum likelihood. The first set of parameters, those that describe the box models, have no intuitive interpretation. They do, however, generate item characteristic curves that are easily displayed. Indeed, because we think these pictures are worth the proverbial thousand words, we content ourselves with graphical displays of this portion of our results. The second set of parameters then has a natural interpretation similar to conventional regression coefficients. Tables of these coefficients, together with the three most conventional ways of estimating their standard errors, are displayed where instructive and appropriate.

We have estimated models for the surveys taken in years 1987, 1988, 1990, 1992, 1993, 1994, 1997, 1999, 2002, 2007, and 2009, contributing eleven years in total. For each of these years, there is a model for economics, a model for culture, and a model for their joint distribution (as explained below). Accordingly, to report one basic version of our completely modeled analysis requires: twenty-two five-panel graphics (five panels since there are five items in each scale); twenty-two coefficient tables for demographic effects; and eleven tables characterizing the estimates of the joint distribution of values. Each of the twenty-two graphics takes about a page, as do the thirty-three tables.

We would be happy to tax the reader with explicit display of all this, were it to be the end of the matter. But depending on the year, there is some variation in the demographic variables available, so that there is both scope and necessity to estimate additional variants of the basic model. These variants take into account further details of educational attainment and religious practice in particular, details that are not available in all years. Model A thus reflects the basic demographic variables available in all years, and is the model of choice for most subsequent analyses. But Models A_1 and A_2 do exist, to reflect those additional details on education and religion respectively. In that sense, they are superior to Model A, though all models tell basically the same story. Accordingly, for the substantive analysis in subsequent chapters, some embellishment is possible in the years with greater detail, and by comparing these with the basic model, the likely variation in interpretation due to differing data availability can be judged.

Below, we present two detailed results for the basic model as estimated from the Pew survey of 1987, for the election year of 1984. We choose this example not only because it opens the Pew Values series, but also because it is the survey that both had the largest sample and was the most carefully conducted. Most surveys, from Pew or elsewhere, are conducted through telephone interviews; the 1987 Pew survey was done face-to-face. Beyond its impressive size and live character, the 1987 survey, as the first of this series, also yields an initial position for American public opinion. The demographic divisions underpinning these models, as reflected in Model A for Tables 2.4 and 2.5, include

- Age, both *age* as a conventional measure (age) and as *age-squared* (agesq.01)
- Race and Ethnicity, as *Black* (black) or *Hispanic* (hispanic), with *Anglo* (that is, non-Hispanic White) as the reference category
- Religious Denomination, as *White Evangelical* (bornagain), *Black Evangelical* (blackbornagain), *Catholic* (rel.catholic), and *Non-Christian* (rel. nonchr), with *Mainstream Protestant* as the reference category
- Educational Attainment, as *high school dropout* (ed.dropout), *some-college* (ed.somecoll), and *college graduate* (ed.collgrad), with *high school graduate* as the reference category
- Family Income, as *low-income* 30 percent (income.1), *upper-middle* 30 percent (income.3), and *upper* 10 percent (income.4), with *middle* 30 percent as the reference category;
- Sex, as *female*, with *male* the reference category;
- Parenthood, that is, those having children at home, as *parent* (parent) with *non-parent* the reference.

The reasoning behind these divisions is elaborated as they are utilized, in Chapter 3. As above, Model A_1 includes Generic Religiosity, as weekly or more, and once or twice a month, with rarely or never as the reference category. Model A_2 includes a revised educational demographic, adding a separate category for *postgraduates* and thereby separating these postgraduates from the college graduates.

Economic Values, Cultural Values, and Their Joint Distribution

Figure 2.2 shows the characteristic five-item response curves defining the economic scale, the curves that are implied by the maximum likelihood estimates of equation (2) using Model A to supply the conditioning variables for this attitude in the 1987 survey. These box models suggest that the first three items, which are direct questions about the role of government in assuring the welfare of the less fortunate—"government guarantees," "caring for the unable," and "running deficits to provide aid"—evoke differential responses throughout the economic scale. The remaining two items show a less sensitive response, though they otherwise differ in an additional

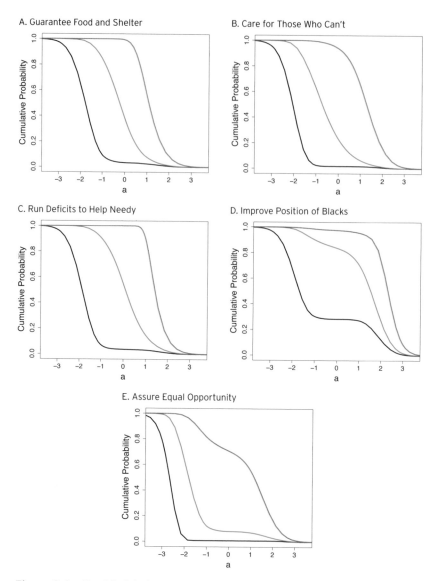

Figure 2.2 Box Models for Items in a Scale of Economic Values

Key: Black = "$r = 1$", Red = "$r = 2$ or less", and Green = "$r = 3$ or less."

major way. From one side, the majority of the respondents are not sympa-thetic to racial preferences.[10] From the other side, guarantees of equal op-portunity command wide assent.

Note that we have no a priori expectation that any item *should* respond more smoothly or gradually to economic or cultural values. Though we can (and do) go on to offer explicit calculations about the informativeness of each, which does depend (among other things) on the response to other items. On the other hand, we would want these items to have relatively similar and stable relationships to the major demographic characteristics across time, and Chapters 3 and 4 will confirm that this is very much the case. Accordingly, Table 2.4 gives the "pseudo-regression" of these economic values on social backgrounds, again as these are enumerated in Model A.

For economic values, race and ethnicity stand out as impressively powerful, more so than social class as measured by either education or income, despite the inherently economic nature of class. Thus a Black American is .72 more liberal than the reference category, rising to .95 if he or she is in addition an Evangelical Protestant, as the smaller half of Blacks in fact are [.95 = +.72 + (+.23)]. For a further contrast, note that a Black Evangelical is 1.10 more liberal than an Anglo Evangelical [1.10 = .95 − (−.15)]. Hispanics display a similar but smaller economic liberality, sitting at .34 in comparison with the standard. With that said, our main indicators of social class, education, and income, do also produce clear relationships to economic

Table 2.4 Pseudo-Regression of Economic Values on Demographic Characteristics

	coefficient	OPG s.e.	Hessian s.e.	Robust s.e.
age	−0.0032	0.0013	0.0013	0.0012
agesq.01	−0.0009	0.0065	0.0063	0.0064
black	0.7228	0.0869	0.0848	0.0879
bornagain	−0.1494	0.0505	0.0485	0.0477
blackbornagain	0.2305	0.1227	0.1264	0.1320
rel.catholic	0.2075	0.0493	0.0470	0.0462
rel.nonchr	0.2164	0.0599	0.0586	0.0585
ed.dropout	0.1946	0.0532	0.0515	0.0506
ed.somecoll	−0.1609	0.0504	0.0496	0.0495
ed.collgrad	−0.1650	0.0519	0.0509	0.0513
income.1	0.1806	0.0499	0.0484	0.0484
income.3	−0.1112	0.0500	0.0483	0.0494
income.4	−0.0887	0.0685	0.0656	0.0654
income.dk	−0.1427	0.0930	0.0934	0.0951
parent	−0.0125	0.0427	0.0421	0.0431
hispanic	0.3430	0.0802	0.0784	0.0783
female	0.0583	0.0368	0.0359	0.0360

values for both Blacks and Hispanics, with education slightly the more important.

Figure 2.3 shifts to the characteristic five-item response curves defining the cultural scale, curves that are likewise implied by the maximum likelihood estimates of equation (4) using Model A to supply the condi-

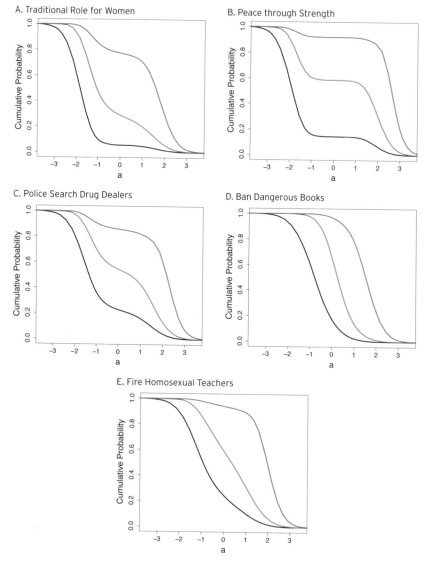

Figure 2.3 Box Models for Items in a Scale of Cultural Values
Key: Black= "*r* = 1", Red= "*r* = 2 or less", and Green= "*r* = 3 or less."

tioning variables for this alternative attitude in the same (1987) survey. This time, the box models show that "ban dangerous books" and "fire gay teachers" are the items evoking differential responses throughout the entire range of cultural values. "Search drug dealers (or terrorists)" and "women in traditional roles" share this quality more modestly. "Peace through strength" is responsive only at the extremes of opinion.

Table 2.5 then gives the "pseudo-regression" of cultural values on social backgrounds. Here, the most notable effects are of religion and education on cultural attitudes. Among religious denominations, Evangelical Protestants are .83 standard deviations (of the referenced subpopulation) more conservative than the most liberal group, the Non-Christians [.83 = +.29 − (−.54)]. Recall that all such statements must be made in the ceteris paribus sense: this is the relationship of Evangelical Protestants to Non-Christians with all other demographic characteristics present in the model. Education appears to have an even stronger effect: the difference is 1.11 between college graduates, the most liberal category, and high -school dropouts, the most conservative [1.11 = .98 − (−.13)].

Table 2.5 Pseudo-Regression of Cultural Values on Demographic Characteristics

	coefficient	OPG s.e.	Hessian s.e.	Robust s.e.
age	−0.0147	0.0015	0.0013	0.0013
agesq.01	0.0084	0.0068	0.0066	0.0069
black	−0.1187	0.0966	0.0897	0.0873
bornagain	−0.5419	0.0544	0.0519	0.0524
blackbornagain	−0.0354	0.1332	0.1337	0.1395
rel.catholic	−0.0275	0.0518	0.0493	0.0496
rel.nonchr	0.2921	0.0614	0.0605	0.0611
ed.dropout	−0.1338	0.0570	0.0547	0.0565
ed.somecoll	0.5121	0.0540	0.0528	0.0534
ed.collgrad	0.9812	0.0575	0.0551	0.0590
income.1	−0.0135	0.0536	0.0506	0.0501
income.3	0.1945	0.0518	0.0509	0.0565
income.4	0.2598	0.0738	0.0686	0.0703
income.dk	−0.0644	0.1035	0.0981	0.0958
parent	−0.1640	0.0462	0.0437	0.0435
hispanic	−0.1077	0.0947	0.0824	0.0725
female	0.1502	0.0397	0.0389	0.0436

A full discussion of the implications of this and similar results is undertaken in Chapters 3 and 4. Here, it is important to note that the effects just calculated are ceteris paribus in a second sense as well: the .84 difference between Evangelical Protestants and Non-Christians indicates the difference in the specific contribution to cultural values of being in one rather than the other demographic category. It does not indicate the full difference between social groups as defined by these categories, since the Non-Christians also tend to be better-educated (and have higher incomes, etc.) than the Evangelical Protestants. Discussion of the first type of effect—individual differences among demographic categories—is taken up in Chapter 3. Discussion of the second type—comprehensive differences among social groups—is taken up in Chapter 4.

Beyond that, note that the direction of these cultural influences is now opposite to their economic counterparts. Respondents of higher social class, with more education and/or more income, tended to be more conservative on the economic dimension, while these same respondents are more liberal on the cultural dimension. And of course vice versa: respondents of lower social class tended to be more liberal in their economic values, while they are more conservative in their cultural preferences.

Estimates in the previous section have assumed a scalar a—that is, a single attitude that underpins the observed response pattern. The reasonableness of this assumption is subject-matter dependent, but in general we will want to assess the impact of multiple attitudes on behaviors. If there is a collection of items with a monotonic scale representation for a single attitude, then proceeding as above for each such collection produces consistent estimates for each individual attitude. But to analyze responses or outcomes that are dependent on multiple attitudes, we will inevitably require at least a simple model of how attitudes are related—that is, jointly distributed.

So, let us divide the total set of item responses such that the first dimension (m) involves economic items, while responses $m+1, \ldots M$ are cultural. If each class of items has a monotonic scale representation in a single attitude, we can write:

$$
\begin{aligned}
p(r_1, r_2, \ldots r_M \mid W) &= \iint p(r_1, r_2, \ldots r_M \mid a_C, a_E) f(a_C, a_E \mid W)\, da_C\, da_E \\
&= \iint p(r_1 \mid a_C), p(r_2 \mid a_C), \ldots p(r_m \mid a_C) p(r_{m+1} \mid a_E), \ldots \\
&\quad p(r_M \mid a_E) f(a_C, a_E \mid W)\, da_C\, da_E
\end{aligned}
\tag{5}
$$

Now, from the scale models already estimated, we have:

$$p(r_1|a_C), p(r_2|a_C), \ldots p(r_m|a_C) \text{ and } p(r_{m+1}|a_E), \ldots p(r_M|a_E).$$

We have already specified $f(a_C, a_E|W)$ as having normal margins. Consequently, we can completely specify $f(a_C, a_E|W)$ by simply supplying the missing covariance between a_C and a_E, which can be made to depend on W. A convenient specification is:

$$\rho(W) = \frac{\exp(W\delta - 1)}{\exp(W\delta + 1)} \tag{6}$$

Lastly, W is here augmented from its previous definition by the inclusion of an intercept, so that the "standard" respondent may have correlation between a_C and a_E. More generally, we could specify the margins as uniform; that is, we could work in terms of what would be called u_C, u_E, and then estimate the density corresponding to the copula $F(u_C, u_E.)$.

An important aspect of the foregoing is that we have not assumed that attitudes or factors are independent. The basic question in our exposition is the dimensionality of a required for the existence of a monotonic scale representation. In principle, if the dimensionality of a has been underspecified, model specification tests derived from the ML or sieve ML framework should detect this. If, in contrast, we treat two item sets as arising from different factors when there is in fact only one—so that, for example, there is not "economic liberalism" and "cultural liberalism" but only "overall liberalism"—then when estimating the above equations (or their more general analogs), the resulting copula should prove to be estimated as large, showing high association.

To supply the raw material for the following section, we estimate equation (5) using the parameters derived from the separately estimated E and C models, so that only δ from equation (6) is being estimated. Figure 2.4 is then the corresponding estimate of the *joint* density of attitudes with uniform marginals.[11] What emerges is a portrait of the national distribution of economic and cultural values jointly, one which is impressively "flat." The two grand political values are nearly independent for the nation as a whole, yet they are not entirely so. There is a modest tendency for those who are strong economic liberals to overpopulate the strongly liberal but especially

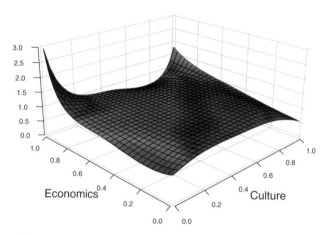

Figure 2.4 Joint Distribution of Cultural and Economic Values, 1984

the strongly conservative extremes of the cultural continuum, along with an even more modest tendency for those who are strong economic conservatives to overpopulate the territory of modest cultural liberalism.

Chapter 5 will revisit this basic distribution as a key tool on the way to the analysis of voting behavior while warning, in particular, against putting too much weight on apparent twists at the ideological extremes, which are more thinly informed numerically and thus less reliably estimated. Here, the function of Figure 2.4, beyond confirming the general independence of the two great valuational dimensions, is just to provide a comparative standard for the situation of social groups that sample and combine these dimensions in a manner clearly different from the national picture.

Soccer Moms and NASCAR Dads

All these aspects of a fresh methodological approach to public opinion data will be deployed in highly systematic fashion in the chapters to follow. Chapter 3 will turn to the great *demographic categories* that have long characterized analyses of social backgrounds, namely social class, race and ethnicity, religious background, and domestic roles. In so doing, it will attempt to isolate the impact of each on economic and cultural values within the general public. Chapter 4 will then turn to the *social groups* that are defined by these demographic cleavages. In any given society, no one can have, say, just an educational background. Those who are high school graduates, for example, must also have an income, an ethnicity, a denominational attachment, a sex, and so on. It is only when these are put back together that the strategic landscape for electoral politics appears, the landscape upon which campaign decisions must be made and from which electoral victory or defeat will emerge.

Yet the approach summarized above can in principle be used to analyze the values and behavior of nearly any demographic category or social group that the analyst can conceive, provided only that this category or group is not too small to be captured by a national sample and that the analyst can convert the available indicators into a theoretically defensible definition, one sufficient to isolate the individuals of interest. Accordingly, it may be helpful, in closing this chapter, to take a couple of journalistic rather than scholarly categories, the "buzz-word groups" that seem to appear with every new presidential election, and apply our systematic method to these idiosyncratic groups. Two popular examples from the period of the Pew surveys are "Soccer Moms" and "NASCAR Dads," though every election seems to produce another aspiring option.[12]

In scholarly terms, the problem with Soccer Moms and NASCAR Dads is twofold. First, they are not ordinarily defined with reference to the standard categories of social background, with the result that each analyst can produce a different incarnation. Worse yet, they are rarely defined explicitly at all, so that individual respondents get ruled in or out according to the whims of the specific analyst. It is as if journalists—and campaign strategists—"know them when they see them." On the other hand, for purposes of methodological exposition, this need not deter us. All that is necessary is a specific demographic translation, with some surface theoretical plausibility. For these purposes, we shall define Soccer Moms as Anglo (White non-Hispanic) college graduate female parents (that is, having children at home), and we shall define NASCAR Dads as Anglo high school graduate male parents.[13]

Table 2.6.A approaches these two putative social types in the most elementary way possible, taking the economic and cultural scores for their four defining demographics in the nation as a whole, and summing these to produce a pair of valuational profiles. Thus, Soccer Moms at the time

Table 2.6   Soccer Moms and NASCAR Dads

A. Isolated by Individual Demographic Characteristics

	Soccer Moms		NASCAR Dads	
	Economics	Culture	Economics	Culture
1984	−.12	+.97	−.01	−.16
2008	−.35	+1.03	−.24	−.13

B. Isolated as Composite Social Groups

	Soccer Moms		NASCAR Dads	
	Economics	Culture	Economics	Culture
1984	+.03	+1.28	+.02	+.07
2008	−.47	+1.15	−.25	+.02

of the 1984 presidential election would have acquired a score of −.12 on economics—they were moderate economic conservatives—which is the additive composite for being Anglo, a college graduate, female, and a parent.[14] At the same time, these Soccer Moms would have had a score of +.97 on culture—they were strong cultural liberals—which is the additive composite of the mean scores of the same demographic categories. The common journalistic assumption that they were modestly conservative on economics but pulled strongly in the opposite direction by their cultural prejudices thus receives support.

When the NASCAR Dads are added to this picture, the two populationss can be readily distinguished by their political values, though not in the sense of being simple opposites, a sense that often characterizes their use in more impressionistic analyses. Approached in the same manner as above, these NASCAR Dads had a composite score of −.01 on economics. They were thus in the dead center of American economic values, making them modestly more liberal on this dimension than the Soccer Moms.[15] A composite score of −.16 on culture would have made them modestly conservative, though this position left them far off to the cultural right of the Soccer Moms. This, too, accorded with orthodox journalistic assumptions. Together, the strategic point is that two populations with these characteristics should have been potentially amenable to the same candidate when economic issues came to the fore in electoral conflict and very hard to attract for the same candidate when cultural issues came to the fore instead.

A revisit to both populations at the presidential election of 2008 then shows elements both of stability and change. Chapters 3 and 4 will confirm that associations between demographic characteristics or social groups and political values are impressively stable over the quarter-century for which we have data, so there is little room for either the Soccer Moms or the NASCAR Dads to reconfigure their economic or cultural preferences in a major way. Yet the changes that do appear when approached through mean scores serve to underline the strategic challenge to candidates for public office which these two populations, together, create. Moreover, these are still ideological positions with regard to reference categories; the *distribution* of preferences for the Soccer Moms and NASCAR Dads at Figures 2.5–2.8 will, if anything, sharpen these differences and their associated strategic challenges.

In any case, the Soccer Moms, when approached through this simple additive measure, moved in the intervening quarter-century from being marginally to clearly conservative in terms of their economic values. This shift from −.12 to −.35 actually took them into very conservative territory by comparison to the array of individual demographic categories that will be examined systematically in Chapter 3. At the same time, they managed to become marginally more liberal in terms of their cultural values, moving from +.97 to +1.03. Having always been strongly liberal by comparison to the rest of society, they had little room for a further leftward shift, yet they managed a modest move in that direction even then.

The NASCAR Dads likewise became more economically conservative over this quarter-century, moving from −.01 to −.24. In the process, they appeared to abandon the economic center of American society. If they were still left of the Soccer Moms, they were now clearly right of the national mean. Like the Soccer Moms, they also moved ever so slightly leftward on culture, from an old mean of −.16 to a new one of −.13. Yet strategically, this amounted to no change at all: the two populations remained about as far apart on cultural values as two such populations could get in American society. The old strategic world constituted by these two, along with its inherent challenge—appeal to both on economics, pit them against each other on culture—was thus alive and well a quarter-century later.

The second half of Table 2.6, however, moving on to look at the mean scores on economics and culture for these two demographic categories as social groups, suggests that any analyst who wants to think about their implications for the structure of political conflict, and thus for the strategies of electoral competition, must attend to this analytic move as well. As noted, Table 2.6.A used a simple additive scoring system:race plus education plus sex plus parenthood. This is what the analyst would want if the question was what each of these defining aspects of social background was contributing individually to the values of those who held all four defining characteristics—those who were either Soccer Moms or NASCAR Dads.

Yet we know at the same time that any given subgroup, as with these Soccer Moms and NASCAR Dads, samples all other aspects of social background simultaneously. So if the defining characteristics of these two journalistic creations (at least when given an explicit definition) are consciously intended not to be a random sample of the nation—this intention is, after all, the reason they are being isolated for attention—it becomes very unlikely that their other demographic characteristics will somehow be just such a random sample. This is the point—and focus—of Table 2.6.B, which converts individual demographic categories into composite social groups. As it turns out, the result is some modest but distinguishable alterations in what each group is now contributing to the ideological landscape for practical politics.

When the actual distribution of their other social characteristics is allowed back into the analysis, then, both the Soccer Moms and the NASCAR Dads actually stood in the center of American society in terms of their economic values in 1984. Associated social characteristics had pulled the Soccer Moms *as a social group* in from the economic right, such that the two groups were effectively indistinguishable, at +.03 and +.02. On the other hand, moving from additive demographic means to composite group scores had little effect on their comparative cultural positions. The Soccer Moms looked even more liberal, at +1.28. The NASCAR Dads actually shifted ever so slightly liberal, too, at +.07. But the distance between them nevertheles increased: cultural-policy promises that pleased the Soccer Moms should have repelled the Soccer Dads, and vice versa.

The story of valuational shifts across time for these two social groups then became one of clear economic change, coupled with a cultural stasis that kept the two groups very distant. By 2008, the Soccer Moms have moved hugely rightward in their economic values—when analyzed not as a demographic category but as a social group. An economic score of +.03 in 1984 had become a score of −.47 in 2008. A weaker echo of the same effect could be found among the NASCAR Dads: +.02 in 1984 to −.25 in 2008. Though note that this opened up some genuine ideological space between the two groups on economics as well. Depending on what other social groups did, economic policy promises pegged to the NASCAR Dads might potentially pick up the Soccer Moms, yet economic promises pegged to the Soccer Moms might now potentially alienate the NASCAR Dads. By contrast, the comparative cultural story remained essentially unchanged. The NASCAR Dads remained close to the cultural center of American society. The Soccer Moms remained wildly off to their left.

Accordingly, Table 2.6.A contributes what is at least an explicit, transparent, and systematic view of two otherwise highly impressionistic, alleged social types. Table 2.6.B contributes what is a comparatively more sophisticated pair of portraits of the same two groups. Yet even these latter portraits remain relatively crude in the sense that each value, economic or cultural, is still defined by a single point, and the two resulting points still take no cognizance of each other. In the real—behavioral and strategic—world of political conflict, every social group actually constitutes (and offers) a distribution of scores on both the economic and the cultural scale, while these economic and cultural values of course occur simultaneously—that is, in the presence of each other.

Figure 2.5 responds to these considerations by showing the joint distribution of values for Soccer Moms at the election of 1984. The figure confirms that the overwhelming valuational characteristic of these Soccer Moms was their cultural liberalism, now plotted visually. There were nearly no cultural conservatives in this population; almost the entire group resided on the liberal half of the cultural scale. Yet at most points on that scale, the Soccer Moms leaned modestly but consistently conservative on economics. Thus at every cultural point, there was a shortage of economic liberals and a surplus of economic conservatives, with one exception: at the high end of the culture scale, Soccer Moms were simultaneously economic liberals.

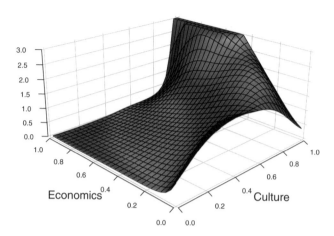

Figure 2.5 Soccer Moms, 1984: Joint Distribution of Attitudes

Figure 2.6 shows that same distribution at the election of 2008. Most of what needs to be said about this figure involves its impressive similarity to the one capturing the world of the Soccer Moms a quarter-century before: same dominant (and liberal) cultural gradient, same conservative economic overlay, same exception to the general pattern among strong cultural liberals. The main element of difference between Figures 2.5 and 2.6 is just a modest reduction of economic liberalism among the more culturally liberal. Among stronger cultural liberals in this social group, of which there are in fact many, the huge previous uptick toward economic liberalism, which was contrary to economic preferences in the rest of the group, had been reduced by 2008, though the direction of the effect remained, and the change should not be overstated.

The NASCAR Dads, at the beginning of this period and in Figure 2.7, were more simply described. Theirs was an opposite but far weaker cultural gradient, rising across-the-board toward the conservative end of the cultural scale. This was coupled with an even more modest economic gradient, edging upward toward the conservative end of the economic scale. But in fact, it might be better to describe the NASCAR Dads as having an essentially flat profile, one that was relatively evenly distributed across both value scales, with two clear exceptions: they featured a downturn among strong economic liberals, and they completely lacked strong cultural liberals. In other words, this group was relatively evenly distributed except at both liberal extremes, where they were largely missing.

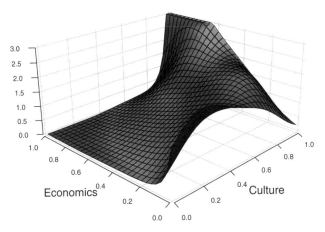

Figure 2.6 Soccer Moms, 2008: Joint Distribution of Attitudes

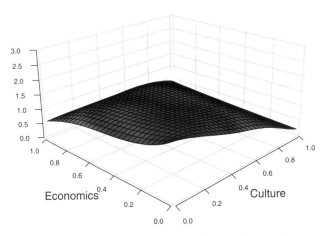

Figure 2.7 NASCAR Dads, 1984: Joint Distribution of Attitudes

This time, however, Figure 2.8 tells a story of ideological evolution.[16] By 2008, while the group remained recognizable from its earlier survey, there were two main points of difference, which made its collective profile look different as well. The more general change was that the cultural gradient had become considerably steeper. Now, in direct contradistinction to the Soccer Moms, the NASCAR Dads had nearly no cultural liberals and more strong cultural conservatives. Yet there was a further twist. For now, there was an additional uptick of economic liberalism among those (ascendant) strong cultural conservatives. This was still not a large

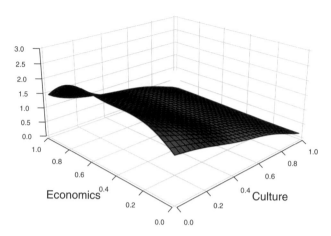

Figure 2.8 NASCAR Dads, 2008: Joint Distribution of Attitudes

subpopulation, but where those residing at this location were once additionally unlikely to be strong economic liberals (as at Figure 2.7), they were now even more likely to be so.

All of which implies different prospects for political strategy. Until we get to Chapters 6 and 8, where we can more easily judge which values matter to a given group, it is not empirically possible to confirm the strategic approaches that do and do not work with any given group. It is still abstractly possible to possess more extreme scores on culture, for example, but to possess economic scores that are more aligned with vote choice. What it is possible to do, courtesy of Figures 2.5, 2.6, 2.7, and 2.8, is to note the available strategic options that are formally inherent in these joint distributions.

In this view, the Soccer Moms look conventionally cross-pressured. They have strong liberal preferences on culture and clear conservative preferences on economics. While there is nothing inconsistent in this pairing—it must certainly seem normal and natural to these Soccer Moms—the pairing becomes problematic for a *party system* where one party is liberal and the other conservative on both dimensions. By contrast, the NASCAR Dads look more conventionally centrist on one dimension but strongly conservative on the other. True economic moderation coupled with clear cultural conservatism should attract them.

Yet when the two social groups inhabit the same political world, the strategic complexities of appealing to their members only grow. Or at least, a cultural liberalism sufficient to energize the Soccer Moms would potentially be a major repellent for these NASCAR Dads, while the economic conservatism sufficient to satisfy the Soccer Moms would strongly alienate a subgroup among the NASCAR Dads and might alienate the entire population. And that is before immersing both groups in a party system built around offering none of these combinations.

3

Structure and Substance

Demographic Cleavages and the Roots of Political Values

Four great cleavages have traditionally been used to describe the social roots of political divisions: social class, race and ethnicity, religious background, and sex and gender.[1] Not all cleavages have been relevant to politics in all nations, just as individual nations have mixed the number and sequence of relevant cleavages in idiosyncratic ways. This historical pattern does not prove that any given cleavage was inconsequential for the nation in question, only that it was not mobilized into politics at a particular point in time. Sometimes, the historical pattern has direct and obvious extrapolations to current political conflicts. Other times, modern politics features newly activated cleavages plus a fresh remix of the old. Regardless, any analysis that seeks to begin with the social bases of political opinion would need to address these "big four" divisions.

Modern American politics certainly partakes of arguments about all four. Social class and the class-differentiated distribution of economic well-being were staples of American politics when the New Deal (and survey research!) arrived on the scene in the 1930s and 1940s. They have seldom been far from political conflict since. Indeed, much research indicates that class is actually on the rise as a cleavage relevant to American politics (Stonecash 2000, Bartels 2008). Although there may be nearly as many indicators of social class as there are students of class phenomena, two indicators that would be accepted as an essential part of almost all definitions are income and education. Because they are related but not nearly identical, because both are available in all the Pew surveys, and, to jump ahead of the story, because they work in distinguishable ways, we utilize both in the analysis that follows.

Race and ethnicity have been central to American politics from at least the moments, respectively, when slavery arrived in what would become the United States and when it became clear that this new nation would be populated, to an impressive degree, by way of immigration. The debate over race policy would be reinvigorated with a veritable civil rights revolution in the 1960s and 1970s (Sitkoff 1974, Graham 1990). Debate over immigration policy—and with it, over the Americanization of immigrants—would rise and fall across time, largely in conjunction with immigrant waves (Portes and Rumbaut 1990, King 2000). In our time, in any case, the inescapable categories are clear enough. Race must take account of Black Americans if it is to have any meaning. Ethnicity must mean Hispanic Americans, first and foremost. The Pew surveys offer both, and we attend explicitly to them.

Religious background can be thought of in the same fashion: present from the creation, rising or falling in political relevance across the years, getting a refreshed and partially new incarnation in modern times. Some (not all) of the American colonies began as explicitly religious experiments, attempts to create a new world according to theological precepts. Religious movements were integral to the great political conflicts of American history that followed, especially to the American Revolution and the Civil War. Policy issues associated with religious traditions went on to dominate American politics in the late nineteenth century, only to recede and then reemerge in the late twentieth (Kohut et al. 2000, Layman 2001). The Pew surveys permit carrying the five great denominational families of American society in all years—Evangelical Protestants, Mainstream Protestants, Black Evangelicals, Catholics, and Non-Christians—along with a more generic religiosity, in the form of church attendance.

Lastly, sex and gender cleavages, conceived in the broadest sense, have attracted some attention in all eras and insistent attention in more recent years. As organizing principles for social life, they have been omnipresent (Klein 1984, Inglehart and Norris 2003). Still, the array of possible aspects of sexual identities and gendered institutions that have made their way into opinion surveys in modern times remains impressive. The Pew surveys allow us to carry two major aspects of what will be translated here as "domestic roles." The first is the basic sex difference, men versus women. The second is a basic household difference, parents versus non-parents, that is, households with and without children. Both cleavages are numerically large but easily distinguished, from other grand cleavages as well as from each other. In addition, the Pew surveys permit us to look for age-related differences, and we have folded them into the section on domestic roles.

Methodologically, it is possible to treat these grand social cleavages, to varying but largely parallel degrees, as "instruments" for the measurement analysis here—that is, as phenomena associated with our central concern, political values, which are nevertheless not shaped reciprocally by them. This is easiest to see—most indisputable—in the cases of race or sex. One might get an individual survey respondent to change answers on questions tapping economic or cultural values, but it is only in rare cases or on the far shores of behavior that one would be changing race or sex as a result. Social class allows a bit more reciprocity in the abstract: a change in economic or cultural values, asserted for a long enough time, just might affect social mobility and thus class position. Yet this could hardly work from one survey to the next on any major scale, so that the overall direction of effect, from social background to political values, should remain clear. The greatest fluidity might thus involve religious background: a change in economic or cultural values might reasonably lead to a switch in denomination. That said, the vast bulk of religious affiliations are inherited, full stop, so that aggregate shifts in the size and composition of the great religious families move only glacially from survey to survey.

Substantively, the story is more varied. Some demographic cleavages are related more strongly to one than to the other of the two great dimensions of political opinion. Some are related about equally to both. For some demographic cleavages, an evident ordinal relationship to economic and/or cultural values appears. For others, because nothing gives their associated categories an inherent order, it makes more sense to address these demographic categories one by one, rather than treating them as components of a social variable. Lastly, some elements of social background drive economic and cultural values in a parallel fashion—that is, liberal or conservative on both; while other elements drive them in opposite directions—liberal on one and conservative on the other. The result is a straightforward but not uncomplicated picture of the links between social cleavages and political values in the United States, yielding the opening contours of an ideological landscape for strategic conflict.

Social Class

Family Income

Social class—the placement of an individual within an economic system and the array of life chances and lifestyles that go with that placement—is one of the great demographic locaters for all individuals, though its relevance to politics can vary enormously. A personal history, a particular period in time, or an idiosyncratic mix with other background characteristics can cause class to be more or less important to any given individual when addressing political conflict. The mobilizing effect of organized intermediaries, most especially political parties and interest groups, can give different collective priorities to class attachments, quite apart from individual preferences. The programmatic substance of the particular policies at the center of political conflict can cause the impact of social class to vary additionally across individuals and groups, and in a partially autonomous fashion.

With that as prologue, Table 3.1 presents coefficients for the first measure of social class, namely family income, in its relationship to economic and cultural values. Table 3.1.A offers these coefficients for every year in which there was a Pew Values survey; Table 3.1.B gathers them by election years. Both are intended to be straightforward and consistent in their interpretation. Family income is divided into rough thirds—terciles— along with a small top category aimed at capturing some distinction (if any) between the wealthy and the rest of the population. Hence the table features the bottom 30 percent as lower-income, the middle 30 percent as middle-income, the next 30 percent as upper-middle, and the top 10 percent as upper-income.

Table 3.1 Social Class and Political Values: Family Income

A. Contributions to Political Values for All Surveys

	Lower-Income		Middle-Income		Upper-Middle		Upper-Income	
	Economic	Cultural	Economic	Cultural	Economic	Cultural	Economic	Cultural
1987	+.18	−.01	.00	.00	−.11	+.19	−.09	+.26
1988	+.12	+.03	.00	.00	−.14	+.15	−.26	+.38
1990	+.22	−.07	.00	.00	−.07	+.27	−.12	+.49
1992	+.11	+.07	.00	.00	−.13	+.29	−.22	+.41
1993	+.22	+.02	.00	.00	−.28	−.02	−.44	+.34
1994	+.41	+.04	.00	.00	−.06	+.29	−.09	+.49
1997	+.08	+.13	.00	.00	−.15	+.19	−.12	+.18
1999	+.22	−.06	.00	.00	−.22	+.33	−.15	+.40
2002	+.17	−.03	.00	.00	−.12	+.23	−.23	+.44
2007	+.18	+.01	.00	.00	−.17	+.22	−.20	+.20
2009	+.18	−.01	.00	.00	−.11	+.20	−.09	+.26
Average	+.19	+.01	.00	.00	−.14	+.20	−.18	+.34
Median	+.18	+.01	.00	.00	−.13	+.22	−.15	+.38

B. Contributions to Political Values by Presidential Election Year

	Lower-Income		Middle-Income		Upper-Middle		Upper-Income	
	Economic	Cultural	Economic	Cultural	Economic	Cultural	Economic	Cultural
1984	+.15	+.01	.00	.00	-.13	+.17	-.18	+.32
1988	+.17	+.00	.00	.00	-.10	+.28	-.17	+.35
1992	+.22	+.03	.00	.00	-.13	+.29	-.09	+.42
1996	+.15	-.03	.00	.00	-.19	+.26	-.14	+.40
2000	+.17	-.03	.00	.00	-.12	+.23	-.23	+.44
2004	+.18	+.01	.00	.00	-.17	+.22	-.20	+.24
2008	+.18	-.01	.00	.00	-.11	+.20	-.09	+.26
Average	+.17	-.00	.00	.00	-.14	+.21	-.16	+.34
Median	+.17	+.00	.00	.00	-.13	+.23	-.17	+.38

Coefficients are presented for relationships between these four categories of family income and economic or cultural values, with the other
major demographic cleavages—race and ethnicity, religious background,
domestic roles—simultaneously in the model. Such coefficients show distance from the reference category, and thus the contribution to economic
and cultural values, that is purely traceable to being in a given demographic category within a given social cleavage. In the case of income,
this reference category is the middle 30 percent of the income distribution, effectively our "middle class." To understand Table 3.1.A, note that
being in the upper-middle category for the survey of 1987 would have
been sufficient, by itself and without regard to any other social characteristics, to pull an individual to the right of the reference category on economics (in the more-conservative direction) by −.11 and to the left of the
reference category on culture (in the more-liberal direction) by +.19.

Similar, comprehensive year-by-year portraits are available for all other
demographic categories within social cleavages. Yet gathering them by
election year in the manner of Table 3.1.B is always more directly relevant
to the structure of the American political landscape as it affects the voting
analysis to follow. Accordingly, Table 3.1.B does this, while dropping the
single largest outlier (the coefficient farthest from the average) from each
of the columns of Table 3.1.A. Both the 1987 and 1988 surveys ask about
presidential vote in 1984, for example, so they are combined to create the
figures for that year, and so on.[2] Counterparts to Table 3.1.B are what will
be used for the analysis of social cleavages in the rest of this chapter.

The resulting Table 3.1.B tells a strongly patterned and impressively
stable story. Being in the bottom category on the income scale pulls an
individual to the left of the reference category on economic values by an
average of +.17 across surveys and a median of +.17. The middle-income
category is the reference category, at .00, though even this reference role
confirms that middle-income status does not pull its denizens into any
automatic coalition with either poorer or richer counterparts. Being in the
upper-middle category pulls residents in an additionally conservative direction, with an average contribution of −.14 and a median contribution
of −.13. And the upper-income category pulls residents ever so slightly
farther to the right, for an average of −.16 and a median of −.17.

Family income and *cultural* values tell a very different story. On culture, the lower- and middle-income categories are effectively indistin-

guishable. The middle-income category is at .00 by virtue of being the reference category, while being lower-income contributes an average score across all surveys of –.00 and a median of +.00. Accordingly, this cross-class convergence is not the result of simple standardization, though it does create an incipient coalition between lower- and middle-income populations. Being in the upper-middle category then pulls members in a more-liberal direction, with an average contribution of +.21 and a median contribution of +.23. Being upper-income makes residents more liberal yet, with an average of +.34 and a median of +.38. As a result, there is a clear overall division between being lower- or middle-income on one side, versus being upper-middle or upper-income on the other, with that additional increment of cultural liberality among the wealthy.

Overall, then, economic conservatism increases with family income and economic liberalism declines, just as cultural liberalism increases with family income and cultural conservatism declines. Said the other way around, economic and cultural values prime these two great dimensions in opposite ideological directions. Wealthier Americans are more liberal on cultural values and more conservative on economic values, just as poorer Americans are more conservative on cultural values and more liberal on economic values. As we shall see, not all social characteristics share this tendency to prime preferences on the two grand domains in opposite ways. On the other hand, both dimensions do still share an ordinal relationship to income, even as this runs in opposite directions. Yet these ordinal relationships themselves differ additionally, and these differences are also consequential.

In this, economic preferences divide income categories—our social classes—into three distinct pieces: lower-income, middle-income, and upper-middle plus upper-income. Because family income is defined by income shares (30/30/30/10), these three pieces represent rough thirds of society. This economic distribution is then roughly symmetric: poor to the left, middle in the middle, upper-middle and upper to the right. By contrast, culture cuts American society into two great pieces, the more and the less advantaged, with an extra increment for the best-off. The marginals color this distribution of cultural preferences in an additional way that might have strategic implications: 60 percent in the first category, 30 percent in the second, 10 percent in the third. There is nothing symmetric about that.

Across Chapters 6, 7, and 8, a very substantial change—a huge shift—will appear in the relationship between political values and the vote. Here, by contrast, when the focus is only the relationship between political values and demographic backgrounds via family income, the theme is impressive stability. There is little evidence even of fluctuation, much less of change, in the underlying relationship between income and economic or cultural values. What appears in Table 3.1 is instead a neatly ordinal and apparently stable relationship for at least a quarter-century between political values and the categories within this first great indicator of social class.

Educational Attainment

Table 3.2 offers essentially the same analysis, using educational attainment rather than family income as the central indicator of class. Recall, however, that just as valuational relationships to family income were derived in the presence of educational attainment, so valuational relationships to education are likewise derived in the presence of income. In any case, the traditional way to handle this social cleavage involves four discrete categories: high school dropouts, high school graduates, some-colleges, and college graduates. The analysis here begins by following tradition, with high school graduates serving as the reference category, standardized at .00.

Economic values prove to be clearly aligned with this second measure of social class and in the same manner as the first (Table 3.2). Being a high school dropout pulls an individual to the left on economics, with an average contribution of +.25 and a median contribution of +.21. High school graduates sit at .00, by assignment. Being in the some-college category pulls an individual to the right, with an average contribution of –.25 and a median of –.25 as well. And being a college graduate makes almost exactly the same economic contribution, with an average of –.24 and a median of –.26.

This is an overall pattern similar to the one involving family income: economic liberalism rising as one goes down the educational scale, economic conservatism rising as one goes up. Within this pattern, there is again a roughly tripartite division—bottom category (high school dropouts), middle category (high school graduates), and upper-middle plus upper categories (some-colleges and college graduates)—although it is worth

Table 3.2 Social Class and Political Values: Educational Attainment

	High School Dropout		High School Graduate		Some-College		College Graduate	
	Economic	Cultural	Economic	Cultural	Economic	Cultural	Economic	Cultural
1984	+.18	–.18	.00	.00	–.21	+.51	–.17	+.98
1988	+.34	–.25	.00	.00	–.25	+.56	–.24	+.92
1992	+.31	–.32	.00	.00	–.26	+.53	–.17	+.89
1996	+.21	–.26	.00	.00	–.29	+.52	–.26	+.84
2000	+.21	–.15	.00	.00	–.31	+.60	–.32	+1.10
2004	+.18	–.30	.00	.00	–.20	+.34	–.29	+.91
2008	+.35	–.37	.00	.00	–.24	+.52	–.26	+.98
Average	+.25	–.26	.00	.00	–.25	+.51	–.24	+.95
Median	+.21	–.26	.00	.00	–.25	+.52	–.26	+.92

noting that the relationship to education is stronger than the relationship to income even when the focus is economic values.

Cultural values prove to be even more strongly aligned with this second measure of social class. Being in the lowest educational category, as a high school dropout, pulls an individual to the right, with an average contribution of −.26 and a median contribution of −.26 as well. High school graduates stand at .00, again by definition. Being in the next category up, as a some-college, pulls an individual considerably more to the left, with an average contribution of +.51 and a median contribution of +.52. And being a college graduate, the highest educational category, pulls an individual yet farther left, with an average of +.95 and a median of +.92.

This relationship, too, shows a basic parallel to family income. Thus, cultural liberalism rises with movement up the educational ladder, while cultural conservatism rises with movement down, though internal alignment *within* this overall relationship is now different. For family income, there was a basic divide between lower- and higher-income categories, with an extra increment of cultural liberalism at the very top. For educational attainment, all four categories are strung out in an individualized fashion, which suggests that education should have a stronger overall relationship to cultural values than does income—like its stronger relationship to economic values only more so. And indeed, every coefficient for cultural values (comparing Tables 3.1 and 3.2) is higher for education than for income—either more conservative or more liberal, depending on the direction of the effect.

Yet this is a realm where a formal difference in the nature of the two indicators interacts with empirical change to reduce parallelism additionally between family income and educational attainment. Recall that family income is measured through proportions of society, else income would not vary in individual years: nearly everyone in 1984 would be poor, and nearly everyone in 2008 would be rich, even controlling for inflation. The income division in these analyses is thus set by definition at 30/30/30/10. By contrast, educational attainment is measured through discrete categories, which can grow and shrink in the quarter-century between the opening and closing Pew surveys—as in fact they do.

In the earliest of these surveys, the modal category was high school graduates, with society divided roughly 20/40/20/20 across the four traditional categories. Candidates whose cultural positions were not attractive to high school graduates (the 40 percent category) should have faced a problem needing compensation elsewhere. In the most recent surveys, the practical onrush of education has altered the underlying distribution, with society now divided roughly 10/30/30/30. Other things being equal, this must make the valuational preferences of high school dropouts much less consequential. More to the strategic point, it makes the optimal ideological position for a candidate less obvious on cultural issues, since rough thirds of American society are in categories pulling them toward roughly equidistant (and quite distant!) positions.

Yet this still understates the change contributed by the spread of educational attainment in society as a whole, by missing the largest single embodiment of that spread. For this growth in education has not only come mainly at the higher end of the educational continuum; it has come disproportionately at the highest end, among those who attain additional degrees beyond the baccalaureate. These are not college graduates but postgraduates. For presidential elections from 1984 through 1992, it is not possible to isolate these individuals. But for presidential elections from 1996 through 2008, it is possible, and it seems formally desirable, since this is a distinct category of educational attainment that produces a clear change in relationships to both economic and cultural values, a change that pulls educational attainment additionally away from previous parallels with family income.

Table 3.3 shows this, facilitating a further comparison among demographic categories as well as between relationships to economics versus culture. Ideological contributions to both economic and cultural values remain essentially unchanged for the three lower educational categories, the high school dropouts, high school graduates, and some-colleges. But the new category, the postgraduates, diverges notably from the previous top category, the college graduates—who are now shown without these postgraduates inside their number. Both valuational continuums are affected, though the nature of the two effects is additionally (and strikingly) different:

- On economics, being a postgraduate, the top of the educational continuum, conduces toward only modest conservatism, with an average

Table 3.3 Social Class and Political Values: Education Revisited

	High School Dropout		High School Graduate		Some-College		College Graduate		Postgraduate	
	Economic	Cultural	Economic	Cultural	Economic	Cultural	Economic	Cultural	Economic	Cultural
1992	+.41	–.23	.00	.00	–.13	+.62	–.14	+.75	–.02	+1.36
1996	+.35	–.25	.00	.00	–.28	+.53	–.31	+.84	–.25	+1.37
2000	+.21	–.19	.00	.00	–.29	+.65	–.39	+.97	–.11	+1.50
2004	+.18	–.31	.00	.00	–.21	+.39	–.33	+.75	–.26	+1.10
2008	+.36	–.37	.00	.00	–.19	+.58	–.25	+.92	–.20	+1.28
Average	+.30	–.27	.00	.00	–.22	+.55	–.28	+.85	–.17	+1.32
Median	+.35	–.25	.00	.00	–.21	+.58	–.31	+.84	–.20	+1.36

contribution of −.17 and a median contribution of −.20. Yet this pulls the postgraduates not toward the high end of the ideological spectrum, but toward the middle, in effective convergence with the some-colleges.[3] If they are still pulled to the right of the high school dropouts and high school graduates, they are now pulled to the left of the college graduates. Along the way, this recalculation makes being a college graduate a slightly more conservatizing experience on economics, converting them into clearly the most-conservative educational category.

- On culture, by contrast, a postgraduate education makes the most liberalizing contribution of all, with an average of +1.32 and a median of +1.36. Not only is this a larger contribution to cultural liberalism than that of being a college graduate, which now averages +.85 with a median of +.84, but the isolation of these postgraduates simultaneously stretches the cultural continuum in an impressive way. In the process, the some-colleges actually become more like the high school graduates than they are like these postgraduates. This does not make the some-colleges any more conservative than they were before, of course. Yet if a candidate succeeded in pleasing the postgraduates, the some-colleges should now be almost as comfortable with the low end as with the high end of the educational continuum.

In that sense, recognizing the postgraduates as a demographic category makes the strategic environment for politics potentially more complex on both great valuational dimensions. They stretch the ideological spectrum on culture, while they disorder it on economics. Moreover, this growing ideological complexity is only magnified when the analysis attends to the distribution of educational attainment in society as a whole. For now, with the postgraduates as a separate category, that distribution of high school dropouts through postgraduates becomes 10/30/30/20/10. In the process, the median educational category from the old world, the high school graduates, is replaced by the some-colleges as the new median.

Race and Ethnicity

Race and ethnicity bring with them a different kind of cleavage pattern. Social class, whether measured through family income or educational attainment, allowed for an ordinal ranking within its confines by levels of income or education. Race and ethnicity are nominal categories; they do not promise comparative levels of the distinguishing phenomenon, and they thus possess no inherent order. Keeping that in mind, it is important to recall that the difference between racial or ethnic categories here is a difference between collectivities that are identical on all other demographic locaters: on family income, educational attainment, denominational attachment, generic religiosity, sex, and parenthood. Said the other way around, individuals who are identical in every regard *except for* race or ethnicity are what is being compared.

Even working with survey data as extensive as those from the Pew Research Center, the analysis of race and political values must in effect be limited to African Americans. It is not possible, for example, to have reliable figures for Native Americans. Likewise, it is necessary to focus ethnic analysis on Hispanics, though this stricture does have the virtue of capturing the major immigrant category of recent years. Older ethnic categories, as with European Americans of all sorts, are no longer asked for their nationalities in national surveys, while newer categories, as with Asian Americans, even aggregated, are not sufficiently numerous to sustain the same kind of analysis. Nevertheless, the payoff from the major available categories remains high. Race and ethnicity in their main contemporary incarnations turn out to matter a great deal to the shaping of political values, hugely so for economics and consistently so for culture as well.

Race actually leads Black Americans to anchor the economic left in the United States, making an average contribution of +.75 and a median contribution of +.77 (Table 3.4). No other category within any social cleavages comes close to this effect, and—again—this is not because Blacks tend to have lower incomes and lower educational levels. They do have both, but neither is reflected in these figures, which deal only with race. Yet being a Black American does makes it more likely that the respondent is both low-education and low-income in class terms. As we have already seen, a Black American who did not complete high school would add +.28 on average to his or her economic score. If he or she was also low-income, they would add a further +.19 on average, for a total shift away from the national mean—race plus income plus education—of +1.20 on economic values.[4]

Table 3.4   Race/Ethnicity and Political Values

	Race: Black		Ethnicity: Hispanic	
	Economic	Cultural	Economic	Cultural
1984	+.67	−.09	+.25	−.16
1988	+.77	−.19	+.21	−.16
1992	+.85	−.18	+.38	−.17
1996	+.82	−.19	+.31	−.03
2000	+.82	−.10	+.19	−.22
2004	+.55	**	+.17	−.12
2008	**	−.22	+.33	−.03
Average	+.75	−.16	+.25	−.15
Median	+.77	−.18	+.25	−.16

** Outlier score for the entire series

In any case, race in the case of Black Americans also proves to be moderately but consistently conservatizing on cultural values, with an average contribution of −.16 and a median contribution of −.18. While these are not large negative scores in any year, they are never positive, and they are actually to the right of the all income groups. In comparison with the Anglos, the non-Black/non-Hispanic category that is the reference group here, race thus pulls Blacks in a far more liberal direction than these Anglos on economics and a reliably more conservative direction on culture.

A more modest version of the same things can be said about Hispanic Americans, the largest contemporary immigrant group. As with race in the case of Blacks, so with ethnicity in the case of Hispanics: being in this category pulls denizens clearly to the left on economic values, with both an average and a median contribution of +.25. These are nowhere near the comparable Black figures, yet they still draw Hispanics to the left of even the lowest income category. On cultural values, ethnicity instead pulls Hispanics moderately but consistently to the right, with an average of −.15 and a median of −.16. This is essentially equivalent to the result for Blacks, keeping Hispanics moderately to the right of Anglos on culture, clearly to the left of Anglos on economics.

One cannot know from these data whether other immigrant groups, more recent or more distant, would have displayed the same pattern of values at the same point in their assimilation. Clear economic liberalism and modest cultural conservatism do seem appropriate to the generic immigrant experience, but we have no historical data to confirm this perception. On the other hand, there surely have been specific groups at particular points in time for which such expectations would have been different. Conversely, we do know (but cannot profit from the fact) that the Hispanic data miss a large further population of undocumented immigrants, whose values might also in principle be different. All that can be said here is that these latter individuals must be almost entirely missing from the voting analysis to follow.

Religious Background

Denominational Attachment

Religious backgrounds can influence political values in a variety of ways. Theologically, different faiths are organized around different central values. In principle, these can provide means for evaluating arguments in all walks of life, including politics. Yet the historical evolution of these faiths also provides them with specific doctrinal demands and prohibitions. These can have immediate relevance when they happen to be engaged by particular public policies or political conflicts. There can also be an organizational (and not just a theological) link from religious background to political values. In this, different organized faiths, that is, different churches, can communicate specific political choices to their assembled congregants in a process whereby a church hierarchy bypasses the indirect shaping of political values and explicitly translates church positions into economic or cultural preferences.

Table 3.5 presents the coefficients for our first measure of religious background, denominational attachment, in its relationship to political values. Religious denominations are classified into five broad families of theological attachment:

- *Catholics* combine Roman Catholic and Eastern Orthodox branches of attachment to the Catholic Church. This puts back together the split in the original Christian church and is the conventional way of proceeding in the literature on religion and politics.

- *Protestants* are further divided into two main branches, sometimes defined as "Pietistic" and "Liturgical" but more commonly encountered as *Evangelical* and *Mainstream*. This division is accomplished through an item in the Pew surveys asking about a "born-again" experience: *Evangelical Protestants* are born again; *Mainstream Protestants* are not. The latter then become our reference category, creating the zero point on both economics and culture.

- The category *Non-Christians* gathers Jews, miscellaneous other identifiers, and those who answer "none" when asked about denominational affiliation. While this is the most theologically heterogeneous category, its individual pieces do reliably co-vary, not just in their values but also (as we shall see) in their voting behavior, and they are otherwise too small individually to offer stable coefficients in the search for the relationship between social background and political values.

- Finally, we acknowledge the distinctive theology characterizing historically Black churches. Black Mainstream Protestants do not look much different from their White brethren in theological terms, and many Black Mainstreams are members of what were historically White congregations. *Black Evangelicals* may not look all that different in terms of church ritual from *White Evangelicals* either. Yet enough of Black Evangelicalism has been built upon the specifically Black experience that it has moved off from generic evangelicalism theologically, most especially through a greater emphasis on liberation theology and social justice.[5]

Table 3.5 once again tells a strongly patterned story. These social categories, too, matter, albeit considerably more for cultural than for economic values. On economics, Evangelical Protestants are pulled evidently and consistently to the right, with an average contribution from their religious category of −.17 and a median contribution of −.15. While not huge, those scores are sufficient to make them the conservative religious pole on economics. Mainstream Protestants stand modestly to their left, as the reference category at .00. Catholics are pulled modestly left, with an average contribution of +.09 and a median of +.08. Non-Christians are drawn slightly farther left, with an average contribution from Non-Christianity of +.14 and a median of +.13. And Black Evangelicals contribute the far economic left, with an average of +.33 and a median of +.27.

Table 3.5 Religious Background and Political Values: Denominational Attachment

	Evangelical Protestant		Mainstream Protestant		Catholic		Non-Christian		Black Evangelical	
	Economic	Cultural	Economic	Cultural	Economic	Cultural	Economic	Cultural	Economic	Cultural
1984	−.09	−.41	.00	.00	+.22	+.09	+.19	+.46	+.39	**
1988*	−.21	−.54	.00	.00	+.04	+.01	+.13	+.49	+.27	−.40
1992	−.05	−.49	.00	.00	+.10	−.01	+.25	+.46	+.55	−.45
1996	−.15	−.35	.00	.00	+.04	+.13	+.08	+.60	**	−.51
2000	−.15	−.50	.00	.00	+.10	+.11	+.08	+.40	+.00	−.58
2004	−.13	−.44	.00	.00	+.06	+.18	+.12	+.65	+.27	−.63
2008	−.38	−.30	.00	.00	+.08	−.05	+.13	+.60	+.48	−.19
Average	−.17	−.43	.00	.00	+.09	+.07	+.14	+.48	+.33	−.46
Median	−.15	−.44	.00	.00	+.08	+.09	+.13	+.49	+.27	−.45

* There was no question tapping generic religiosity for the 1988 election, so religiosity is not in the model for that year.
** Outlier score for the entire series

On culture, Evangelical Protestants are again drawn conservative—very strongly conservative—with an average contribution from their denominational family of −.43 and a median contribution of −.44. But this time, it is the Non-Christians who anchor the liberal end of the (cultural) continuum, every bit as strongly as their opposite numbers, the Evangelical Protestants, at +.48 for the Non-Christian average and +.49 for the Non-Christian median. And this time, the Black Evangelicals join their White denominational brethren at the far conservative pole, through an average contribution of −.46 and a median of −.45. The Mainstream Protestants, as the reference category (at .00), are a nearly perfect midpoint between these conservative and liberal extremes, but so are the Catholics, with an average contribution from Catholicism of +.07 and a median contribution of +.09. Note that this convergence between Catholics and Mainstream Protestants in the true ideological center cannot be chalked up to the reference status of the latter.

All four of these great religious families exhibit stability in both economic and cultural values across the years for which there are Pew Values surveys, with perhaps the greatest year-by-year fluidity among the (reliably moderate) Catholics. Overall, the spectrum of average economic values by religious denomination is actually as large as that spectrum by educational attainment, and larger than the counterpart spectrum from family income. Economically, this denominational spectrum is otherwise most noteworthy for its very gradual but neatly ordinal arrangement, from Evangelical Protestants to Mainstream Protestants to Catholics to Non-Christians to Black Evangelicals.

Denominational attachments add (or subtract) much more to cultural than to economic values, not only in the sense that the ideologically extreme religious families are much farther apart on culture than on economics, but also in the way that three of these great families—Evangelical Protestants, Black Evangelicals, and Non-Christians—show a much greater internal group effect on cultural than on economic values. On the other hand, this augmented effect of denomination on culture is itself not uniform. Both the Mainstream Protestants, for whom a moderating effect might be argued to be statistically definitional, and the Catholics, for whom it is most clearly not, show a rough equivalence between their internal contribution to economic and culture values.

Generic Religiosity

A different aspect of religious attachment, with a potentially different relationship to economic or cultural values, involves generic *religiosity*.
Where denominational attachment features beliefs and practices within
distinct theological traditions, religiosity is the intensity of religious practice, quite apart from the denomination within which this practice occurs.
Measured here as the regularity of church attendance, generic religiosity is
differentially distributed across the various denominations, with Evangelicals, White or Black, the most regular attendees and Non-Christians the
least regular. This alone would make it necessary to distinguish denomination from religiosity, to be sure that the apparent effect of denominational attachment was not simply due to generic religiosity.

Yet once this is done, the prospect immediately arises for religiosity to
interact with denomination in two very different ways. On the one hand,
the analyst might expect that those who practice their religious faith on a
regular basis would be more likely to absorb the particular values that go
with their denomination. This would make religiosity an extrapolation,
not an alternative, to denominational attachment. On the other hand,
generic religiosity might instead unite those at various levels of religious
commitment *across* denominations. That would make religiosity an alternative principle of religious organization—and an alternative embodiment of the contribution of religious background to political values.

The Pew Values surveys did ask about church attendance in at least one
survey tapping presidential elections for every contest except that of 1988.
Available categories for an answer changed in 1997, going from six to
seven alternatives and mixing them somewhat differently. Yet if we take
the category "once or twice a month," which is asked in that form in all
surveys, and make it the midpoint of any attendance scale, it is possible to
have the same measure in all years when the question was asked. Accordingly, Table 3.6 shows the result of dividing respondents into the religious
(attending almost once a week or more), the marginally religious (attending once or twice a month), and the irreligious (attending a few times a
year or less). Because it is not good practice to take the least frequent response as the reference category, we have given the irreligious the standardized score of .00. The result, while not as powerful as Table 3.5 on

Table 3.6   Religious Background and Political Values: Generic Religiosity

	Religious		Marginally Religious		Irreligious	
	Economic	Cultural	Economic	Cultural	Economic	Cultural
1984	−.18	−.33	−.03	−.18	.00	.00
1992	−.10	−.41	+.03	−.25	.00	.00
1996	−.25	−.46	−.05	−.06	.00	.00
2000	−.12	−.41	−.16	−.04	.00	.00
2004	−.12	−.25	+.02	−.01	.00	.00
2008	−.19	−.26	−.02	−.03	.00	.00
Average	−.16	−.35	−.04	−.10	.00	.00
Median	−.18	−.33	−.05	−.06	.00	.00

denominational attachment, is nonetheless additionally instructive, with a story all its own.

On economics, there is a regular but modest distinction between the *religious* (weekly or more) and the *irreligious* (rarely or never). Religiosity opens up an average gap of .16 and a median gap of .18 between the two demographic categories, with the former more conservative and the latter more liberal. This gap is not always large, but it always appears, and it always appears in the same direction. On average, the middle category (occasionally) falls between these two, though it wanders sufficiently on a year-by-year basis to make this finding less meaningful than others. The main relationship between the extremes, then, is jumbled a bit when the middle category on religiosity is allowed into the analysis, though note that the extremes do comprise more than 85 percent of the sample.

The situation with regard to cultural values is very different. Religiosity opens up an average gap of .35 and a median gap of .33 between the religious and the irreligious, with the former again more conservative and the latter again more liberal. This gap is not as large as the one between Evangelicals and Non-Christians on culture, but it is large in absolute terms. Moreover, for culture, the middle category, *marginal religiosity*, performs as a generic middle should, yielding a contribution to cultural values that always falls between the religious and the irreligious, albeit reliably more like the latter than the former. This is another strongly patterned and highly regular set of relationships between religious background and cultural values.

The two main indicators of religious background thus interact—recall again that each effect exists in the presence of the other—in an especially idiosyncratic way. Religiosity is most conducive to economic and cultural conservatism. Irreligiosity is most conducive to economic and cultural liberalism. Evangelical Protestantism and Non-Christianity work in the same way, with the former driving in the conservative direction on both economics and culture and the latter driving in the liberal direction on both. Yet Mainstream Protestantism plus Catholicism pull their adherents toward the middle ground on both dimensions, with religiosity or irreligiosity then pulling these identifiers additionally right or left. Black Evangelicalism, finally, draws adherents left on economics and right on culture, while religiosity simultaneously pulls them to the right on both.

Note also how different these valuational relationships to the main indicators of religious background are, when compared with the same valuational relationships to the main indicators of social class. For both family income and educational attainment, overall relationships drove in opposite ideological directions: either more liberal on economics and more conservative on culture or more conservative on economics and more liberal on culture. Yet for everyone except the Black Evangelicals, denominational attachment and generic religiosity drive in the *same* ideological direction: either more liberal, more conservative, or more moderate on both economics and culture.

Domestic Roles

Social class, race and ethnicity, and religious background are all classic demographic locaters in social science research. The fourth of the big four, domestic roles, brings with it a myriad of further prospects for shaping political values, though within these, certain bedrock aspects are inescapable. First comes the straightforward sex difference: men versus women. All the Pew surveys are able to track this particular distinction. Next follows perhaps the leading distinction in family structure: whether there are dependent children within the household and thus whether adult respondents are functioning as parents or not. This, too, is available in every Pew Values survey. Age then falls in a category all its own: we group it with this last set of social cleavages purely for convenience.

It is possible that age has a direct relationship to economic or cultural values, by way of life stages or by way of cohort differences. All the Pew surveys allow us to hunt for these. It is also possible that particular age bands, the young or the old in particular, differ in their economic or cultural values. We can easily test this possibility, too. Yet those who use age as a demographic influence also conventionally suspect that a simple year-by-year progression may not capture the relevant effects: the impact of age 90 is not double the impact of age 45, to take a crude example. Thus conventional users often include "age-squared" (age^2) as a second definition of the variable; we follow their lead. Accordingly, Table 3.7 looks at females, with males as the reference category; at parents, with the childless as a reference category; and at age, both in its own right and squared.

Sex does contribute modest but clear differences on both economic and cultural values. Women are regularly pulled toward greater liberalism on economics, with an average score of +.11 and a median of +.13, just as they are regularly pulled toward greater liberalism on culture, with an average of +.18 and a median of +.16. While both differences are modest, they do run in the same direction in every available year. Being modest, they might still be the result of some other, stable, social distinction not in the model. What can be said with certainty is that social class, race and ethnicity, and religious background are definitely in this model; as is that other major aspect of domestic roles, namely parenthood; as is age. At the very least, women are pulled modestly more liberal than men on both economics and culture in the presence of all that.

Parenthood offers a similar story. Having children at home draws parents toward a very modest conservatism on economic values, with an average score of –.08 and a median score of –.10, and having children at home draws parents toward a slightly less modest conservatism on cultural values, with an average of –.18 and a median of –.19. As with sex, so with parenthood: both impacts are modest. Yet they, too, run in the same direction in every year. Under the general rubric of family structure, we also looked at the never-married, the divorced-but-not-remarried, and the widowed, but results were variously undersampled, unstable, or not obviously different from .00. Among these possibilities, then, parenthood remains the most apparently consequential, when the focus is its relationship to political values.

Table 3.7 Domestic Roles and Political Values: Sex, Parenthood, Age, and Age^2

	Female		Parent		Age		Age^2	
	Economic	Cultural	Economic	Cultural	Economic	Cultural	Economic	Cultural
1984	+.12	+.19	−.01	−.15	−.01	−.02	+.00	+.01
1988	+.14	+.20	−.05	−.19	−.01	−.02	+.00	+.01
1992	+.14	+.14	−.10	−.20	−.01	−.02	−.00	+.00
1996	+.13	+.16	−.16	−.14	−.01	−.02	−.01	+.01
2000	+.15	+.07	−.13	−.15	−.00	−.02	−.02	+.03
2004	+.01	+.16	−.02	−.21	+.01	+.01	−.00	−.00
2008	+.05	+.31	−.12	−.22	−.00	−.01	−.00	+.02
Average	+.11	+.18	−.08	−.18	−.00	−.01	−.00	+.01
Median	+.13	+.16	−.10	−.19	−.01	−.02	−.00	+.01

The drama in valuational links to age comes instead from the lack of any relationship to economic or cultural values. For economics, age contributes an average score of $-.00$ and a median of $-.01$. For culture, it contributes an average of $-.01$ and a median of $-.02$. Squaring age offers no evident improvement. For economics, age^2 has both an average and a median score of $-.00$. For culture, it has both an average and a median of $+.01$. We did test two other dichotomies: greater or less than age 65, and greater or less than age 30. Neither showed any sizable and stable relationship to economic or cultural values.

Accordingly, in this fourth great realm of social cleavages, sex has a modest but clear relationship to both valuational dimensions. With men as the reference category, women are drawn modestly toward the more liberal position on both economics and culture. Parenthood, too, has a modest but clear relationship to both economic and cultural values. With households currently lacking dependent children as the reference category, parents are drawn modestly toward the more conservative position on both economics and culture. Age and age^2, finally, add little to the story. There may be life-stage effects on political values; there may be cohort effects on political values—we suspect that there are. But age as a variable in any straightforward sense, running across the full age spectrum or comparing just the top or the bottom against the rest, does not capture these.

Social Backgrounds and Political Values, Revisited

It should come as no surprise that the great social cleavages—social class, race and ethnicity, religious background, and domestic roles—demonstrate, with their familiar demographic categories, powerful influences on incipiently political values. If these are indeed the great demographic locaters of social life, they ought to provide comparable *experiences* for those in similar locations. At the same time, if these are the great demographic locaters, they ought to provide similar *interests* for those with comparable experiences. As indeed they do:

- Social class does so with sufficient power that major alternative aspects of class, such as family income and educational attainment, make their own, partially independent, additive contributions to political values.

- Race and ethnicity do the same, at least for the leading American division on race, Black versus non-Black, and the leading contemporary division on ethnicity, Hispanic versus non-Hispanic.
- Religious background does the same, both for denominational attachment and for generic religiosity, though these alternative aspects of religion make their own, partially independent, *interactive* contributions to political values this time.
- And domestic roles do so, too, both for straightforward sex differences, women versus men, and for bedrock differences in family structure, parents versus non-parents—as ever, with both aspects of these roles in the model simultaneously.

Most of these relationships are straightforward, in the sense that individual categories within grand cleavages can be given an ordinal array, in terms of their varying liberal or conservative contributions to economic and cultural values. Yet note that this masks two very different types of valuational ordering. Social class (as measured by either family income or educational attainment) along with generic religiosity have an inherent metric to their internal categories, from high to low or low to high. By contrast, race and ethnicity, denominational attachment, and domestic roles (as measured by either sex or parenthood) achieve an internal order to their political values in the absence of any obvious ordinal metric to their internal categories.

This does not mean that differences among categories within family income, for example, do not reveal further differences in both economic and cultural values. Nor does it mean that the categories that make up denominational attachments do not have some inherent organizing principle associated with them. It is just that if the rich are more conservative and the poor more liberal on economics—controlling for all other available social characteristics—this is a relationship that appears to follow more or less directly from the natural order of these social categories. Yet if Evangelical Protestants are more conservative and Mainstream Protestants more liberal on economics—again, everything else being equal— this order, too, might still follow from some social principle that is inherent to the two categories. It is just that this principle has no obvious metric from which to derive it: the analyst arrays these categories by their political values, rather than arraying those values by the apparently definitional order of the categories.[6]

Regardless, the picture that these relationships between social backgrounds and political values present for American society as a whole is straightforward but complex, in the sense that none of these demographic contributions to political values are simply subsumed by any of the others. This picture becomes additionally complicated by the fact that some grand cleavages, as with religious backgrounds or domestic roles, are associated with these values in a parallel ideological direction: they push individuals left or right on both economics and culture simultaneously. Meanwhile other, equally grand cleavages, as with social class or race and ethnicity, are associated with these values in *opposite* ideological directions: they push individuals left on one and right on the other. And to top it all off, there are major individual categories within these cleavages—the Black Evangelicals and the Postgraduates spring immediately to mind—that shape political values in additionally idiosyncratic ways.

The implications of these facts for the strategic landscape of American politics are potentially huge, though these cannot be explored directly until Chapters 6, 7, and 8. Here, let it just be noted that whether one underlying cleavage rather than the other is activated in practical politics should have a great deal to do with the political coalitions that emerge. Or, alternatively, the political coalitions that exist should have a great deal to do with what programs can and cannot be put together in the realms of economic and cultural policy. Either way, the strategic imperatives from these facts must be additionally complex when fundamental social cleavages do not align policy preferences in parallel ways. By extension, the strategic landscape of American politics must be substantially different from that of any nation where the underlying social cleavages *do* align values in essentially parallel ways or, more practically, where one or the other of these cleavages has a very different importance to politics than it does in the United States.

Chapter 4 will shift the analysis from *demographic categories* within these grand social cleavages to the *social groups* that are constituted by them, and the distinction is important. Chapter 3 has been concerned with the specific contribution to political values of the major categories within each of these grand cleavages—in the presence of all other categories and thus in the absence of contamination by them. In effect, it has asked, "What is the contribution to economic and political values of being, say, a high school graduate, controlling for every other aspect of social background?" It is impossible to make sense of the links between social backgrounds, political values, and voting behavior without being able to answer that question.

Yet specific categories within these grand cleavages are not—most definitely not—randomly related to each other in any actual society. Racial and ethnic groups are not a random sample of the income distribution in society; income groups are not a random sample of the denominational distribution in society; denominational groups are not a random sample of the racial and ethnic distribution in society; and round and round. As a result, knowing that a postgraduate education conduces toward certain economic and cultural values does not imply that the further contribution to group values among those who are postgraduates will be constituted from a random sample of income, racial and ethnic, or religious characteristics. Rather, precisely because particular categories within a given social cleavage tend disproportionately to tap other categories from other cleavages, the question of the association between social characteristics becomes additionally important for understanding the ideological landscape for electoral politics. This movement from demographic categories to social groups in their relationship to economic and cultural values is the purpose of Chapter 4.

4

Structure and Substance
Social Groups and the Incarnation
of Political Values

The great social cleavages are recognized as such in part because they have proved capable, over the generations, of shaping the political values of those who can be categorized by them. Any analysis of the roots of public preferences must thus begin with these bedrock divisions. Moreover, social class, race and ethnicity, religious background, and domestic roles work in impressively different ways in shaping political values, so that only an approach that can separate them out can hope to tie public preferences back to social backgrounds, before taking these preferences forward to political behavior.

On the one hand, then, it is essential to be able to examine each of these demographic relationships in isolation, one by one, in order to see what each separately is contributing. On the other hand, social cleavages do not actually occur this way. That is to say: any given individual, much less any collective group, is inevitably some mix of social characteristics, and it is this mix—in three distinguishable senses—that really determines the relevance to electoral politics of social backgrounds and their associated political values.

The first of these mixes is effectively automatic, though no less practically important for that. Every individual can (and must) be located on each of these basic background characteristics *simultaneously*. None actually occurs in isolation; every individual is some combination of them all. When the political analyst wants to examine—or the campaign strategist wants to address—female adults with children at home, for example, all such female parents also have a social class, a race and ethnicity, plus a religious background. It is necessary to attend to these latter characteristics in conjunction with the one that is the focus, precisely because they inevitably occur together.

The second sense in which demographic characteristics are inherently blended in their relationships to political values follows more or less naturally from this focus on the individual. When a given characteristic is instead used to define a social group, by which we mean the collectivity of individuals that have this characteristic in common, the same logic applies. The group may be isolated by means of a given social cleavage, or even a specific demographic category within it: high school graduates, Hispanics, Evangelical Protestants, men. But the members of that group simultaneously possess a mix of other social characteristics, and these too will be important in determining the diagnostic values of group members.[1]

This would not matter if most social characteristics were uncorrelated, that is, if they combined in essentially random fashion. But of course they do not. This is true even *inside* the great social cleavages. High-income people, for example, are very likely to be college graduates. Yet college graduates are not reliably high-income. This same nonrandom pattern of association is even truer *across* the great cleavages. Hispanics, for example, are very likely to be Catholics. Yet the modal Catholic is not Hispanic. Needless to say, the presence of both types of groups in American society—some of which have associated characteristics that are highly correlated and others of which feature only general tendencies within the group—adds another layer of complexity to the picture of cleavages and values.

Yet there is a flip side to these same patterns of association, and it contributes the third sense in which social characteristics are inherently blended in their relationship to political values. In this, if every individual and every group contributes some inescapable combination of economic and cultural values, then every valuational mix itself becomes a diagnostic characteristic. Indeed, it is this mix that in some sense contributes—constitutes—the ideological landscape for electoral politics, though to make the matter more complicated and contingent, a precisely measured blend of economic and cultural values contains no guarantee of their comparative weight in shaping political behavior.

Finally, note also that in this third sense—of a mix of values as itself a social characteristic—the internal patterns of interaction for these economic and cultural values can differ even among social groups that show similar overall preferences. That is to say: an identical summary number for two social groups can hide quite different internal distributions, especially when two ideological dimensions are being considered at once, as they must always be when practical politics is the focus. It is really this *joint* distribution of values that constitutes the political landscape. Chapter 4 is devoted to eliciting this landscape, in its full, rich, group-based complexity.

Social Groups by Social Class

Family Income

It is not that a focus on groups and their memberships as opposed to cleavages and their categories produces a fundamentally different picture of the links between social backgrounds and political values. Social cleavages are, after all, achieving their influence within social groups. It is rather that a focus on groups inevitably channels (and in that sense modifies) the apparent impact of cleavages on political values, magnifying some relationships while moderating others. And social class—by which we mean, this time, social *groups* defined by class characteristics—is as good a place as any to observe these changes. Accordingly, Table 4.1 presents the economic and cultural values of the collections of individuals who are variously lower-class, middle-class, upper-middle, and upper-class. Table 4.1.A arrays these results by election year; Table 4.1.B compares average positions by social category *versus* social group for these seven elections.

On economic values, the story derived from a focus on social cleavages (in Chapter 3) is repeated through a focus on social groups, but in a reinforced and expanded fashion. Table 4.1.A attests to the continued stability of relationships between social class and political values, now as seen by

Table 4.1 Family Income and Political Values: Income Categories as Social Groups

A. Contributions to Political Values by Presidential Election Year

	Lower-Income		Middle-Income		Upper-Middle		Upper-Income	
	Economic	Cultural	Economic	Cultural	Economic	Cultural	Economic	Cultural
1984	+.26	-.36	+.00	-.12	-.18	+.25	-.25	+.66
1988	+.35	-.41	+.02	-.22	-.17	+.26	-.31	+.67
1992	+.44	-.28	+.03	-.13	-.19	+.11	-.34	+.66
1996	+.33	-.35	+.08	-.17	-.24	+.32	-.17	+.41
2000	+.35	-.41	+.03	-.17	-.16	+.30	-.31	+.67
2004	+.33	-.35	+.01	-.03	-.23	+.43	-.26	+.49
2008	+.46	-.44	+.01	-.01	-.34	+.43	-.11	+.45
Average	+.36	-.37	+.03	-.12	-.22	+.30	-.25	+.57
Median	+.35	-.36	+.02	-.13	-.19	+.30	-.26	+.66

B. Contributions to Political Values for Demographic Categories *versus* Social Groups

	Lower-Income		Middle-Income		Upper-Middle		Upper-Income	
	Economic	Cultural	Economic	Cultural	Economic	Cultural	Economic	Cultural
Category	+.17	+.00	.00	.00	-.14	+.21	-.16	+.36
Group	+.36	-.37	+.03	-.12	-.22	+.30	-.25	+.57

Note: Table entries are average scores for the elections of 1984–2008 unless otherwise noted.

way of social groups: low-income on the left, upper-income on the right, upper-middle aligned closely with upper-income, and middle-income positioned neatly in the middle. Yet Table 4.1.B demonstrates the *ideological expansion* accompanying this shift of analytic focus. The low-income group moves clearly leftward in its economic values. The high-income group moves rightward, accompanied by the upper-middle group. And the middle-income group still sits resolutely in the middle, between the rich and the poor, though note that this is no longer the product of its being a reference category but results instead from the way that members sample other social categories.

While this is the same overall relationship between political values and social groups as it was between political values and demographic categories, the valuational continuum—the spread of those values from the most liberal to the most conservative—is now much wider, roughly double what it was when social cleavages in isolation were the focus. It is of course the demographic characteristics associated with group membership that explains this expansion. For example, low-income groups are more likely to be low education, and to be Black or Hispanic. High-income groups are more likely to be high education, and to be White non-Hispanic (Anglo).[2]

The coalitional picture derived from this array of economic values by income group likewise remains similar to the coalitional picture derived from economic values arrayed by income category: low-income versus middle-income versus upper-middle plus upper-income. Tilt sufficiently to the right, and the middle-income group becomes aligned with their lower-income counterparts; tilt sufficiently to the left, and the opposite occurs. Yet now, the augmented distance *between* social groups must increase the likelihood that victory or defeat, to the extent that it was tied to policy promises, would turn on the decisions of (and divisions within) the middle-income group, our middle class, at least when family income was relevant to voting behavior.

On cultural values, the story is similar: social groups foster an expansion of the ideological continuum among members isolated by family income (Table 4.1.B). In this, the low-income group moves the most, thereby contributing the most to this expansive effect. Its members stand out as clearly conservative on cultural values, rather than sitting at the same place as middle-income members. In turn, the latter now appear as evident but moderate cultural conservatives. They too move rightward in this analytic shift, just not as much. The upper-middle group remains clearly liberal on culture, becoming only more so in the shift from a focus on demographic categories to a focus on social groups. On its own terms, this is a moderate leftward shift, like the moderate rightward shift in the middle-income group. Yet the result is a doubling of the previous distance between middle-income and upper-middle. The upper-income group then moves additionally leftward, thereby anchoring the left on culture in newly extreme territory.

It is again the other social characteristics associated with being in one or another income group that pull members additionally away from the ideological center.[3] And again, there are coalitional implications to this newly refined valuational landscape. Family income as a social cleavage featured an implicit cultural coalition that pitted lower-income and middle-income Americans against upper-middle plus upper-income counterparts, where the cultural right was numerically dominant. Yet this alignment becomes more complex when family income becomes the delineator of social groups. It is not only that every group has pulled farther away from the center with this shift of focus; every group has also pulled farther away from every other group. Moreover, the specific values associated with group membership now paint a noticeably amended picture. Seen by way of social cleavages, the conservative side of this cultural coalition looked very moderate; it was the liberal side that tailed away to the left. Seen by way of social groups, however, the lower-income group can be seen to be clearly conservative and the middle-income group moderately so, at the same time as the upper-income group tails even more solidly off to the left.

Two characteristics of this picture of social groups delineated by family income will prove to be generalizable to all of the other cleavages and groups considered here. Together, they permit a more condensed presentation of the data behind these individual group portraits. In the first, as Table 4.1.A suggests, there is an impressive stability to the link between political values and group membership, as there was between political values and demographic categories. And in the second, as Table 4.1.B suggests, the key message about the shift from a focus on demographic categories to a focus on social groups is best isolated—precisely because the year-by-year figures are impressively stable—by comparing category versus group means on economic and political values for this time period as a whole, the quarter-century bracketed by the elections of 1984 and 2008. The remainder of this chapter will thus focus on these comparative means.

Educational Attainment

With that said, family income is only one aspect of social class, albeit a major one. Educational attainment is another, with its own long history of political impact. It too is easily tapped by the Pew surveys. From one side, these two key aspects of social class should not be radically at variance in terms of their impact on political values. Yet from the other side, income and education are not the *same* social characteristic, even in the abstract, so that the presence of one should not eliminate the impact of the other—and did not do so when social class was approached through the demographic categories for family income and educational attainment in Chapter 3. They will likewise prove to be not the same when treated as bases for distinguishing social groups in Chapter 4.

On economic values, the shift from social *cleavage* to social *group* by educational attainment makes the bottom group, the high school dropouts, strongly liberal, moving it off to the left in a fashion that is not echoed in the other direction by the top group, the college graduates, who look much as they did before (Table 4.2). The some-colleges remain conservative but look less so with this shift in focus, while the high school graduates now appear as clearly but modestly liberal. On the one hand, this is a neater ordering for the impact of educational attainment on economic values, since the top group, the college graduates, now occupies the clear economic right. On the other hand, the major change is within the bottom group, the high school dropouts, who move sharply to the left, a bigger shift than with any other educational group.

This shift from social cleavage to social group works in an additionally different fashion for education as compared with income. With groups delineated by family income, the bottom group was strongly liberal, the middle-income group was truly in the middle, and the top group was joined by the upper-middle as clearly conservative. With groups delineated by educational attainment, all four groups are instead strung out across the economic spectrum, with an extra increment of economic liberalism for

Table 4.2   Educational Attainment and Political Values:
              Educational Categories as Social Groups

	High School Dropout	
	Economic	Cultural
Category	+.25	−.26
Group	+.48	−.83

	High School Graduate	
	Economic	Cultural
Category	.00	.00
Group	+.13	−.42

	Some College	
	Economic	Cultural
Category	−.25	+.51
Group	−.13	+.17

	College Graduate	
	Economic	Cultural
Category	−.24	+.95
Group	−.22	+.68

the high school dropouts. For education, this produces a strategic landscape for electoral politics that is both more complex than the one identified by demographic categories examined in isolation and more complex than the counterpart group alignment for family income.

On cultural values, the shift from social cleavage to social group as delineated by educational attainment moves every group in a more conservative direction. The biggest movement again occurs among the high school dropouts. Though note that the result is now *two* culturally extreme groups, these high school dropouts on the right and the college graduates on the left. High school graduates stand revealed as being strongly conservative, courtesy of being more likely to be lower-income, to be racial or ethnic minorities, and to be Protestant Evangelicals, White or Black. The some-colleges are clearly but only modestly liberal, being somewhat less likely to be all those other demographic things. In the process, the cultural spectrum, like the economic spectrum, is stretched by re-immersing educational attainment in it full social context.

As with family income, so with educational attainment, then: the other background characteristics associated with education are creating a noticeably different picture of the ideological landscape for electoral conflict. Judged through demographic categories, the high school dropouts and high school graduates appeared likely to make common cause on cultural values, so that the strategic question was whether the some-colleges would join a countervailing coalition with the college graduates or whether they would instead serve as the fulcrum for electoral conflict. Judged through social groups however, the four educational groups are now arrayed along the ideological continuum at roughly equal distances. Coalitional possibilities are thus sharply increased, for an array that brings with it no inherently obvious resolution.

Where educational attainment was most different from family income in Chapter 3 was in its shifting composition within society over time. While part of this was definitional—income was examined through proportionate shares, education through discrete categories—educational growth actually shifted not only total membership in these categories but also the appropriate nature of the categories themselves. In turn, this change had both direct effects—by virtue of the explosive growth of a new category, the postgraduates—and indirect effects, through changing marginals that affect the entire indicator. In Chapter 3, this growth exaggerated the dispersion of ideological contributions to political values from educational categories, with the postgraduates introducing a new left on culture while breaking up the old alignment on economics.

Yet when the postgraduates are given their full set of associated characteristics as a comprehensive social group, with the college graduates simultaneously adjusted to remove postgraduates from their ranks, both of these effects disappear (Table 4.3). That is to say: the postgraduates move to the position on economics that an ordinal ranking by educational attainment would suggest: they stand revealed as the most economically conservative educational group. At the same time, the apparent difference of these postgraduates from the college graduates on culture, marking them off as far more liberal, shrinks to the vanishing point. There is no serious cultural distinction remaining between the two high-education groups.

Table 4.3   Social Groups and Political Values: Education Revisited

| | High School Dropout | |
	Economic	Cultural
Category	+.33	−.27
Group	+.52	−.84

| | High School Graduate | |
	Economic	Cultural
Category	.00	.00
Group	+.15	−.46

| | Some College | |
	Economic	Cultural
Category	−.22	+.55
Group	−.11	+.10

| | College Graduate | |
	Economic	Cultural
Category	−.28	+.85
Group	−.18	+.62

| | Postgraduate | |
	Economic	Cultural
Category	−.17	+1.32
Group	−.25	+.64

On economic values, the postgraduates—unlike every other social group delineated by education—move in the ideologically conservative direction when their income, race and ethnicity, and religious background are added to the picture. Indeed, they move sufficiently rightward to anchor the conservative economic pole among educational groups. The high school dropouts still anchor the ideological left, even more so. The high school graduates stand revealed as modestly liberal on economics and the some-colleges as modestly conservative. And the college graduates are now modestly to their right, flanked only (and likewise modestly) by the postgraduates. The ideological spectrum for educational attainment is thus neat and orderly, with an extra increment of liberalism for the high school dropouts.

On cultural values, allowing the postgraduates to have their full array of social characteristics—once more, postgraduates as social group rather than as demographic category—causes everything to look different. The postgraduates remain the far cultural left, but only trivially; they are essentially indistinguishable from the college graduates. The some-colleges remain marginally liberal on culture, but they are now nearly as close to the high school graduates as they are to the college graduates. These high school graduates are now solidly conservative. And the high school dropouts still anchor the cultural right, more—far more—than they previously appeared to do.

Accordingly, if the individuals who inhabit these educational categories need to be addressed in their full social contexts—if it were not possible, as it normally is not, to address them purely as educational products, such that they could be convinced to ignore their income, their race, their religion, and such—then the addition of the postgraduate category (as well as the adjustment it creates in the college graduate category) is of relatively little consequence. Where the postgraduates initially looked more liberal than the college graduates (not to mention the some-colleges) on economic values, they now stand revealed as more conservative, which education as an indicator of social class would predict. Where once these postgraduates seemed much more liberal than the college graduates on cultural values, they now appear essentially indistinguishable.

Social Groups by Race and Ethnicity

As with social class, so with race and ethnicity: the story derived from a focus on social cleavages in Chapter 3 is roughly recapitulated by a focus on social groups instead. Blacks still look extremely and Hispanics solidly liberal on economics. Blacks still look clearly and Hispanics modestly conservative on culture. The shift in analytic focus does take both groups farther to the left on economics, a change that is somewhat more consequential for Hispanics than for Blacks. On the other hand, embedding political values in the social groups that actually embody them now distinguishes Blacks from Hispanics on culture: the two racial/ethnic categories do not move similarly when transformed into social groups. As a result, some of the previous relationships between social class and race/ethnicity are modified—altered—as well.

Little is changed on economics by considering Black or Hispanic Americans as social groups, rather than as demographic categories within a social cleavage (Table 4.4). Both look additionally liberal in their economic values. Sharing a roughly similar profile on social class—being weighted strongly toward the bottom on both family income and educational attainment—they should both move left with the shift of focus from social cleavage to social group. Both do. Compared with each other, Blacks are slightly advantaged on education while Hispanics are slightly advantaged on income, so that there is little to encourage further distinction, and none in fact occurs. However, the proportionate increase is greater for Hispanics in this shift from demographic category to social group.

On culture, the two groups then diverge modestly. Hispanics look essentially as they did before, while Blacks look additionally conservative. Social class, through both income and education, helps to hold both groups on the cultural right. But religious background distinguishes them. Being disproportionately Evangelical, Blacks are drawn additionally to the right on culture. Being overwhelmingly Catholic, Hispanics are instead pulled modestly to the left. Year after year, then, Black Americans remain extremely liberal on economics and consistently conservative on culture, while Hispanic Americans remain reliably liberal on economics and waveringly conservative on culture (Table 4.4).

Table 4.4   Race, Ethnicity, and Political Values:
Racial and Ethnic Categories as Social Groups

| | Race: Black | |
	Economic	Cultural
Category	+.75	−.16
Group	+.82	−.30

| | Ethnicity: Hispanic | |
	Economic	Cultural
Category	+.25	−.15
Group	+.32	−.12

If the comparison is instead between social groups from the domain of race and ethnicity versus groups delineated by social class, a number of simple, further distinctions stand out. Blacks as a social group end up well to the economic left of the bottom category on either family income or educational attainment, while Hispanics lie over *toward* those two bottoms categories, but are not quite as liberal as either. In turn, Blacks as a social group remain well over to the cultural right, though not as far over as the bottom categories on either measure of social class, while Hispanics, albeit remaining modestly conservative, are now in the center of the continuum of income or educational groups.

Social Groups by Religious Background

Denominational Attachment

With a shift of analytic focus from the relationship between social *cleavages* and political values to the relationship between social *groups* and those values, the picture looks different yet again when examined through religious background. Denominational attachment samples the previous demographic cleavages, social class and race/ethnicity, in a manner that distinguishes the great religious families more or less idiosyncratically, rather than imparting a simple expansion (or contraction) of the ideological spectrum, while generic religiosity actually samples those cleavages in such a way as to shrink this spectrum. Denominational attachment thus makes the strategic challenges of electoral politics more complex by making them more specifically group-based, while generic religiosity makes these challenges a bit less daunting overall.

On economics, the five great religious families still stand in the same ideological order through the lens of social groups as they did (in Chapter 3) through the lens of demographic categories (Table 4.5). Right to left, they remain: Evangelical Protestants, Mainstream Protestants, Catholics, Non-Christians, and Black Evangelicals. On the other hand, the four majority-White families all look slightly more conservative when portrayed this way. Thus, while Evangelical Protestants still anchor the economic right, Mainstream Protestants now look modestly conservative, Catholics are even more modestly liberal, and Non-Christians are the slightest bit more liberal yet. Black Evangelicals then anchor the economic left—and it is the

Table 4.5 Religious Denomination and Political Values:
The Great Religious Families as Social Groups

	Evangelical Protestants	
	Economic	Cultural
Category	−.17	−.43
Group	−.23	−.61

	Mainstream Protestants	
	Economic	Cultural
Category	.00	.00
Group	−.14	+.13

	Catholics	
	Economic	Cultural
Category	+.09	+.07
Group	+.06	+.11

	Non-Christians	
	Economic	Cultural
Category	+.14	+.48
Group	+.09	+.77

	Black Evangelicals	
	Economic	Cultural
Category	+.33	−.46
Group	+.85	−.66

far left—being farther from the next-most-liberal group, the Non-Christians, than those Non-Christians are from the Evangelical Protestants at the other pole.

Being disproportionately lower income, disproportionately lower education, and, of course, disproportionately Black, Black Evangelicals do move much farther left in the transition from demographic category to social group. Indeed, the huge difference in political values by category versus group for Black Evangelicalism is essentially the reason why the other four religious families appear to move modestly to the right with this change of focus. Without Black Evangelicals in the picture, the ideological spectrum for economic values, running from Evangelical Protestants through Non-Christians, is actually no broader for social groups than for demographic categories. With Black Evangelicals in the picture, the ideological spectrum is effectively doubled by the same analytic shift.

On culture, the ideological extremes for denominational groups remain as they were for demographic categories, with the Evangelicals, Black and White, anchoring the cultural right and the Non-Christians holding down the cultural left. Catholics and Mainstream Protestants do swap their order, but since they remain clustered at the center (and far away from both extremes), this swap seems inconsequential. On the other hand, the extremes move substantially farther out in this analytic shift—rightward for both Evangelical families, leftward for the Non-Christians—which makes the Catholics and Mainstream Protestants farther away from both ends of the ideological continuum.

This time, however, the Black Evangelicals do nothing that requires specific comment about any further exception. On culture, they were essentially indistinguishable from Evangelical Protestants—that is, White Evangelicals—when the focus was demographic categories. They remain essentially indistinguishable when the focus is social groups. In this, the same associated social characteristics that moved them sharply leftward on economics, namely lower income, lower education, and racial minority status—augmented, as we shall see, by generic religiosity—move them consistently rightward on culture. They are thus always by themselves on the far economic left and always joined with Evangelical Protestants on the far cultural right.

To say the same thing differently: Evangelical Protestants, both White and Black, anchor the conservative end of the ideological spectrum on culture. Both groups are similarly conservative, and both are *very* conservative. Yet they part ways on economics, where they anchor the opposite ends of the ideological spectrum: Evangelical Protestants to the right, Black Evangelicals to the left. There is little to separate the Catholics and Non-Christians on economics, where both are modestly liberal, in contrast to the Mainstream Protestants who are modestly conservative. And there is little to separate the Catholics and Mainstream Protestants on culture, where both are modestly liberal, in contrast to the Non-Christians who are extremely so.

Generic Religiosity

Generic religiosity then offers the first group embodiment of a grand social cleavage that actually shrinks the ideological spectrum in the process
of being translated from an abstract demographic category into a concrete
social group. Because methodological considerations dictated using an
ideologically extreme rather than an ideologically central category as the
reference group when religiosity was considered in isolation (in Chapter 3),
it is necessary to shift and assign the central category a score of .00 on
both economics and culture, in order to be able to compare the three demographic categories with their counterpart social groups—and hence to
be able to see this shrinkage. Yet this transformation is easily accomplished, and Table 4.6, for the social groups created by the devotional
categories in our scale of religiosity, is the result.

On economics, the highly religious, the marginally religious, and the
evidently irreligious now cluster near zero (Table 4.6). Social groups delineated by religiosity thus contribute next to nothing to economic values.
Said the other way around, the resulting scores are both tiny and have no
ordinal relationship that can be linked to religiosity. On culture, the marginally religious and the irreligious continue to reside where they did
when examined through religiosity in isolation, while the previously more
extreme category of high religiosity creates a social group that moves away
from the conservative pole and toward the ideological center (Table 4.6).
The propensity of religiosity to sample both indicators of social class in a
roughly equivalent way has much to do with this lack of any great movement, even on culture.

Table 4.6   Generic Religiosity and Political Values:
            Devotional Categories as Social Groups

	Religious		Marginally Religious		Irreligious	
	Economic	Cultural	Economic	Cultural	Economic	Cultural
Category*	−.12	−.25	+.00	+.00	+.04	+.10
Group	−.06	−.19	+.04	+.01	+.02	+.12

*Scores adjusted to put the centrist category in the middle.

On economics, then, there remains no serious difference (nor even any obvious order) among the three categories of religiosity when they are converted into social groups. What looked to contain some modest strategic options and possibilities when analyzed as demographic categories loses that potential when translated into social groups. On culture, by contrast, the religious remain more conservative, the irreligious more liberal, with the marginally religious still in the middle, which appears to mean that when religiosity itself has something to contribute to the potential coalitions of electoral politics, it must come by way of culture and not economics.

In truth, the same could be said of the two extreme groups by denominational attachment, the Evangelical Protestants and the Non-Christians: a much stronger relationship to culture than to economics, and thus presumably more strategic leverage over these denominational groups by way of cultural rather than economic policy, though economics is not irrelevant to either. Yet the parallels then break down, and in two ways. First, the Black Evangelicals, despite their extreme cultural conservatism, must still be described the other way around, as having an even stronger relationship to economic values. And second, the Mainstream Protestants and Catholics must be seen as different yet again. While they are united in being comparatively moderate—centrist—on both economics and culture, they are actually converging on culture but diverging on economics in the course of a shift from demographic category to social group.

Social Groups by Domestic Role

Domestic roles as a principle of social division tell yet a different story from all of the preceding. When sex and parenthood, the main available indicators here, are used to create two vast pairs of social groups rather than to isolate the specific impact of demographic categories, the apparent contribution of the latter to political values disappears entirely. By category, Chapter 3 showed women to be modestly more liberal than men on both economic and cultural values, with parents modestly more conservative than non-parents on the same two dimensions. By social group, Chapter 4 introduces four collectivities that, with one modest exception, just collapse to the midpoint on both ideological dimensions.

Women remain a bit more liberal than men on economics—or men a bit more conservative, in what is only a two-group comparison—and this difference, though modest, does appear to be stable (Table 4.7). In the full catalog of economic scores by presidential election (table not shown), women are left of men and men right of women in every election year. On the other hand, the previous difference on culture falls away entirely. As a result, the more impressive cultural liberalism apparent when women are treated as a social category is simply gone when they are analyzed as a social group, while the more modest economic liberalism apparent from their treatment as a social category is further reduced.

The situation is even more stark with parenthood, where the average difference on both economics *and* culture is now effectively zero for parents versus non-parents (Table 4.7). Worse yet, the full catalog of cultural scores by presidential year (table not shown) would confirm that this tiny difference has become wobbly. It is more often positive than negative for both economic and cultural values, but it can be negative in individual years. Accordingly, both the stronger cultural conservatism that appeared when parents were treated as a demographic category and the more modest economic conservatism that was at least consistently present disappear when parents are treated as a social group.

Both pairs of groups, women versus men and parents versus non-parents, are vast. Women contributed about 51 percent of the total sample for the Pew surveys; parents contributed about 39 percent. Apparently, the associated sampling of the other main social indicators (for class, race/ethnicity, and religion) is nearly sufficient to eliminate modest prior differences on economic and cultural values, completely so in the case of culture, nearly so with economics. It is not statistically impossible for groups this large to move off from the national average, if they sample other social character-

Table 4.7 Domestic Roles and Political Values: Social Groups by Sex and Parenthood

	Female		Parent	
	Economic	Cultural	Economic	Cultural
Category	+.11	+.18	−.08	−.18
Group	+.07	+.01	+.01	+.01

istics distinctively and if these distinctions cumulate. In the case of these two groups, they obviously do not.

On the other hand, what appears as a reduction (indeed, a disappearance) of substantive findings in the case of both groups is a fact with practical implications not only for group behavior but also for strategic approaches to political conflict. In this, strategies premised on the modest but real contribution to economic and cultural values of female or male identity, as well as parental or non-parental status, immediately run up against a situation in which actual females and males, as well as actual parents and non-parents, can be expected to have associated characteristics that defuse the impact of such strategies. The real people in these social groups are not in the positions suggested by the demographic categories used to delineate them.

Social Groups and Political Values, Revisited

The analytic shift from a focus on demographic cleavages to a focus on social groups is a crucial step in the move from social backgrounds through political values to voting behavior. A focus on demographic cleavages remains the essential first step in understanding the translation of social background into political values. That is to say: the categories within these cleavages, categories of social class, race and ethnicity, religious background, and domestic roles, must first be understood in isolation, so that their impact is not contaminated by categories from the other grand cleavages, categories that are always present in any composite human being. Yet once the impact of these demographic categories is understood in isolation, it is essential to move past them, by reimmersing them in the social groups they constitute—and within which they actually reside.

In this next analytic step, no individual fails to be a mix of social backgrounds on all four of the great principles of social division used here, and each background aspect has implications for that person's political values. As a result, social groups, too, are necessarily a mix of influences from the specific category that is used to define the group plus the other social categories that every member of the group brings with them in their very persons. Seen the other way around, the valuational patterns that result— the combinations of economic and cultural values that characterize these social groups—are themselves always a mix. If every individual and every group has positions on both economics and culture simultaneously, then the product must perforce be some *joint* distribution of those preferences.

Describing a social group by its mean scores on economic and cultural values goes a long way toward providing its ideological profile, and thus a long way toward establishing the ideological landscape on which electoral conflict occurs. Tables 4.1–4.7 have done this for the major social groups in American society, as derived from the major demographic cleavages that have traditionally been used to address political conflict. Taken together, those tables attest to huge variation in the ideological profiles characterizing these groups, and this variation needs to be brought back together in summary pictures here. But before that, it is worth resurveying the simple (and likewise highly varied) differences among these principles of social division that were uncovered in the process of moving from demographic cleavages to social groups.

When social class is the focus, this analytic move actually expands the ideological spectrum. Because many (though not all) demographic cleavages are cumulative in their relationship to social class, class *groups* stand even farther apart on economic and cultural values than they appeared to do when class *categories* were examined in isolation. Thus the rich and the poor are not only more likely to be more and less educated respectively—they are also likely to have different racial/ethnic and religious backgrounds. Family income testifies to this effect in a very straightforward way, as every income group moves farther from the ideological center on both economics and culture, either farther left or farther right, when income is examined not in isolation but as a means of delineating income groups (Table 4.1).

The same can be said of educational attainment. It, too, stretches the ideological spectrum for political conflict (Table 4.2). Yet the analytic difference between a demographic cleavage and a social group becomes additionally important for education, in a way that it did not for income, because the growth sector of educational attainment behaves so very differently under the two analytic approaches. This growth sector, the postgraduates, is the middle category on economics and the far left on culture when examined in isolation, as a demographic category. But it becomes the far right on economics, while collapsing back to an essential unity with the college graduates on culture, when it is instead used to distinguish a social group (Table 4.3).

On the other hand, the same analytic move shrinks the ideological spectrum when domestic roles are the focus. Seen as demographic categories, in isolation, sex and parenthood create modest but consistent valuational differences. Women are more liberal than men (and/or men more conservative than women) on both economics and culture when the issue is what sex alone contributes to political values, just as parents are more conservative than non-parents (and/or non-parents more liberal than parents) on both economics and culture when the issue is what parenthood in isolation contributes to political values. But once these demographic categories are used instead to create social *groups*, asking about the economic and cultural values of women and men or parents and non-parents as a collectivity, these modest differences collapse (Table 4.7).

Religious background tells yet a different story. Both indicators of religious background do sustain a crude version of the original relationships, derived by considering denominational attachment and generic religiosity in isolation, when these indicators are used instead to create social groups. Yet the groups defined by denomination look increasingly idiosyncratic under this treatment (Table 4.5), while the groups defined by religiosity contract the ideological spectrum sharply for economics, though not for culture (Table 4.6). The one place in either indicator where something more noteworthy occurs is with Black Evangelicalism, the fifth great religious family in American society. When Black Evangelicals are considered, not in demographic isolation but as a social group, they prove to be far more liberal on economics and considerably more conservative on culture than an initial demographic measure would suggest.

Race and ethnicity, finally, are different yet again. The main racial and ethnic divides in American society, involving Black and Hispanic Americans respectively, are similar to each other (and distinct from non-Hispanic Whites) when analyzed as demographic categories, pulling strongly liberal on economics and mildly conservative on culture. Yet considered as fully developed social groups, immersed in the real sample of demographic backgrounds that race and ethnicity as categories bring with them on the group landscape, they cohere in part and diverge in part. In the obvious continued coherence, both move left in their economic values. But in a previously hidden difference, Blacks become considerably more conservative in their cultural values while Hispanics do not, thereby changing their relationship not only to each other, but also to groups defined by class or religion (Table 4.4).

Social Groups and Ideological Profiles

Both sets of analyses, from demographic cleavages and social groups, suggest a society with a wide diversity of views, not only on the individual dimensions created by economics and culture but also on the resulting combinations of the two. In the crudest sense, albeit one in which this diversity already shines through, it is worth noting that different principles of social division continue to put economic and cultural values together in different—indeed, increasingly different—ways, when the analytic focus shifts from individual categories to collective groups:

- Family income, for example, puts them together in *opposite* ideological ways. Those higher up the income scale are more conservative on economics and more liberal on culture, just as those lower down the income scale are more liberal on economics and more conservative on culture.
- By contrast, denominational attachment puts these values together in *parallel* ways. The most theologically fundamentalist are conservative on both, the least theologically fundamentalist are liberal on both, and the theologically in-between are moderate on both—though the great exception remains those Black Evangelicals, who are very liberal on economics and very conservative on culture.
- What domestic roles do with social groups as a focus, which is once again different in kind, is to bring all groups not just toward the ideological center but to the point of overwhelming (and indistinguishable) moderation.
- Finally and conversely, what the two main racial and ethnic groups do is to insist on idiosyncrasy, that is, to effects specific to the group, rather than offering any general move in opposite, parallel, or middling directions.

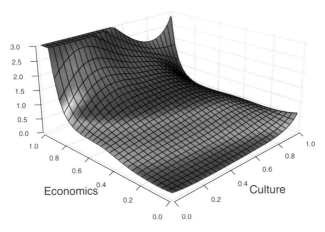

Figure 4.1 The Political Landscape, 1984: Joint Distribution of Attitudes
for Black Americans

Even this, however, does not fully capture—because it does not fully
picture—the complexity of the ideological landscape fostered by social
groups through their political values. Much of this complexity will be unpacked through systematic analysis of the relationship between political
values and voting behavior *within* social groups, especially in Chapters 6
and 8. Yet, in part because the social heterogeneity of the resulting ideological landscape is so central to the strategic possibilities that follow from
it, but also in part because mean scores on economic and cultural values
for disparate social groups can still mask substantial diversity around these
means, it seems worth closing Chapter 4 with a small set of examples—
ideological pictures—of the distribution of political values inside selected
groups.

Figure 4.1 and all subsequent figures in this chapter use the very first
Pew Values survey, the one whose detailed analysis will be the center-
piece of Chapter 6. Recall, however, that the tables in Chapters 3 and 4
have confirmed that there was very little change in the relationship between economic and cultural values by social group across the entire
span of Pew surveys. But note that this implies neither that social groups
retain the same internal priority for economic versus cultural values in
the voting behavior of their members, nor that the members of these
groups connect up their remarkably stable value patterns to the two political parties in the same way across time. Chapters 7 and 8 will confirm

that neither of these static possibilities is characteristic of American politics.

In any case, Figure 4.1 offers the joint distribution of economic and cultural values for a social group that is much more powerfully colored by one of the two main dimensions of opinion. That group is Black Americans, and its critical organizing dimension is economics. This is a group whose internal ideological landscape rises sharply from economic conservatism to economic liberalism, such that the vast bulk of the group is concentrated on the economic left. There is some further terrain contributed by culture, where this same internal landscape rises modestly but reliably from the cultural left to the cultural right at every level of economic liberalism or conservatism. Yet it is economic liberalism that contributes the dominant character of this group-based ideological map.

Figure 4.2 offers another social group whose joint distribution of economic and cultural values is more powerfully colored by one of the two main dimensions of opinion. But this time, the group is a religious and not a racial one, the Non-Christians, and this time, the critical dimension is culture and not economics. These Non-Christians feature an internal ideological landscape that rises sharply from cultural conservatism to cultural liberalism, such that the obvious bulk of the group is well left of the cultural midpoint in American society. In their case, there is some

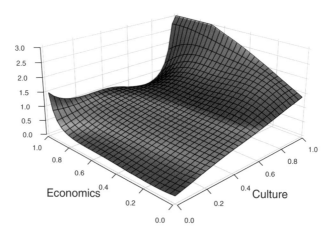

Figure 4.2   The Political Landscape, 1984: Joint Distribution of Attitudes for Non-Christians

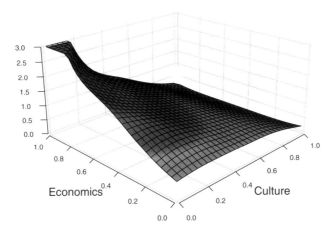

Figure 4.3 The Political Landscape, 1984: Joint Distribution of Attitudes for High School Dropouts

further terrain contributed by economics, as this same internal landscape rises modestly from the economic right to the economic left, again at every level of cultural liberalism or conservatism. Yet it is cultural liberalism this time that contributes the dominant character of this group-based ideological map.

Figure 4.3 contributes a very different kind of ideological profile, where both valuational domains contribute seriously to defining the internal landscape characterizing the group. The social group in question is high school dropouts, the bottom educational category, who become more and more prominent—they contribute more and more of the ideological terrain—as the focus moves from economic conservatism to economic liberalism and from cultural liberalism to economic conservatism simultaneously. As an overall description, this was true of Black Americans as well. Yet the resulting pictures are very different, courtesy of the much greater power of cultural values to describe the high school dropouts as a social group. As a result, they cluster much more in one corner of the ideological landscape, residing very disproportionately at the joint extremes of economic liberalism and cultural conservatism.

The Evangelical Protestants offer the same sort of profile, in the sense of rising or falling neatly on both valuational dimensions and of ending up concentrated in one corner of the ideological landscape (Figure 4.4). Yet they are hugely different on the specifics, while they come with an

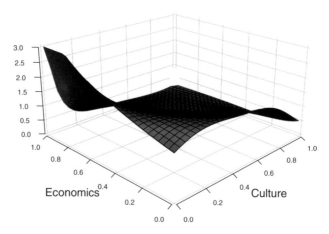

Figure 4.4 The Political Landscape, 1984: Joint Distribution of Attitudes for White Evangelicals

important secondary twist. For the group as a whole, there is a pronounced and increasing gradient from one joint ideological extreme to the other. There are almost no group members who are jointly liberal on economics and culture, while the modal member is clearly and jointly conservative. Yet there is an important secondary twist to this joint distribution, in the form of an uptick of group members who are extremely conservative on culture but extremely liberal on economics, coupled with a shortage of members who are extremely liberal on culture but extremely conservative on economics. Table 4.5 in both Chapters 3 and 4 confirmed that the group as a whole was conservative on both economics and culture. But nothing in either table hints at this secondary twist, privileging one off-diagonal while depopulating its opposite number.

To elaborate the heterogeneity of this political landscape, consider the ideological profile of a further social group, the one contributed by college graduates (Figure 4.5). Again, there is a dominant organizing dimension, culture. On it, the group rises sharply from cultural conservatism to cultural liberalism, much as the Non-Christians did. Yet where the Non-Christian landscape also rose modestly from economic conservatism to economic liberalism, the college graduate landscape is the reverse, rising clearly from economic liberalism to economic conservatism at every point on the cultural continuum. Until the far cultural left—this is the addi-

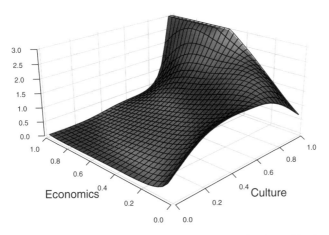

Figure 4.5 The Political Landscape, 1984: Joint Distribution of Attitudes for College Graduates

tional twist characterizing college graduates as a group—where the landscape instead rises from economic conservatism to economic liberalism.

Lest this seem to imply that every demographic category, when converted into a social group, presents an ideological profile that is distinctive by being dramatically skewed in its economic and/or cultural values, Figure 4.6 offers the middle-income group, our "middle class." For its members, the overwhelming impression is of an essentially flat internal landscape: the middle class is quite evenly distributed across both the economic and cultural domains. This is close to being a graphical picture of what it means to be "middling," though even here there are twists. The middle class is short of individuals who are extremely conservative on economics and extremely liberal on culture, while it has a modest and compensating excess of individuals who are extremely conservative on both economics and culture.[4]

The statistical setup for this analysis makes no inherent assumptions about, and thus contributes no methodological constraints on, the pictures of these group preferences. The wild diversity of relationships that actually surface for major social groups makes it clear that there is likewise no inherent empirical drive toward parallel associations between economic and cultural values for major subsets of the population. As a result, one huge fact about American society, with even larger implications for American politics, does not change in the shift from a focus on demographic cleavages to a focus on social groups.

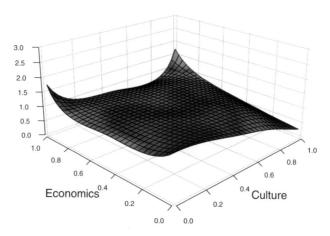

Figure 4.6 The Political Landscape, 1984: Joint Distribution of Attitudes for the Middle-Income

Chapter 3 closed by emphasizing the complexity of political values inherent in this society, when it was characterized by the grand and gross cleavages that would have been relevant to the analysis of politics in nearly any nation for generations—namely social class, race and ethnicity, religious background, and domestic roles. Chapter 4 closes with, in effect, the same point. Even more than at the end of Chapter 3, there is a wide variety of strategic possibilities—and by extension, alternative outcomes—inherent in this group-based picture of the link between social backgrounds and political values.

It is always possible that the great apparent variety in this ideological terrain can still be reduced to a mental map of two normal distributions for economics and culture in their actual application to voting behavior. A remarkable number of analysts, especially among social scientists and, less commonly, among campaign strategists, appear to carry this map (or something even simpler) in their heads. But it is also possible that the variety of three-dimensional pictures—the maps—necessary to capture the political values of major groups in American society go on to create a world in which the strategic options resulting from these combinations of economic and cultural preferences are much broader than that.

Only an examination of the next link in the chain, between political values and voting behavior, can comment on these very different possibilities. Only the actual outcome of key elections during the years of the Pew surveys—not in the persons of their winners and losers but in the links manifested between political values and candidate choice—can distinguish between these very different maps of the structure of mass politics in the United States.

5

Mapping the Political Landscape Three Routes across Ideological Terrain

Chapter 2 introduced our method of measuring political values, along with specific measures for public preferences on economic and cultural policy. Chapter 3 then went in search of the contribution of major demographic cleavages—by social class, race and ethnicity, religious background, and domestic roles—to these political values. Chapter 4 shifted the focus to embed these values in social groups rather than demographic categories, thereby attempting to display them as they actually occur in American society. Chapters 6, 7, and 8 will go on to examine relationships among social backgrounds, political values, and the archetypal incarnation of political behavior in a democratic society—namely, the vote.

Accordingly, Chapter 5 must introduce the methods for moving from groups and values to the vote. Sometimes these methods will be used to produce a picture of the ideological landscape for electoral politics in the nation as a whole. Sometimes they will be used to produce a picture of the contributions of various subgroups to that landscape. Either way, three types of graphic displays will be central to the analysis:

- The first type involves the relationships between economic or cultural values separately and the vote. This is surely the most common form of voting analysis in the scholarly literature, and sometimes— when one domain clearly dominates the other—it is the crucial form for campaign strategists as well.
- The second type involves the relationships between economic and cultural values jointly with the vote. This is the way that social scientists most commonly distinguish the impact of one or another domain when both are influential, and it is closer to the picture of the world as campaign strategists ordinarily encounter it in our time.
- The third type of graphic display moves away from relationships and toward distributions. In effect, it looks underneath these voting relationships, at the actual clustering of voters on the ideological landscape. It is the approach least common among social scientists and most critical to campaign strategists. As such, it is the key to misunderstandings between scholars and practitioners.

The results can probably be best summarized, methodologically, as "thick description" rather than as comprehensive causal argument. We ourselves are attracted by (and may someday attempt) a truly causal account of the effect of attitudes on the vote or on other political behaviors. We do not put that goal front and center here for three reasons. First and generically, the statistical techniques for analyzing a discrete outcome that depends causally on directly observable endogenous covariates are themselves in a parlous state, and this disarray reaches far more areas than just political strategy. Second and concretely, even if the requisite assumptions could be met generically, they might not apply to the specific case. These assumptions require, among other things, the existence of additional covariates that are correlated with the explanatory variables, yet themselves play no explanatory role. We were more comfortable with this prospect in Chapters 3 and 4, where social backgrounds and political values could be studied in isolation. We are less comfortable in Chapters 6, 7, and 8, where voting behavior is added to the mix. Third and finally, this still does not confront the difficulty that, in our case, some of the presumed explanatory covariates—the attitudes—are not even directly observed.

On the other hand, it would be difficult to evaluate or understand the outcome of any causal analysis without its logically prior description, and that is what we attempt here. Note, however, an implicit but inescapable implication: when the intent is to describe comprehensively the ideological landscape for electoral politics in the United States, theory and method quickly impinge on real-world arguments about political strategy, where social scientists meet campaign strategists once again. Social scientists *must* have such a description in order to move forward. Campaign strategists always *do* have at least an implicit description in their heads, however it may be derived. Moreover, many of the arguments from both over campaign strategy are explicitly causal, taking the form of "If the campaign would only do (or had only done) *this*, then what would result (or would have resulted) is surely *that*." Many—perhaps most?—such causal arguments become instantly implausible in the face of an accurate description of the strategic landscape for electoral conflict.

The Statistical Mechanics of a "Thick Description"

Conditioning on the Observed Vote

Chapter 2 developed methods for measuring the attitudes E and C based on the item responses r plus demographic characteristics of each respondent. Since the item responses are coarse and the relation between attitude and response stochastic, the best one can hope to do in measuring the attitudes of any particular individual is to derive a *posterior density* for the attitude based on the information available. To that end, the attitude's distribution is derived from the equation:

$$f(a|r,W) = \frac{f(a,r|W)}{p(r|W)} = \frac{p(r|a,W)f(a|W)}{p(r|W)} = \frac{p(r|a)f(a|W)}{p(r|W)} \tag{1}$$

The first two steps in the formula are analytical. The final step reflects the assumption that item responses are independent of demographic characteristics once underlying (latent) attitudes have been taken into account.[1] This formulation explicitly represents the uncertainty we have about the valuational position of a particular respondent. It should also be recognized that (in the limit) this distribution is in fact how attitudes are distributed for those with given values of r and W.

Throughout Chapters 1 to 4, we have not considered political behavior (including the vote) in any way. One reason for avoiding this was to insulate the description of attitudinal variations across social groups from their political expression. What people value was analyzed without regard to their behavior, to allow the possibility that this behavior is by some standard unrelated to, even inconsistent with, underlying values. We now introduce a step that may initially appear counterintuitive: we condition our inferences about attitudes on the observed (self-reported) vote.[2]

Formally, it is easy to do this: treat V as an element of W. We offer two arguments for doing so in the current analysis. The first is heuristic. Imagine a population all members of which have given the response "$2, 4, 3, 3, 4$" and that consists of people with exactly the same value of W. Some of these people, despite being observationally equivalent in demographic terms and having responded to the five items in precisely the same way, will be more liberal than others. If there were no connection between political values and the vote, then within this (r, W) sub-universe, those voting Republican would have the same distribution of attitudes as those voting Democratic (and of those choosing every other alternative.)

Yet we do not actually expect this. Instead, we expect that in such sub-populations, those who are more liberal will still be more likely to vote Democratic. The vote is thus informative in this thought experiment in assessing the distribution of attitudes. The second argument is then simply a formalization of the first: Conditioning our posterior assessment of attitude on the observed vote necessarily increases the asymptotic accuracy of the assessment. Hence, if the object of inquiry is the distribution of attitudes, this conditioning is actively indicated. A more perspicuous notation in pursuit of this is to rewrite equation (1) as:

$$f(a \mid r, W, V) = \frac{f(a, r \mid W, V)}{p(r \mid W, V)} = \frac{p(r \mid a, W, V) f(a \mid W, V)}{p(r \mid W, V)}$$
$$= \frac{p(r \mid a) f(a \mid W, V)}{p(r \mid W, V)} \tag{2}$$

The components of the numerator of equation (2)—$p(r|a)$ and $f(a|W,V)$—are directly estimated by the methods outlined in Chapter 2. The denominator—$p(r|W,V)$—is the integral of the numerator over the two components of the attitude vector. Consequently, we can directly calculate the posterior density of attitudes corresponding to each observation. The models from Chapter 2 produce estimates that allow the characterization of attitudes on a scale that is standard normal $N(0,1)$ for the subpopulation upon which we arbitrarily standardize. In Chapters 6, 7, and 8, the analysis will be conducted entirely upon renormalized attitude scales that are standard uniform $U(0,1)$. This means that all attitudes are characterized in terms of percentiles of the population. Thus, someone who has an attitude of 0.7 on the cultural scale is more liberal than 70 percent of the population and less liberal than the remaining 30 percent. Because the analysis is presented entirely in graphs using these measurement units, it is convenient to have their construction outlined explicitly by way of some examples.

Accordingly, the very first observation of the 1987 Pew Values survey was a 27-year-old childless male Catholic with a college degree and a middling income (Respondent No. 1). His responses to the economic items were 3, 3, 3, 2, 2 (where 4 is the most liberal response) and to the cultural items were 4, 3, 3, 4, 3. Respondent No. 1 is thus, on the face of these responses, economically moderate and culturally liberal. Yet we also know that he voted for Reagan. Using the model estimated for Chapter 2, we can compute a posterior for the joint distribution of his attitudes in the a scale (the normal or Gaussian style score) and the u scale (the percentile score). These are portrayed in the two left-hand panels of Figure 5.1. Corresponding to this are estimates that are derived from models that additionally condition on the respondent's vote. These are represented in the two right-hand panels.

Figures 5.1.A and 5.1.B, while they appear to be identical, are not strictly so. The $N(0,1)$ subpopulation in Figure 5.1.A is White, male, middle-income, high school graduate, Catholic, and childless, whereas the $N(0,1)$ population in Figure 5.1.B adds to these characteristics "voted for Reagan." Yet two further observations follow. In the first, Figures 5.1.C and 5.1.D *are* formally comparable: the economic and cultural coordinates are scaled so that the population is $U(0,1)$ on each coordinate separately. In the

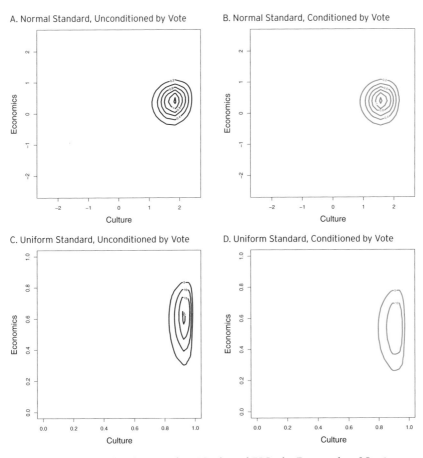

Figure 5.1   Political Values on the *A* Scale and *U* Scale: Respondent No. 1

second, a notable further feature of these figures is that contours in *a* scale are nearly circular, whereas contours in *u* scale are considerably flattened on the right side where they approach 1 on the x-axis.

In examining Figure 5.1.B, we see that the contours are centered at a point on the cultural scale equal to about 1.5. Values greater than this are in the right-hand tail of the "normal-esque"[3] distribution. Consequently, values ranging from 1.5 to 2.0 take in a smaller proportion of the population than values ranging from 1.0 to 1.5. This means that the "*u*" representation will be compressed on the right (toward $x = 1$) and stretched out to the left (toward $x = 0$). While the *u* representation may not be as visually pleasant as the *a*, the *u* representation guarantees comparability across subsamples drawn from the same parent sample. Moreover, the effect of conditioning the inference of an attitude distribution on the reported vote is generally small, as seen in this and the following example. In general, the effect is to increase the estimated precision of the attitude measure when the respondent votes as would be expected from his item responses and characteristics, and to decrease that precision when the voting decision is surprising.

Respondent No. 2 in the 1987 sample was a 23-year-old female with children at home, a middle-income, White, Mainstream Protestant, high school graduate who also voted for Reagan. Her responses on economics are 4,3,2,1,4 and on culture 4,3,1,3,1. These responses are more variable than those of Respondent No. 1, so there is considerable uncertainty as to her true position, but the responses make her appear to be moderately liberal on economics and slightly liberal on culture. The posterior estimate of her position is given in Figure 5.2. Most comparisons among the panels of this figure can be described in a roughly similar way to those of Figure 5.1. Yet because the mass of probability occurs roughly in the middle of the range of both valuational dimensions for Respondent No. 2, the corresponding contours in Figures 5.2.C and 5.2.D are relatively symmetric this time: the contour flattening that occurred for Respondent No. 1 because of his liberal cultural position is largely absent.

Ideological Contours for Social Groups

An important aspect of the posterior densities that have been illustrated is that they represent not only our uncertainty in placing a particular respondent in valuational space, but also the estimate of the values that a "clone population," consisting of many individuals with exactly the same observable attributes, would have. Were we to have an infinite population of people exactly like Respondent No. 2, for example, their actual values would be distributed as Figure 5.2 depicts. In practice, of course, we *see* only one person who is exactly like Respondent No. 2. Yet we are not exclusively interested in populations that clone this respondent, but rather in various populations that *resemble* No. 2: females who are White, Mainstream Protestant, high school graduates with children at home, and who voted for Reagan. Other elements of the sample fulfill these criteria and represent variations within the relevant subpopulation.

To estimate the distribution of attitudes within a subpopulation, then, we find the elements of the sample that correspond to that population and

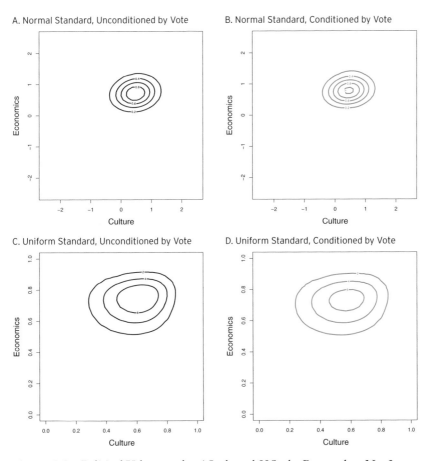

Figure 5.2 Political Values on the *A* Scale and *U* Scale: Respondent No. 2

we average the estimates of attitudes corresponding to each such element. Averaging Respondents No. 1 and No. 2 would thus yield Figure 5.3, where the influence of the two observations is apparent. Adding more observations automatically smoothes out the idiosyncratic attitude positions of particular respondents. If a sufficiently large sample of the target subpopulation is available, the idiosyncrasies are attenuated and the "true" distribution emerges.

The results of averaging over all respondents voting for Reagan are thus seen in Figure 5.4. Note that the similarity of the panels in the left and right columns (Figures 5.4.A versus 5.4.B or 5.4.C versus 5.4.D) shows that the overall result is very similar *regardless of whether one conditions inference*

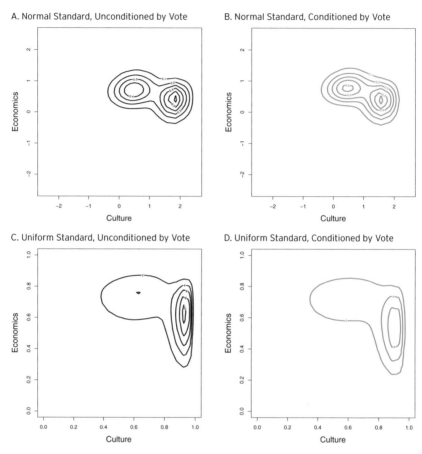

Figure 5.3 Political Values on the *A* Scale and *U* Scale: Aggregate Position of First Two Respondents

on the vote or not. The inference is not dramatically different between the left and right panels. However, the relationship between the top and bottom panels (Figures 5.4.A and 5.4.B versus 5.4.C and 5.4.D) is now not at all obvious. The bottom panels still are, in effect, alternative representations of the top. On the other hand, the *u*–scale representations of the bottom panels contain a wealth of information that is difficult if not impossible to glean from the *a*–scale panels above. This striking visual difference—and more importantly, the associated major gain in information—stems from the fact that the normative, uniform *u* scale of Figures 5.4.C and 5.4.D contains one new slice of information that is not possible to gain from the *a* scale in Figures 5.4.A and 5.4.B.

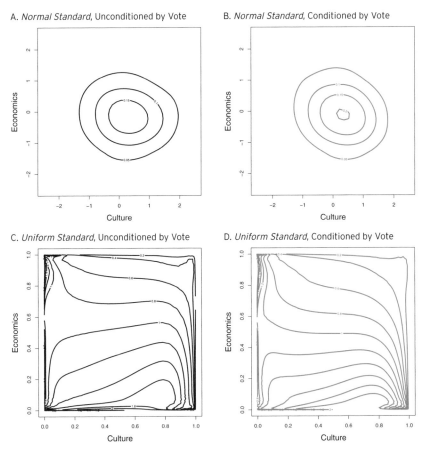

Figure 5.4 Aggregate Political Values of All Respondents Voting for Reagan

Initially, the distribution of Reagan voters from the top panels is transformed to their relative ordering along each axis for the bottom panels. Percentiles along each axis are now the scale. But what really distinguishes the visual presentations of this transformation is that they now depict the relative likelihood that a randomly picked Reagan voter would be resident at each (E) and (C) coordinate—where the contour 1.1, for example, represents a 10 percent greater likelihood that a Reagan voter would reside at that location than at a point chosen at random from the unit square. In short, this map now designates where Reagan voters are most likely to live. The result is an additionally compelling picture of Reaganite voting behavior, to such an extent that Figure 5.4.D now represents our preferred procedure. In effect, it continues to condition the inference of individual values on the vote, while rescaling Figure 5.4.B to a percentile representation and displaying the results as the likelihood of a Reagan vote at any given place on the ideological landscape.

Accordingly, we extract that panel as a separate exhibit at Figure 5.5 and consider it in detail. Now, the higher-valued contours, which correspond to the greatest density of Reagan–voting respondents, occur at the bottom of the figure. Reagan voters tend, perhaps unsurprisingly, to be economic conservatives. However, these contours are largely flat on the other dimension except at the extremes, indicating that among economic conservatives voting for Reagan, there exists a broad array of cultural views. These extend from about the fifth to the eighty-fifth percentile, and there is even evidence of a bulge of opinion at relatively high levels of cultural liberalism (around the seventy-fifth percentile). Otherwise, there is very little density, as might be expected, in the "liberal, liberal" upper-right corner, while the irregular and crowded contours in the upper-left corner correspond to a small clump of supporters who are simultaneously very liberal on economics yet very conservative on culture.

Effects at the edges and especially the corners of these plots are ordinarily estimated from tiny amounts of data. Heuristically, a point in the center

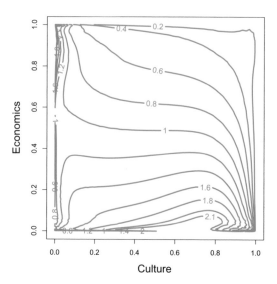

Figure 5.5 All Respondents Voting for Reagan: *U* Scale, Conditioned by the Vote

of the plot draws information from all the individuals around it, effectively drawing from data in a circle around itself, whereas corner points draw from a much more limited region. To make the effects at corners and edges easier to interpret and to eliminate some of the noise inherent in the raw picture, we introduce some smoothing. Since we are working with random variables with bounded support (economic and cultural values expressed as percentiles relative to the total population), the distributions we seek are completely characterized by their sequence of moments. Our estimates calculated from the sample give estimates of these moments. Roughly speaking, higher-order moments, which are inaccurately estimated, make disproportionate contributions to irregular behavior, particularly at edges and corners. The effect of our smoothing procedure is to de-emphasize the effects of these noisily estimated moments.[4]

Just as we can construct the distribution of values for Reagan voters and portray its smoothed density in a contour plot, we can construct densities for the values of Mondale voters, Non voters, and, of course, their sum: all respondents. The national distribution of values (that is, the distribution of the values of all respondents), is related to the mutually exclusive and jointly exhaustive components for Reagan, Mondale, and Non vote by the equation:

$$f(E, C) = f(E, C \mid \text{``}R\text{''}) p(\text{``}R\text{''}) + f(E, C \mid \text{``}M\text{''}) p(\text{``}M\text{''})$$
$$+ f(E, C \mid \text{``}NV\text{''}) p(\text{``}NV\text{''}) \tag{3}$$

Figure 5.6 shows the estimated density for each voting category and their sum as computed by equation (3). These will receive much more extensive investigation in Chapter 6. Here, they serve largely to demonstrate how to read similar displays, while suggesting the inherent variety among them.

Figure 5.6.A shows, as above, that Reagan voters were most often economic conservatives but that they were spread over a large range of cultural values. The contour with value 1.5, for example, contains the most economically conservative 20 percent of the sample (economic values of 0.0 to 0.2) but almost the full range of cultural values (0.1 to 0.9). The modal Reagan voter was thus a solid economic conservative who was a moderate liberal on culture. A secondary concentration of opinion among strong

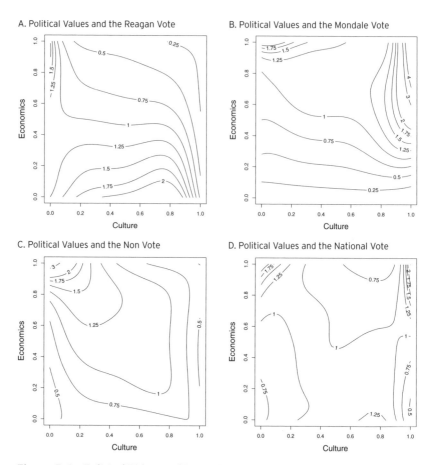

Figure 5.6   Political Values and Voter Categories

economic liberals who are strong cultural conservatives is so tiny as to risk being artifactual.

In contrast, Figure 5.6.B shows that Mondale voters had two noteworthy ideological clumps, where the contour with value 1.25 can be used to isolate both. The larger of the two is constituted from the most culturally liberal 20 percent of the sample (cultural values of 0.8 to 1.0) but with economic views that cover a broad range, including even some moderate economic conservatives (0.3 to 1.0). The secondary concentration, much smaller but more important and less easily dismissed for Mondale than for Reagan, consists of strong economic liberals (0.9 to 1.0), whose cultural views range from conservative to moderate (0.0 to 0.5). Here again, the u scale has the great benefit of focusing attention on places where real voters actually reside, rather than on a range of possibilities that lacks many living, breathing respondents.

Lastly, Figure 5.6.C locates a plurality of Non voters in roughly the same ideological territory as the secondary Mondale concentration: economic liberals (0.6 to 1.0) who were cultural conservatives (0.0 to 0.4). Note that the Non cluster is considerably larger than the Mondale cluster in this ideological terrain. Note also that Non voters are rare in the other three corners of the plot, making both "aligned" combinations rare in this group (that is, either strongly conservative or strongly liberal on both economics and culture), along with the combination that is culturally liberal but economically conservative.

When these three voting categories are brought back together, Figure 5.6.D results: the composite national picture for the full sample of respondents. The dominant fact about Figure 5.6.D is that its contour lines, inevitably for a fully national picture, are much less impressive— flatter—than for its component subpopulations, the Reagan, Mondale, and Non voting categories. Three residual value clumps remain: one economically very liberal but culturally very conservative; one economically and culturally very liberal; and one economically very conservative but moderately liberal on culture—in that order of numerical importance. Yet none of these clusterings is of any size, and, more to the practical point, none is as strong in the overall populace as it is in one or another of the constituent voting categories.[5]

In any case (and to jump well ahead of the story), this was the situation with regard to the 1984 election. As Chapter 8 will ultimately demonstrate in detail, this picture was destined to shift substantially over the next quarter-century, with major impacts on the strategic environment for electoral politics. In other words, Figure 5.6 is helpful in demonstrating how to read similar displays. Yet it is most definitely not the unchanging template for them, and would be very unhelpful as a description of modern American politics.

Graphical Strategies for Understanding the Vote

Density Plots and Probability Plots

As we saw above in equation (3), the density of the total population's attitude at a given point in attitude (E, C) space is the weighted sum of each
constituent population's density at that point, where the weights are the
proportion within each constituent group. Consequently, when we fix a
point in (E, C) space and consider the proportion of the total density that
is contributed by a particular group, that proportion is the probability at
that point in space of being a member of that group. In this context, to be
a member of the Reagan group means to have voted for Reagan, so we
have found the probability of voting Reagan at a particular point in (E, C)
space. As an equation we have:

$$p(R|E,C) = \frac{f(E,C,R)}{f(E,C)} = \frac{f(E,C|R)p(R)}{f(E,C)} \tag{4}$$

The denominator of equation (4) is now given by equation (3). This construction guarantees—as it must—that probabilities are positive and sum
to 1, because the denominator is simply the sum of numerator terms that
correspond to the totality of voting alternatives, and each of the components of the numerator is nonnegative by definition.

Figure 5.7 shows the vote probabilities that are obtained from the densities of Figure 5.6 by using the sample voting proportions as the population voting proportions. In interpreting these plots, it is useful to remember that if contours are strictly horizontal, then vote probabilities vary
with economic attitudes only, while if contours are strictly vertical, vote
probabilities vary only with culture. A plot with contours of both types
shows a transition of behaviors consistent with a change of salience at the
points in attitude space where the contours change orientation. In short,
the direction (and shape) of contour lines has a very powerful interpretation. Those that are horizontal signal a division of the vote along economic lines; those that are vertical signal a division of the vote along cultural lines; and various mixes signal various, changing combinations.

With this in mind, one can see that the Reagan plot, Figure 5.7.A, features long horizontal segments throughout. This confirms that the Rea-

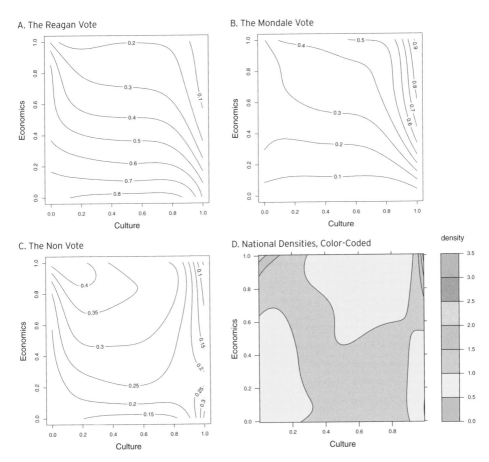

Figure 5.7 Vote Probabilities and Value Densities

gan vote is heavily conditioned by economic values and is in fact largely invariant to culture except at the liberal extremes (greater than 0.8). Conversely, one can see that the Mondale plot, Figure 5.7.B, features much more of a mix of horizontal and vertical segments but with an increased probability of voting for Mondale associated with cultural values, to the exclusion of economics in the prominent upper-right corner of the figure. And Figure 5.7.C, the Non plot, is characterized neither by horizontal nor vertical segments, but instead shows nonvoting behavior to be most prevalent among economic liberals who are cultural conservatives, while falling away (and hence turnout rising) both toward economic conservatism and toward cultural liberalism.

Figure 5.7.D reassembles the Reagan, Mondale, and Non plots in the manner introduced previously at Figure 5.6.D. As such, the plot brings back the distribution of attitudes for the country as a whole, but now with prospective implications for the interpretation of both national and sub-group plots of those choosing Reagan, Mondale, or Non voting. The value range for Figure 5.7.D is color-coded this time, as in the key to the right of the plot. In mechanical terms, the contour "1.0" separates a green area where there are somewhat more respondents than the national average (representing the value 1.0 to 1.5) from a tan area where there are somewhat fewer respondents than that same national average (representing values 0.5 to 1.0). Color-coding makes this (and similar) figures additionally easy to read. Otherwise, this national picture has little substantive message when considered solely on its own.

We have already noted that the distribution of national opinion is such that the *density* of respondents is not dramatically different from the average value of 1.0 over vast areas. Figure 5.7.D, with color, makes this finding even more inescapable: almost the entire plot is green or tan—slightly more or slightly less than 1.0. Yet what this figure can now be used to do is to underline the way in which national opinion is different from the opinion of Reagan voters, or of college graduates, or of just about any group that the analyst might choose—even, if one wished to revert to the journalistic examples of Chapter 2, those so-called Soccer Moms and NASCAR Dads. On purely national terms, the color key in Figure 5.7.D might appear to be wasteful, because only two colors occur in any substantial portion of the plot. Yet this provides the comparative underlay of colored contours for most of the analysis to follow, where the underlays characteristic of individual social groups will often differ impressively from this national picture.

Figure 5.8 goes on to combine filled color underlays with conventional contour plots to convey two relations simultaneously. One reason this can be done productively is that these relations always have the same axes. The x axis is cultural values measured in full population percentiles, while the y axis is the corresponding measure of economic values. Figure 5.8 is straightforwardly produced by laying Figures 5.7.A–C, in turn, over Figure 5.7.D. The panels of Figure 5.8 allow us to see the probability of Reagan, Mondale, and Non votes as they vary in attitude space, while

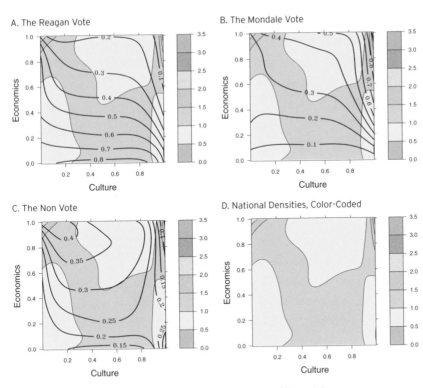

Figure 5.8 Vote Probabilities Overlaid on National Densities

simultaneously allowing us to see which areas of that space are densely populated for the relevant population and which are sparsely populated instead.

The difference in perspective produced by providing the underlay of the probability density of values then gains a powerful further utility—this is the primary point of the preceding setup—when examining the voting behavior of subgroups. As an example, Figure 5.9 is in effect the three voting panels of Figure 5.8, but replacing "all respondents" with "Evangelical Protestants"; that is, the social group comprised of non-Black adherents to one of the Evangelical Protestant denominations. Two things stand out about the voting behavior of these White Evangelicals, courtesy of this ability to impose voting contours on an underlying density map.

On the one hand, the voting relationships portrayed by the dark contour lines in the foreground of this figure are not qualitatively different from the national patterns represented in Figure 5.7. The Reagan vote is

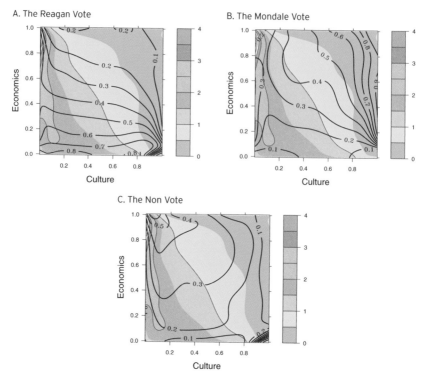

Figure 5.9 Vote Probabilities Overlaid on National Densities: The Evangelical Protestants

largely structured by economic values, and is largely unresponsive to culture (Figure 5.9.A). The Mondale vote loses some of this economic structure, while being more heavily influenced by cultural values (Figure 5.9.B). And the Non vote is concentrated among strong economic liberals who are strong cultural conservatives, while falling away as economic conservatism and cultural liberalism increase (Figure 5.9.C). The patterns of voting behavior that characterize the national sample—the relationships between political values jointly and voter choice—obviously infuse the Evangelical Protestants as a subsample.

On the other hand, the implications of these patterns for partisan outcomes are now strikingly different, courtesy of the comprehensive profile of these Evangelical Protestants that is provided by combining their valuational underlay, that is, the distribution of economic and cultural values within the group as a whole, with their voting plots. Because this underlay (at Figure 5.9) is impressively different from the national underlay (at Figure 5.8), so are the implications of overlaying the Reagan, the Mondale, and the Non vote upon it:

- Economic conservatives remain strongly attracted to Reagan, within the group as for the nation as a whole. That does not change. But now, the point is that this social group is in fact disproportionately located on the terrain of economic conservatism.
- Cultural liberals remain even more strongly attracted to Mondale, within the group as they are in the nation. But here, the point is that few members of the group reside in this territory. Mondale harvests those who do, but that is a trivial asset among White Evangelicals.
- Not surprisingly, then, Reagan carries the Evangelical Protestant vote overwhelmingly, to an extent consistent with the group's ideological position: 55.7 percent Reagan versus 20.4 percent Mondale versus 23.9 percent Non. Reagan wins a genuine majority. Mondale actually manages to come in third.

Univariate Implications of the Bivariate Analysis

The bivariate representation of a probability density contains each of the corresponding univariate densities. Accordingly, the probability density of economic values among Evangelical Protestants, to stay with our example, is derivable from the joint density of economic and cultural values. The calculation is carried out, point-wise, at each value e that E can take, and if we are interested in the density of E for these Evangelicals, it is given by the formula:

$$f(E = e|\text{Evangelical}) = \int_0^1 f(C = c, E = e|\text{Evangelical})\, dc.$$

The corresponding calculation to find the density of C at value c is given by:

$$f(C = c|\text{Evangelical}) = \int_0^1 f(C = c, E = e|\text{Evangelical})\, de.$$

Applying these formulas to the bivariate density of values among Evangelical Protestants produces Figures 5.10.A and 5.10.B, for economics and culture, respectively. These display, in units of percentile rank compared with the full sample, the probability density function of a political value among all Protestant Evangelicals. As a composite social group, these Evangelicals tilt clearly conservative on economics, but are actually well represented at nearly every point on the economic continuum except the far left. This is the message of Figure 5.10.A. In contrast, Evangelical Protestants are much more heavily concentrated on the cultural right. Strong cultural conservatives are the dominant ideological tendency within the group; even moderate cultural liberals are comparatively scarce. This is the message of Figure 5.10.B. By national standards, Evangelical Protestants are very conservative culturally and moderately conservative economically.

Figures 5.10.C and 5.10.D then present the (estimated) probability density functions for economic and cultural values among Protestant Evangelicals who voted for Reagan (the blue line), who voted for Mondale (the red line), and who did not vote (the green line). Figure 5.10.C shows the Reagan vote to be heavily concentrated among economic conservatives. Both the Mondale vote and the Non vote are then much more weakly concentrated in the opposite direction. In sharp contrast, Figure 5.10.D shows the Reagan, the Mondale, and the Non vote—the entire voting universe—to have probability density functions that are nearly identical in their cultural preferences. The valuational distributions for the three voting categories are close to being overlaps, with some residual distinction among strong liberals and strong conservatives. In other words, the distribution of economic values within the group (at Figure 5.10.A), while tilted conservative, coincides with real economic distinctions among the three voting categories (at Figure 5.10.C). Yet the distribution of *cultural* values (at Figure 5.10.B), being sharply tilted in the conservative direction, leaves little room for real distinctions (at Figure 5.10.D).

By definition, the true distribution of attitudes among Protestant Evangelicals as a whole must obey a "sum of the parts" condition. The density of the attitudes of Reagan voters weighted by the proportion of the population that voted for Reagan, plus the density of the attitudes of Mondale voters weighted by the proportion of the population that voted for Mondale, plus the density of the attitudes of Non voters weighted by the proportion of the population that did not vote, must equal the density of the total population. It follows that fixing a value of "economics" or "culture"

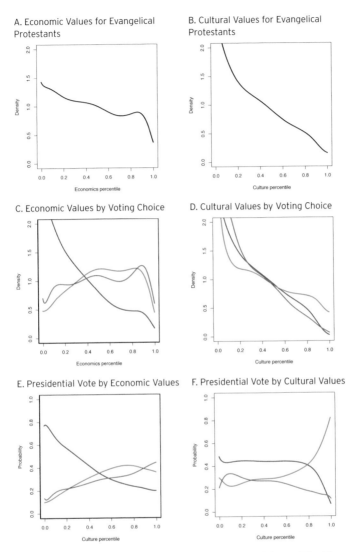

Figure 5.10   Univariate Value Densities and Vote Probabilities: The Evangelical
Protestants

Key: Blue = Reagan, Red = Mondale, Green = Non Voters.

for the contribution made by Reagan voters to the whole density of that
point is the proportion of Reagan voters (among the relevant group) times
the density at that point, and that the ratio of this quantity to the total of
all density contributions is the probability of voting Reagan at this point
in attitude space.

In effect, then, the lines of the second row of plots (Figures 5.10.C and 5.10.D) divided by the lines of the first row of plots (Figures 5.10.A and 5.10.B) yield—after multiplication by a constant equal to the probability of voting Reagan, Mondale, or Non—the plots of the third row, at Figures 5.10.E and 5.10.F. From this perspective, the shapes of the probability density of a value conditional on the vote determine the particular shape of the probability of the vote given the value. If the distribution of a value varies greatly across voter categories, then the probability of the voting outcomes is highly responsive to that value. Conversely, if the distribution of a value is effectively the *same* across voting groups, then the probability of the voting outcomes is invariant to that value. In the case of Evangelical Protestants, this latter condition is untrue for economics, nearly true for culture.

For economics, the distribution of the political value in question is clearly *not* the same among Reagan, Mondale, and Non voters (Figure 5.10.C). The first group is powerfully constituted from economic conservatives, while the latter two are more weakly constituted from economic liberals. As a result, this economic distribution is much more clearly related to the vote than is its cultural counterpart. Figure 5.10.E confirms this with an equivalent representation of these densities, showing voter probability among Evangelical Protestants conditioned on economic values. The Reagan line declines steeply from strong economic conservatism through strong economic liberalism. The Mondale and Non lines rise more modestly in the opposite direction.

An equivalent representation of these densities[6] is Figure 5.10.F, which shows the vote probability among Evangelical Protestants conditioned on culture instead. Because the cultural values of those Evangelicals voting Reagan are not very different from Evangelicals voting Mondale or not voting at all, the line representing the probability of voting Reagan is almost perfectly flat over most its course: from 0.0 to 0.8 there is effectively nothing additional to say. The Reagan line then ticks sharply downward around the eightieth percentile of cultural values, while the Mondale line ticks sharply upward. These latter are features that both share with most other groups, and they will be extensively analyzed in Chapter 6.

Three Approaches to the Vote

Chapters 6, 7, and 8 present a recurrent and systematized variety of graphical analyses similar to those sketched by example here. *Univariate* plots have one basic type, involving the probability of vote alternatives as a function of economic or cultural values individually, though very occasionally they are also used to investigate the density of either one or the other set of values individually, when this is what distinguishes a particular social group. *Bivariate* plots are of two basic types: (1) *Vote probability* as a joint function of economic and cultural values; this produces the classic voting relationships that are much-loved in conventional vote analysis; (2) *Probability density* as a function of both economic and cultural values; this produces the density maps that are much closer to the approach of campaign strategists, identifying where people are inside those voting relationships—that is, where they actually reside in attitude space.

In contrast to the first part of the book, these analyses will be conducted exclusively in terms of values measured against the national percentile distribution within each survey year. Until this point, we have been concerned with seeing how the values of social groups were related to their constituent social characteristics. Henceforth, we are instead concerned with how the relative valuational positions of each social group are related to how that group votes, or with the extent to which partisan voting divisions within a social group correspond to valuational divisions.

Although univariate densities and probability functions are derived ultimately from bivariate density estimates, the starting point for an analysis is often a univariate plot. Univariate plots are not only easier to understand, but also present salient facts more directly. In addition, they permit comparison of voting relationships across different subcategories of the group under examination. It is possible, for example, to use a univariate graph to show the relationship between cultural values and the probability of a Reagan vote among Evangelical Protestants, broken into four income groups or four education groups. Four lines can tell this story. By contrast, with a single bivariate plot, the limit is a single set of line contours over a set of color-filled contours. Anything beyond that is too cluttered to be translated visually.

In the previous section, to continue the example, we saw that Evangelical Protestants in the 1984 survey had both economic and cultural attitudes that differed from the population at large. Among these Protestant Evangelicals, the cultural attitudes of Reagan, Mondale, and Non voters were basically the same; it was their economic values that differed. Consequently, considering Evangelicals only, it is difficult not to conclude that economic values were what distinguished, say, the Reagan vote. We will thus say that economic values align the Evangelical Reagan vote over the entire spectrum of economic attitudes, while this same Evangelical vote is not very responsive to cultural values until the eightieth national percentile is reached—a point at which there are very few Evangelical Protestants. This will provide a verbal way of indicating that the slope of the "probability of vote" lines is substantial for the economics plot, while the cultural plot is largely flat.

While univariate plots can be powerful, there are some further aspects—essential aspects—that they cannot represent. A recurring motif in our analysis will be the *joint* economic and cultural values of a social group, and of the various voting categories within that group. How are college-educated Reagan voters different from college-educated Mondale voters? In answering, it is useful to imagine a room filled with members of just such groups. What are now the characteristic combinations of values in the room? Any answer to such questions requires a bivariate density plot, along with some definition of the "high ground" within it. We shall ordinarily use a standard of 1.5—more than half-again as likely to be in this position when compared with the national picture—as a definition of this electoral high ground.

Bivariate probability plots provide a second aspect of the link between political values and voting behavior that is not available in univariate plots. This is the trade-off between economic and cultural values within this link. We saw previously that if lines are nearly horizontal, as they are for much of the vote for Reagan by political values in Figure 5.8.A, then the vote differs principally by economic values. If these lines feature more verticality, as they do for the Mondale vote by political values in Figure

5.8.B, then the vote differs increasingly by culture. The further point here is that evolution in the shape of these contours over time, as well as differences among social groups, indicates differences in the relative importance—the relative aligning power—of these values to the vote.

Because we do regard the resulting data displays as a clear improvement on the usual analysis of voting behavior in key regards, it is tempting to go on and suggest that they bring us closer to a full-blown causal explanation. Yet a great deal of related research sows implicit mischief by not addressing its own limitations—most commonly in the social sciences by treating even simple regression analyses as if they had dynamic (and therefore causal) implications. What we would like to do here is to assert some methodological improvements without falling into the same trap. So we should probably close this chapter with a few words on what the resulting "thick description" can and cannot do in causal terms.

Higher-quality description can in fact provide some support (and/or some real difficulties) for a variety of existing generalizations and may—we believe it does—prove very problematic for some existing causal arguments. In this sense, thick description can provide a range of theoretical disconfirmations, as, for example, with any argument asserting that cultural values are what disproportionately motivate the vote among Evangelical Protestants: clearly false when confronted with Figure 5.10. Numerous further distributions of social backgrounds, political values, and voting behaviors from Chapters 6, 7, and 8 will likewise be evidently inconsistent with further (and familiar) lines of argument, assertions that characterize both the professional literature in the social sciences and the received lore among campaign strategists.

The comprehensive thrust of an argument from the thick description of Chapters 6, 7, and 8 is likewise inconsistent with some major perspectives on voting behavior generally. Most conspicuously, the resulting story line of presidential elections across time and among social groups is very hard to square with what are often gathered as "median voter theories."[7] Thus there will be obvious social bases for stratifying the vote that do *not* encourage strategic moves toward the ideological center. These are, in effect, social principles of stratification that actually empty out the middle, just as there will be evident distributions of political values that, in association with partisanship, promise punishment rather than reward to candidates who nevertheless seek the center. If the resulting analyses of Chapters 6, 7, and 8 are not themselves a full-blown causal explanation of voting behavior, then, they can still be very hard on individual and collective, implicit and explicit, causal alternatives.

6

Political Values and Presidential Votes
A Benchmark Year

Certain social characteristics are conducive to certain political values, such that different demographic backgrounds beget different policy preferences. That was the message of Chapter 3. Yet while these same characteristics can be used additionally to distinguish social groups, the members of these groups inevitably offer a further mix of demographic characteristics, which simultaneously shape their policy preferences. That was the message of Chapter 4. Moreover, demographic characteristics as embedded in social groups conduce toward varying combinations of economic and cultural values. In so doing, these groups provide a social structure that imparts an impressive stability to these valuational combinations.

Analytically, for social scientists, the result deserves to be thought of as the "ideological structure" of American politics. Practically, for campaign strategists, this structure constitutes the "electoral landscape" upon which they must fashion their candidate appeals. Chapter 6 must thus be concerned with sketching the basics of this landscape. To that end, a single, early, large, and substantively rich survey from the sequence of Pew Values surveys will be used to establish a comprehensive benchmark. Obviously, the ultimate purpose of having such a benchmark is to be able to watch the relationship among social backgrounds, political values, and voting behavior evolve—change or not—over time.

Yet even at the start, building on just this one year, it is important to note two further fundamental aspects of any such picture. In one, social groups may—and will—differ in the degree to which they reflect national relationships. Said the other way around, the national picture can be a composite of very different group-based portraits. In the process, social groups will differ additionally among themselves when examined for the way group membership and political values are connected to voting behavior. Or, said the other way around once again, the strategic landscape for electoral politics gains complexity from the fact that social groups vary not only in their political values but also in the way they link these up to political behavior.

The great register of mass political behavior in a democracy is the general election vote, and the capstone incarnation of that vote in the United States is the vote for president. Accordingly, our examination of the place of public preferences in shaping political behavior will concentrate on the presidential vote in the period for which we have parallel polling data, the quarter-century from 1984 to 2008. Chapter 6 will begin with relationships among social backgrounds, political values, and voting behavior in the opening election covered by the Pew Values surveys, namely 1984. Chapter 7 will then attend to the evolution of the national picture for these relationships through the election of 2008. And Chapter 8 will track the evolution of the group relationships beneath this national picture during the same period.

The National Story in a Baseline Election

This analysis begins with the first of these Pew surveys, the one covering the presidential election of 1984, not only because it is first but also because it is especially large and unusually careful in its execution, being an extended, in-person, national sample. In the abstract, 1984 might seem to suffer as a benchmark by being a landslide reelection, where divisions between the two major-party candidates are in that sense distorted. Yet for most of what follows, it is not the precise numbers in this division that matter but the associations underneath them—that is, in regression-speak, not the intercept but the relationships. Moreover, the presence of comparable analyses for every presidential election thereafter, up to and including 2008, more or less guarantees that any distortions that are limited to 1984 will be revealed in the subsequent analysis.[1]

As a route into understanding the result, this analysis begins with the univariate plots, that is, the relationship to the vote of economic and cultural values individually; then shifts to a consideration of the bivariate vote probabilities, that is, the relationship to the vote of economic and cultural values jointly; and closes by turning away from all such relationships and toward the bivariate density plots, and hence to the question of where the voters generating those relationships actually reside—are concentrated—on the ideological landscape. Because some of these results have already been used in Chapter 5 (at Figures 5.6–5.8) to exemplify our analytic approaches, the national picture can be presented here (in Figures 6.1–6.3) in a very condensed manner.

Accordingly, Figure 6.1 shows, first, the relationship between economic values and the Reagan vote, the Mondale vote, and the Non vote in 1984, followed by the relationship between cultural values and those same three options. What this suggests is that the general election vote for Ronald Reagan, the incumbent president and Republican nominee for reelection, was strongly related to economic values (Figure 6.1.A). Conservatives disproportionately supported him, liberals disproportionately avoided him, and moderates fell neatly in between. The vote for his major-party opponent, Walter Mondale, former vice president under President Jimmy Carter and the Democratic challenger, was likewise related to economic values across their full distribution, though less strongly and in the opposite direction (Figure 6.1.B). Economic liberals preferred Mondale, economic conservatives resisted him, and economic moderates again fell in between.

For 1984, these comparative relationships were much more advantageous to Reagan, since both his best and his worst performances were significantly better than the best and the worst performances by Mondale. Recall, however, that the same relationships, anchored at different levels of support, could in principle produce a different ultimate outcome. Move that strong economic relationship for Reagan downward and the weaker economic relationship for Mondale upward, and Mondale wins the contest. In any case, there was an even more modest relationship to the Non

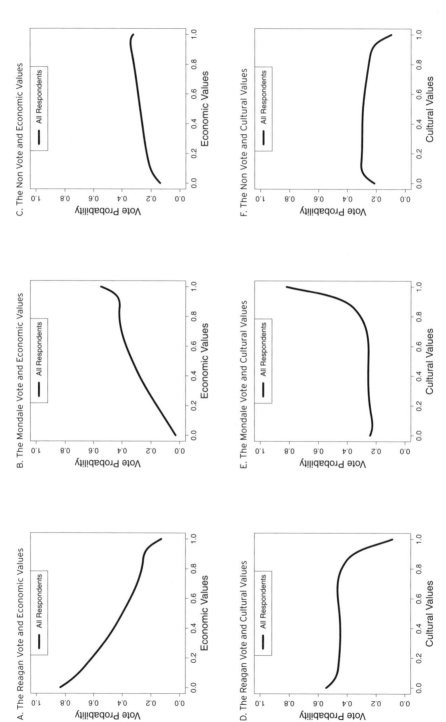

Figure 6.1 Political Values and Voting Behavior: The Nation as a Whole, 1984

vote for economic values, weaker than the relationships to either the Reagan or the Mondale vote, though more like the latter. Economic liberals were more inclined to skip the vote and economic conservatives less inclined to do so (Figure 6.1.C). Note that nothing about this relationship suggests that a higher turnout would have produced a different outcome, though note again that in a sufficiently close year, this could be less true.

The story of cultural values in the 1984 election, seen in isolation, was strikingly different. The Reagan vote for president was effectively unresponsive to cultural preferences for the vast majority of the public, being essentially flat for the range from strong cultural conservatism (0.0) through moderate cultural liberalism (0.8) (Figure 6.1.D). Only at the far liberal end of this distribution was there an impact, and there, the Reagan vote plunged. Conversely, the Mondale vote was equally flat across the vast bulk of this cultural distribution (likewise 0.0 to 0.8), before jumping up sharply among the same strong liberals (Figure 6.1.E).

For 1984, this sharp division among cultural liberals was not nearly sufficient to overcome the huge advantage to Reagan (and disadvantage to Mondale) everywhere else on the cultural continuum: the vote line was almost twice as high for the former as for the latter across most of the cultural spectrum. In the abstract, however, one could again imagine a year in which the same pattern, anchored at different levels of support, would allow the distinctive behavior of cultural liberals to determine the outcome. Nonvoters then showed the very slightest tendency for conservatives to skip the vote more often than liberals across the cultural continuum as a whole. Though what was more visually striking about this line of cultural voting, albeit involving only a small share of the total American public, was the propensity of the cultural extremes, both liberal and conservative, to turn out more than the vast cultural middle (Figure 6.1.F).

Figure 6.2 puts the two valuational dimensions back together and considers them simultaneously, that is, by way of relationships to the vote when both economic and cultural values are on display. For some social groups within American society, as we shall see, this joint picture adds important twists to voting relationships elicited by considering the two valuational dimensions in isolation. For other social groups, the implications of a group portrait developed from the two dimensions individually are so straightforward that the joint picture need not even be presented. For

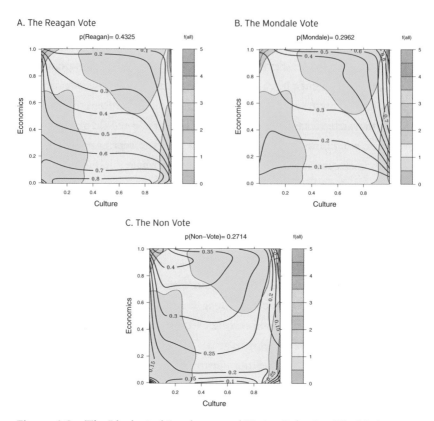

Figure 6.2 The Ideological Landscape and Voting Behavior: The Nation as a Whole, 1984

society as a whole, Figure 6.2 falls somewhere in between, adding nuances but suggesting that the story of voting relationships in the 1984 election, when approached through economic and cultural values individually, is largely confirmed when they are put back together.

Thus the vote for Ronald Reagan, the Republican nominee, remains a strongly economic vote, essentially rising with economic conservatism across the board (Figure 6.2.A). Indeed, for the bulk of the cultural continuum, there is nearly nothing in play *except* economic values. The Reagan vote is thus confirmed as being heavily conditioned by economic values, while remaining largely invariant to culture except at the liberal extremes. By contrast, while the Mondale vote likewise shows a clear and substantial association with economics, it is considerably more influenced by cultural preferences as well (Figure 6.2.B). Across the middle of the cultural distribution, the Mondale vote, like the Reagan vote but opposite to it, rises neatly with economic liberalism and falls correspondingly with economic conservatism. Yet Mondale's counterpart *increment* among cultural liberals begins earlier and rises faster than the opposite decrement for Reagan.

More than the Reagan vote, then, the Mondale vote partakes of some association with both valuational domains. The nuance that is most different when the focus shifts from individual to joint policy relationships actually arrives with the final voting category, the Non vote. Economics still trumps culture in shaping this joint relationship, as evidenced by the fact that nonvoting is more narrowly concentrated among economic liberals than among cultural conservatives. On the other hand, the Non vote now appears even more clearly associated with one particular combination of political values, the combination of strong economic liberalism with strong cultural conservatism, such that this Non vote now declines neatly with both greater economic conservatism and greater cultural liberalism (Figure 6.2.C).

What is less obvious from either Figure 6.1 or Figure 6.2 is the way that these relationships anchor the Reagan, the Mondale, or the Non vote in very different places on the ideological landscape. To that end, Figure 6.3 offers a map of the ideological density of these three votes: that is, the share of the three electorates actually residing at various combinations of economic and cultural values. In the abstract, such maps can have major strategic consequences. A voting relationship that features a modest decrement at one level of preference on one of the two great valuational dimensions, plus a large increment at one level of preference on the other great dimension, can be completely undone in its strategic implications by the actual density of these values in society—if, in this example, there are many people holding the first set of values and few holding the second set.

For most social groups in American society, these densities are in fact highly varied, and this variance will prove to have important practical implications. For the nation as a whole—considered as a composite— these densities are less varied than they can ever be for specific subgroups, since the statistical setup arrays the total population evenly from most to least conservative on both dimensions. Nevertheless, as Figure 6.3 forcefully suggests, the actual populations ending up in the Reagan, the

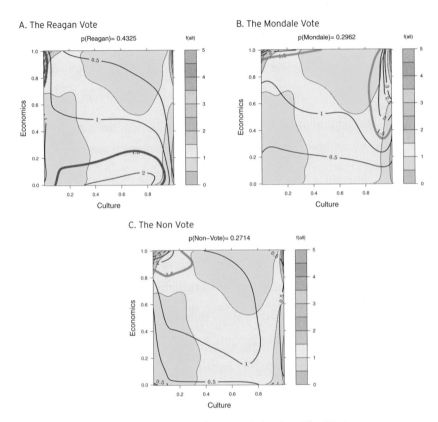

Figure 6.3 Ideological Density and Voting Behavior: The Nation as a Whole, 1984

Mondale, or the Non vote categories in 1984 could still be quite different. Figure 6.3 presents the full distribution of densities for the three voting categories, but highlights areas of the ideological landscape that were more than half-again as likely to choose a Reagan, Mondale, or Non vote than was the nation as a whole.

The result raises a set of strategic choices for electoral combatants that were not obvious when the focus was voting relationships, individually or jointly. In this, Reagan voters were most common among those who were strong economic conservatives but moderate cultural liberals. Voting relationships were in a sense masking this fact (Figure 6.3.A). By contrast, Mondale voters were most common among those who were strong cultural liberals, with economic preferences that varied from strong liberalism to true centrism. Only the strong economic conservatives were missing from this electoral high ground (Figure 6.3.B). Non voters, finally, were concentrated among strong economic liberals who were simultaneously strong cultural conservatives. For them, joint voting relationships already suggested as much, and their density map merely underlines the situation (Figure 6.3.C).

The attitudinal characteristics of the three voting categories were therefore quite distinctive. Said differently, each category was headquartered in a different ideological location on the political landscape. The conventional way to think about a strategic map is to say that one or the other candidate could be clearly advantaged by moving toward the joint ideological center. Ronald Reagan should thus move left on economics (Figure 6.3.A). Walter Mondale should thus move right on culture (Figure 6.3.B). Yet what the highlighted portions of Figure 6.3 suggest at a minimum is that the most common Reagan *and* the most common Mondale voters might well be opposed to these strategic moves. The candidates, after all, are being asked to move away from the populations to which they were disproportionately attractive. Moreover, in the American context, if the most common Reagan and Mondale voters in the general election were an even larger part of the *primary* electorate, they might well think of themselves as a duly constituted nominating majority, democratically entitled to these policy positions.

Even more provocatively, Figure 6.3 can be read to underline a strategic risk of a different sort from this conventional advice, since the ideological terrain that is being recommended constitutes an area of the strategic landscape that was much less successful in generating Republican *or* Democratic votes than was the Reagan or the Mondale "high ground." Seen optimistically, moving there is what it would take to generate just such a vote. But seen pessimistically, this strategy actually counsels candidates to leave areas where they have strong support and go to areas that are less inclined to vote for them—and may well be less likely to vote at all. If those with more liberal or more conservative views on economics or culture were simultaneously more intense in the holding of these views, or even just more attentive to candidate positions on them, this strategic advice would be especially chancy.

Figure 6.3.C, the density map for the Non vote, makes the problem even more stark. Among those who are strong economic liberals and strong cultural conservatives, there is in fact a territory of disproportionately concentrated nonvoters. Attracting them could thus, in principle, pay disproportionate dividends for one candidate or the other. Yet the policy moves that would be required to reach them are massively distant from both the Republican and the Democratic homelands. And beyond this small but distant concentrated realm, the Non vote is spread almost evenly across the ideological landscape. This means that there are no potentially disproportionate gains in attracting these dispersed nonvoters. At the same time, it means that there could well be disproportionate losses in trying to attract their concentrated brethren, if residents of party homelands were likely to defect in response; Chapter 7 will argue that these are precisely the individuals most likely to defect on policy grounds.

Social Class and the Vote

Family Income

Nothing in our methodological setup guarantees that the social groups that make up this national portrait will simply replicate it within their individual memberships, and nearly everything in the empirical results from Chapters 3 and 4 suggests that they will not. For most groups, voting relationships do at least parallel the national picture, merely being anchored by group membership at differing levels of voting and nonvoting, and of partisan support. For a minority of groups, even these initial parallels are missing. Yet even for those groups with relationships that do parallel the national picture, the density of the values underpinning such relationships still varies widely. Recall that two groups can show the same overall relationship to the Reagan vote, for example—economic conservatives swelling that vote and economic liberals deflating it—while the practical consequence of this link varies substantially because one group is economically conservative and the other is economically liberal.

In any case, the analysis of demographic categories in Chapter 3 and of social groups in Chapter 4 began with social class, and Chapter 6 should do the same. Figures 6.4.A–C thus look at the relationship between economic values and voting behavior for the first great measure of social class used here, namely family income—social groups defined by lower, middle, upper-middle, and upper incomes—while Figures 6.4.D–F look at the relationship between cultural values and the vote for these same groups. Income groups do have a kind of natural order to them, from richest to poorest or vice versa, and because the four groups must sum to the national total, voting relationships should roughly mimic national patterns, as in fact they do.

Thus, for economic values among income groups, their relationship to a Reagan vote is strongest, with conservatives attracted and liberals repelled (Figure 6.4.A). Their relationship to a Mondale vote is less strong but still clear, albeit in the opposite direction, with liberals attracted and conservatives repelled (Figure 6.4.B). And their relationship to a Non vote is now nearly flat for all but the upper-middle group, where turnout rises with economic conservatism and falls with economic liberalism (Figure 6.4.C). For cultural values, the relationship of income groups to a Reagan vote is roughly flat across the vast bulk of society, before dropping sharply among those strong liberals (Figure 6.4.D). This group relationship to a Mondale vote is the reverse, still roughly flat across the vast bulk of society, while jumping up sharply among strong liberals (Figure 6.4.E). And the group relationship to a Non vote now appears essentially flat, with a tendency for all but the high-income group to feature greater turnout at both cultural extremes, among the most conservative and the most liberal (Figure 6.4.F).

These relationships, in their rough parallelism across all four income groups, do look very much like national patterns, with the odd group-specific twist here or there. Group-based distinctions are then to be found in the way that group membership anchors these relationships at different comparative levels of support. For voter turnout, stratified by either economic or cultural values, there is a neat hierarchy in the propensity to vote, with the high-income group most likely, the upper-middle group next, the middle-income group next, and the low-income group least likely to turn out (Figures 6.4.C and 6.4.F).

For the Reagan vote, again stratified by either economics or culture, there is a parallel hierarchy of support. The voting relationship is pitched highest for the high-income group, with the upper-middle group next, the middle-income group next, and the low-income group coming in at the bottom (Figures 6.4.A and 4.D). The reverse can then be said for the Mondale vote when stratified by culture: same hierarchy, opposite direction.

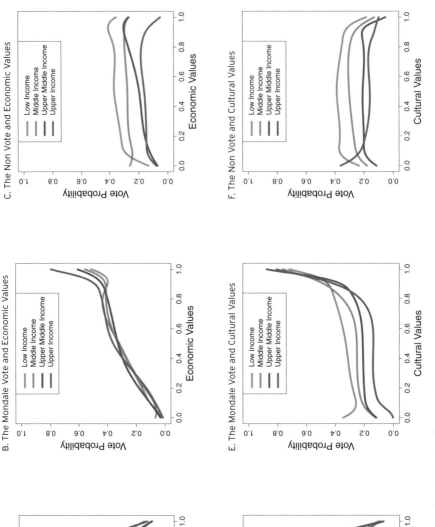

Figure 6.4   Political Values and Voting Behavior: Income Groups, 1984

This voting relationship is pitched highest for the low-income group, next-highest for the middle-income group, next for the upper-middle group, and at the bottom for the high-income group (Figure 6.4.E).

An apparent exception to this income-based patterning comes when the Mondale vote is stratified by economic values: no group-related hierarchy appears. Voting relationships between economics and a Mondale vote are effectively overlaid for all four income groups (Figure 6.4.B). Yet even this superficial exception is really a reflection of two other regularities in these group relationships. For both economics and culture, group membership contributes greater distinctions among Republican than among Democratic voters. For both Republicans and Democrats, group membership contributes greater distinctions when stratified by cultural than by economic values. By the time these regularities are embodied in the Democratic vote by economic values, then, there are just no intergroup differences remaining.[2]

A different way to analyze the same relationships is to ask neither about their overall form nor about whether they are parallel or divergent across income groups, but rather about the comparative power of political values *versus* group membership when social class is the focus. This brings a very different aspect of the story to the fore:

- At one extreme among actual voters, political values trump group membership most dramatically among Mondale voters stratified by their economic values (Figure 6.4.B). Policy preferences are the entire explanation of their voting behavior. Group membership (as delineated by income) contributes nothing.
- At the other extreme, group membership has its most dominating performance among Reagan voters stratified by culture (Figure 6.4.D). Seen this way, intergroup differences are huge. Only among strong cultural liberals does policy preference matter much at all, through there, all four groups do converge to a common point.
- The Reagan vote stratified by economics then privileges policy preference over group membership (Figure 6.4.A). Both influences are visible, but the difference by income group at any given level of economic preference is small compared with the difference *within* each income group between conservatives and liberals.

A. Low-Income Reagan Voters

p(Reagan)= 0.3085   f(income.1)

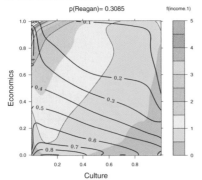

B. Low-Income Mondale Voters

p(Mondale)= 0.3289   f(income.1)

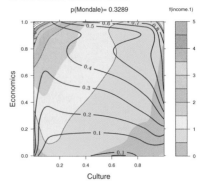

C. Middle-Income Reagan Voters

p(Reagan)= 0.4286   f(income.2)

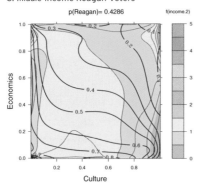

D. Middle-Income Mondale Voters

p(Mondale)= 0.291   f(income.2)

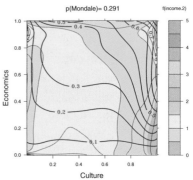

E. Upper-Middle Reagan Voters

p(Reagan)= 0.5272   f(income.3)

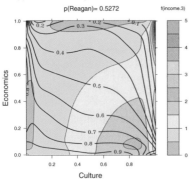

F. Upper-Middle Mondale Voters

p(Mondale)= 0.2765   f(income.3)

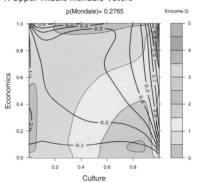

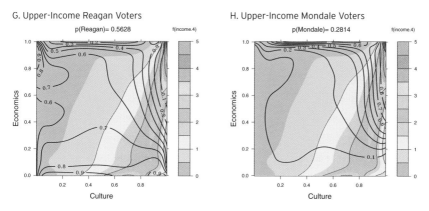

Figure 6.5 The Ideological Landscape and Voting Behavior: Income Groups, 1984

- In turn, the Mondale vote stratified by culture privileges group membership over policy preference (Figure 6.4.E). Group membership dominates the vast bulk of the cultural continuum. Policy preference takes over only among strong liberals, though these preferences largely eliminate the influence of group membership there.

- Yet the real group-based extreme arrives with the Non vote, when approached through either economics or culture (Figure 6.4.C and 6.4.F). For them, group membership is nearly everything, policy preference nearly nothing.[3] The turnout difference across groups is reliably greater than the turnout difference across ideologies, conservative versus liberal, on both economic and cultural values.

Figure 6.5 puts these patterns back together, to consider relationships between economic and cultural values simultaneously with the vote, now paying special attention to voters rather than nonvoters. Each of the component parts of Figure 6.5—Republican versus Democratic voters within the four income groups—has its individual story, and these have the virtue of putting the social group front and center. It is easier to see, for example, what the middle-income group is doing through its partisan choices when presented this way than when the group is embedded in three other groups and then stratified by economic or cultural values singly. Figure 6.5 offers these group-specific stories for each of the four social groups delineated by family income.

Yet this focus on individual groups risks masking two further, dominant patterns running across all eight parts of Figure 6.5. First, among both Reagan and Mondale voters, the relationship between economic values and the vote rises as income falls and falls as income rises. Economics is thus most related to the vote of the poor, least related the vote of the rich. Conversely, among both Reagan and Mondale voters, the relationship between cultural values and the vote rises as income *rises* and *falls* as income falls. Culture is thus most related to the vote of the rich, least related to the vote of the poor. (To see this most clearly, compare Figure 6.5.A with 6.5.C with 6.5.E with 6.5.G and Figure 6.5.B with 6.5.D with 6.5.F with 6.5.H.)

But second and equally noteworthy, the relationship between economic values and the vote is stronger among Reagan than among Mondale voters *within every income group*. Economics is just more related to the vote of the Reaganites, less related to the vote of the Mondalites. Conversely, the relationship between cultural values and the vote is stronger among Mondale than among Reagan voters within every income group. Thus culture is related more to the vote of the Mondalites and less to the vote of the Reaganites, quite apart from group membership. (To see this most clearly, compare Figure 6.5.A with 6.5.B, 6.5.C with 6.5.D, 6.5.E with 6.5.F, and 6.5.G with 6.5.H.)

Yet the practical—the strategic—impact of these economic and cultural preferences, even considered jointly, is the product not only of their joint voting relationships but also of the actual distribution of political values within the four income groups. Indeed, the moment the analyst considers where the bulk of group members actually reside, the strategic landscape for electoral politics is elaborated in consequential ways. Unlike the national composite, the distribution of economic or cultural values within each of these groups is free to vary: it is not constructed to be uniform. And in point of fact, the mix of these values does differ notably from group to group. This is a story first told in Chapter 4, where income proved to be differentially related to both economic and cultural values. Yet here, when those who are disproportionately Reagan or Mondale voters among the four income groups are presented by way of density maps rather than median scores—where "disproportion" is measured as being at least 50 percent more likely than the national average to be in one or another of our voting categories—an additionally complex strategic landscape is revealed.

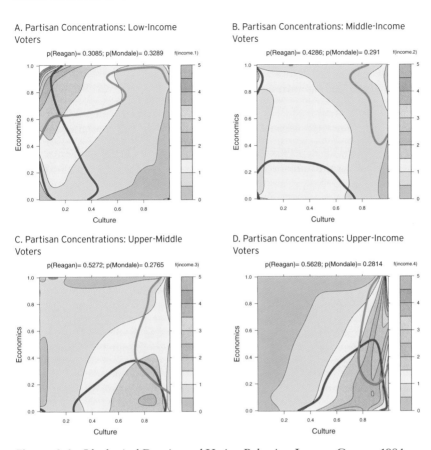

Figure 6.6 Ideological Density and Voting Behavior: Income Groups, 1984

In this, low-income voters for Ronald Reagan or Walter Mondale are seen to be united by cultural conservatism and divided by their economic preferences, with conservatives going to Reagan and liberals going to Mondale (Figure 6.7.A). The fact that disproportionate Reagan voters in this low-income group are concentrated on culture but dispersed on economics suggests that it is their cultural conservatism that fits them into the Reagan camp, while the fact that disproportionate Mondale voters within the low-income group are concentrated on economics and dispersed on culture suggests that it is their economic liberalism that fits them into the Mondale camp. Where the two voting categories actually overlap, of course, is among strong economic liberals who are strong cultural conservatives, and this is precisely the terrain where members of the low-income group are most commonly found.

Disproportionate Reagan and Mondale voters within the middle-income group show no counterpart similarity of values on either dimension, and no resulting overlap on the ideological landscape as a result (Figure 6.7.B). Middle-income Reaganites are strong economic conservatives, who vary from strongly conservative to truly centrist on culture. Unlike their low-income counterparts, *economics* defines these overrepresented Reagan voters. Middle-income Mondalites, by comparison, are strong cultural liberals, who vary from strongly liberal to truly centrist on economics. Unlike their low-income counterparts, *culture* defines these overrepresented Mondale voters. The overrepresented Reagan versus Mondale voters within the middle-income group thus inhabit a stark—nonoverlapping—ideological world.

The overrepresented Reagan and Mondale voters among the upper-middle group shift back toward being united by culture and divided by economics (Figure 6.7.C). There is a healthy leaven of cultural moderates within their disproportionate Reagan vote, as well as a healthy leaven of economic liberals within their disproportionate Mondale vote. Yet the many moderate cultural liberals within the Reagan vote in this upper-middle group, plus the many economic moderates (as well as a genuine body of moderate economic conservatives) within the Mondale vote here, do restore some slight overlap in ideological terrain. Otherwise, it is economics that unites middle-income and upper-middle Reaganites, culture that unites middle-income and upper-middle Mondalites.

The upper-income group is then a stereotypical opposite to its lower-income counterparts, being once again neatly united on culture and divided on economics (Figure 6.7.D). Cultural unification among overrepresented Reagan and Mondale voters comes this time from cultural liberalism, not conservatism, though the economic divide remains where it resides within every income group: conservatives Republican and liberals Democratic. Nevertheless, the cultural overlap is sufficient to restore some ideological overlap, among upper-income Reaganites who are strong cultural liberals and upper-income Mondalites who are moderate to moderately conservative on economics.

Accordingly, the simplest way to describe the strategic landscape for electoral politics when income groups are the focus is to say three things. First, the same basic relationships between the vote and economic or cultural values actually characterize all of these income groups. Group membership does not much alter voting relationships in and of itself (Figure 6.4). Second, economics is more tightly related to the vote among lower-income groups, while culture is more tightly related among higher-income groups, just as economics is more tightly related to the vote among Reagan voters, while culture is more tightly related to the vote among Mondale voters (Figure 6.5). Third and last, the differential presence of these values in the four income groups means that their Reagan and their Mondale voters are nevertheless concentrated in additionally different places (Figure 7.6).

Parallel relationships to the vote by economic or cultural values can thus manage to look very different when encountered as partisan factions within social groups. The major strategic challenge for both parties, then, lies in finding a common national program that can hold all four groups together. Group portraits of the two major parties do echo the national picture: Republicans united on economics but divided on culture, Democrats united on culture but divided on economics. Yet each party sees its overall divisions exacerbated when viewed through the lens of income groups. And each has a dissident group that does not even echo the unifying elements of the national picture.

For Republican voters, there is a cultural split down the middle of their chosen party: low- and middle-income groups have a very different profile from upper-middle and upper-income groups on culture. There is also a small overrepresented faction of strong cultural conservatives who are moderate to strong economic liberals, which is additionally out of step with the general party consensus. For Democrats, the cultural divide is less striking, pitting only low-income voters against the rest. Yet the economic divide is more pronounced, with substantial numbers of economic moderates and even economic conservatives in the upper-middle and upper-income groups. And the overrepresented faction that is additionally out of step with the general party consensus, found among strong economic liberals who are strong cultural conservatives, is much larger than its Republican counterpart.

Educational Attainment

Chapter 3, on the contribution of social class to economic and cultural values, and Chapter 4, on the economic and cultural values of social groups created by class, considered two major class aspects, namely family income and educational attainment. The two are often treated as alternatives, even used as substitutes, and Chapters 3 and 4 did show roughly similar relationships to political values for both aspects of class. On the other hand, both aspects retained their relationships to political values in the presence of the other. At no point did the analysis suggest that one or the other set of relationships was spurious. Moreover, the two operated in distinguishable ways, most especially in the realm of culture, where education was much more strongly related to cultural values than was income. As a result, any benchmark consideration of social class must retain educational attainment as an alternative indicator.

Social groups constructed from educational attainment do show much the same voting relationships to economic and cultural values individually as did social groups constructed from family income, at least in the benchmark year of 1984, so there seems little point in presenting for a second time what are close to being the same exhibits. Economic values remain strongly related to a Reagan vote and clearly if less strongly related to a Mondale vote, albeit in the opposite direction, while the Non vote alignment is a weak echo of the Mondale relationship. Cultural values show the same flat trajectory across most of the ideological spectrum, coupled with the same strong dip in Reagan support and the same strong surge in Mondale support among strong cultural liberals, along with a roughly flat relationship among nonvoters. Group membership—for educational groups this time—still anchors both economic and cultural relationships more strongly among nonvoters than among voters, and more strongly for the Reagan than the Mondale electorate (tables not shown).[4]

When the focus shifts to *joint* voting relationships, social groups constructed from educational attainment still show much the same linkage to political values as did social groups constructed from family income. The same two key effects appear. In the first, the power of economic values falls with educational attainment and rises as education falls, while the power of cultural values rises with educational attainment and falls as education falls, within both the Reagan and the Mondale vote. In the second continuing effect, the Reagan vote is always more tied to economics and the Mondale vote to culture, now within each educational (and not just income) group (figures again not shown).[5]

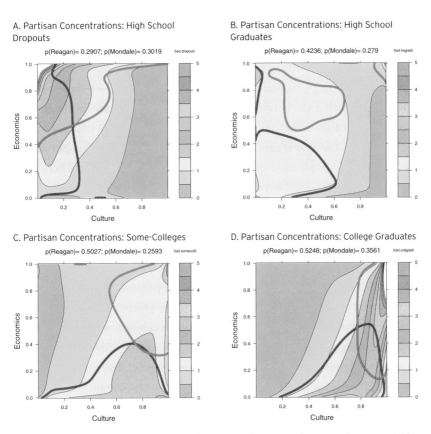

Figure 6.7   Ideological Density and Voting Behavior: Education Groups, 1984

Even the density maps for economic and cultural values jointly are similar in many regards for groups delineated by family income and educational attainment. Yet here there is a striking difference, characterizing the largest educational group. And by virtue of those factors—a big ideological difference in a big social group—this difference alters the strategic calculus that would apply whenever voters were influenced more by their educational than their income levels. The group in question is high school graduates, a middling educational category that forms what was actually the modal educational group in the United States in 1984. Yet it not only differs sharply from the middling income group, our "middle class"; this difference also has major potential strategic consequences.

The shift in the ideology of overrepresented Republicans as seen through these two middling groups—Figure 6.6.B versus Figure 6.7.B—is clear but modest. High school graduate Republican voters are more economically moderate and more culturally conservative than middle-income Republican voters. Yet the shift in the ideology of overrepresented Democrats is striking, with the potential to make a key segment of class-based politics operate differently. Economic values do not change much between high school graduate and middle-income Democratic voters. But where the over-represented Democrats from the middle-income tercile were concentrated in the terrain of strong cultural liberalism, overrepresented Democrats among high school graduates live all the way across the center of the ideological spectrum, in the land of moderate cultural conservatism.

As a result, the overrepresented Democratic faction within the high school graduate group is additionally distinguished from the overrepresented Democratic faction within the middle-income group by the absence of any overlap between the two. Moreover, the resulting divergence is so large that it imposes a whole different strategic perspective—or at least, a different set of strategic options—on campaign strategists addressing social groups delineated by class. Together, the overrepresented Democratic and Republican middle classes had anchored the ideological cores of the two political parties for the nation as a whole, biasing them toward uniformly liberal or uniformly conservative positions on economics and culture (Figure 6.6.B). Now, when educational attainment is the focus, the middling factions, these overrepresented Democratic and Republican high school graduates, are united by culture but divided by economics, the precise same thing that can be said about the high school dropouts (Figure 6.7.B).

In the process, a major additional fissure has opened up inside the Democratic Party. The Reagan coalition, the aggregation that voted disproportionately for Ronald Reagan, was mainly unified by economics and stressed by culture when voters were aligned through their income groups (Figure 6.6). This remains true when the Reagan coalition is realigned through their educational groups (Figure 6.7). By contrast, the Mondale coalition, the aggregation that voted disproportionately for Walter Mondale, was mainly unified by culture and stressed by economics when its voters were aligned through their income groups. Yet now, the Mondale coalition has acquired a huge cultural fissure when aligned by its educational groups. Indeed, its lone previously dissident faction, that cluster of overrepresented Democrats who were strongly liberal on economics but strongly conservative on culture, has been joined by the modal educational group in all of American society, the high school graduates.

Both parties face evident strategic challenges in such an environment. For Republicans, the superficially easy way to unify voting groups stratified by social class—emphasize economics and de-emphasize culture—gets harder to execute with the shift from family income to educational attainment as the lead indicator of class. Those overrepresented Republican voters who were strongly conservative on culture but moderately to strongly liberal on economics were a strategic puzzle even when social groups were stratified by income. When these groups are instead stratified by education, the middling educational group, those high school graduate Republicans, has moved modestly but clearly to the right on cultural values, providing aid and comfort to the previous Republican dissidents.

The only way to hold these dissident voters in the coalition—the national Republican Party can hardly offer them economic liberalism—is through policy promises featuring strong cultural conservatism. This is, after all, the only thing that makes them Republican. Yet they obviously *can* be secured as part of the coalition, so writing them off would be a huge opening injury for any national campaign. Moreover, the overrepresented high school graduate Republicans should be happy with this strategy. On the other hand, offering the necessary cultural conservatism means risking offense to the overrepresented Republicans among both the some-colleges and the college graduates. The members of these groups are not only more numerous in the Republican than in the Democratic Party—they also have higher voting turnout *and* they are better equipped, precisely by way of their education, to notice policies that do not accord with their own wishes.

If the Republican coalition that formed around Ronald Reagan appears challenging when stratified by educational attainment, however, the Democratic coalition that formed around Walter Mondale appears increasingly incoherent when the focus changes from income to education as the lead indicator of social class. This Democratic coalition had major economic tensions when income groups were the focus, and these tensions do not disappear when educational groups are the focus instead. Yet the Mondale coalition is now stressed by culture as well, pitting high school dropouts plus high school graduates against some-colleges plus college graduates.

When social groups were stratified by income, this cultural problem was limited to the low-income group against all others. Now, it is instead a major split down the middle of the party. Yet an attempt to finesse this division through a return to strongly liberal economics highlights those clusters of overrepresented Democrats who were already in tension with their party on economics, namely those among the some-colleges and college graduates who are extremely liberal on culture but true centrists or moderate conservatives on economics. On the one hand, they are less numerous than their economically more liberal but culturally more conservative internal party opponents. On the other hand, and very much mirroring the internal Republican situation, they have the same higher turnout and the same greater chance of noticing policies that do not accord with their wishes.

Race, Ethnicity, and the Vote

Nothing requires the patterning of relationships between political values and a presidential vote for other social cleavages to be even parallel, much less identical, to the patterning associated with social class. And nothing exemplifies this potential for difference as much as the shift from social class to race and ethnicity as a focus of analysis:

- Within this shift, the largest racial minority in the United States, Black Americans, shows nearly no relationship between policy preferences on either economics or culture and the vote for president. Blacks are thus the great social group in all of American society that is linked to electoral politics by social identity and not by policy preference.
- At first blush, the largest immigrant group, Hispanic Americans, looks different, showing relationships to the vote that resemble those of non-Hispanic Whites. Yet when it is possible to see where the Hispanic vote actually resides, in terms of political values but by way of density maps, this vote proves to have some similarities to both Blacks and Anglos, while actually being closer to the former.
- Along the way, it becomes possible to remove both social groups from the analysis and reconsider relationships among the Anglo majority, now itself defined as a racial and ethnic group.

In pursuit of those findings, Figure 6.8 offers the Reagan, the Mondale, and the Non vote, by economic and then cultural values, for Black, Hispanic, and Anglo Americans. In analyzing this figure, it is important to keep in mind that there are nearly no economic conservatives of any sort (<0.4) among Blacks and very few strong cultural liberals (>0.8) among either Blacks or Hispanics. Apart from that, for social groups that represented 8.9 percent and 6.4 percent respectively of the total sample in 1984, it would be unwise to attribute much consequence—or indeed, much reliability—to the most conservative or the most liberal 10 percent of either group. Yet despite these limitations and exceptions, Figure 6.8 manages to sketch three very different racial and ethnic patterns, with very different links between political values and voting behavior.

It is a commonplace to note that Blacks stand out from other major groups in American society in terms of the partisan balance in their vote—really the partisan imbalance—and 1984 was no exception. Black Americans offered the strongest Mondale (62.9 percent) and the weakest Reagan (7.7 percent) vote among all such groups. This tiny Reagan vote was further distinguished by the fact that political values were obviously unrelated to it from the start, on either economics or culture (Figures 6.8.A and 6.8.D). The Black Non vote, considerably healthier than the Reagan vote at 29.4 percent, was likewise nearly unrelated to political values, once it is recalled that there are very few economic conservatives of any sort and few strong cultural liberals within this group (Figures 6.8.C and 6.8.F). The Mondale vote does give an initial semblance of a policy relationship, but once the same ideological sectors are discounted ($<.04$ on economics, >0.8 on culture), this, too, simply disappears (Figures 6.8.B and 6.8.E).

Hispanic voters in 1984 featured a more even division of their tally, albeit with the Non vote as the plurality choice[6]: 45.1 percent Non, 28.9 percent Reagan, and 26.0 percent Mondale votes. Yet while this is a huge distance from the Anglo tally,[7] Hispanic Americans do appear to feature voting relationships that are closer to those of Anglos than of Blacks. For economic values, and ignoring the tiny handful of extreme conservatives in this population, Hispanics appear to parallel the voting relationships of Anglos. Underperforming these Anglos in voter turnout, they of course underperform in aggregate contributions to both the Reagan and the Mondale vote. Yet the *form* of that vote—its relationship to economic

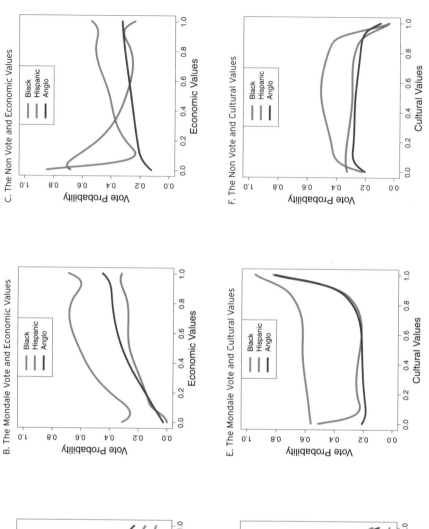

Figure 6.8 Political Values and Voting Behavior: Racial and Ethnic Groups, 1984

values—looks quite similar to the Anglo form (Figures 6.8.A–C). For cultural values, the story is somewhat different. Here, Hispanics fall neatly between Blacks and Anglos among Reagan voters, copy the Anglos and not the Blacks among Mondale voters, and lag both Blacks and Anglos in voter turnout (Figures 6.8.D–F).

In some ways, the Anglos are—and must be—a less interesting counterpoint. Being 85 percent of the total sample, they must largely recapitulate the national picture. For economic values, there is the same strong negative relationship to the Reagan vote (Figure 6.8.A); a clear, less strong, but opposite relationship to the Mondale vote (Figure 6.8.B); and a pale copy of this Democratic relationship among the Non vote (Figure 6.8.C). For cultural values, there is the same flat relationship to both the Reagan and the Mondale votes across most of the ideological spectrum, before plunging for Reagan and jumping up for Mondale among strong liberals (Figures 6.8.D and 6.8.E), along with a nearly flat relationship to the Non vote across the bulk of the cultural continuum, before declining among extreme conservatives *and* extreme liberals, both of whom are more likely to vote (Figure 6.8.F).

For a group that is 85 percent of the total sample, the question of where members of the specifically Anglo group reside is relatively inconsequential. With a setup that distributes the entire sample evenly across the full economic and cultural continuums, a subsample this large cannot get too far from the national picture on this measure either, and Anglos are indeed well represented everywhere. But for Black and Hispanic Americans—small social groups with concentrated policy preferences—that is much less the case. Figure 6.9 offers the distribution of political values for the three voting categories (Reagan, Mondale, and Non), broken out for the three racial and ethnic groups (Blacks, Hispanics, and Anglos), showing the situation for economic and then cultural values. These are, in effect, density maps by individual policy dimension.

The main contribution from the Anglos in this story is just to confirm how different the density maps underneath the Reagan, the Mondale, and the Non vote can be (Figure 6.9.C). On economics, distinctions are stark: conservatives contribute the vast bulk of the Reagan vote, while liberals make up a clear majority of Mondale support. On culture, there is the familiar pattern of little difference throughout most of the cultural continuum.

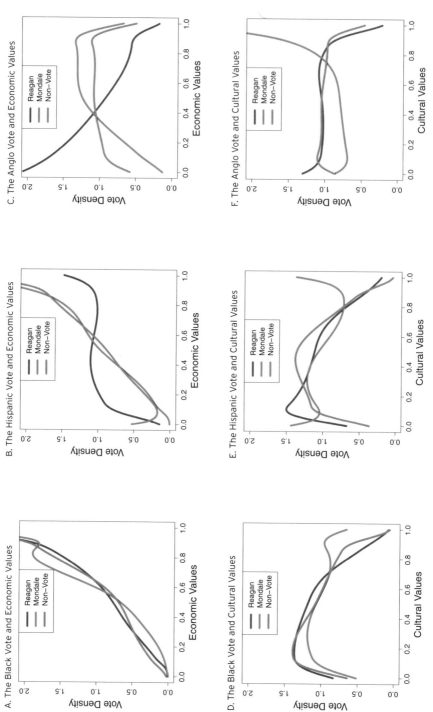

Figure 6.9 Ideological Density and Voting Behavior, Individual Dimensions: Race and Ethnicity, 1984

Yet among strong liberals, the Reagan and Mondale bases diverge sharply—and unlike the situation with Blacks and Hispanics, there are many such individuals among these Anglos.

The new, different, and consequential points in Figure 6.9 are, first, the essential disappearance of valuational differences among Black voting categories and, second, the effective decline of previously apparent relationships among Hispanics. For Blacks more than any other group in American society, the Reagan vote, the Mondale vote, and the Non vote are constituted from essentially identical preference distributions. With regard to economic values, these distributions are truly identical (Figure 6.9.A). With regard to culture, they are identical among all but strong cultural liberals—of whom there are very few in the Black population (Figure 6.9.D). Policy preferences are simply not shaping the Black vote.

Among Hispanics, lesser elements of distinction among the Reagan, Mondale, and Non votes do remain, though they look different through the lens of ideological density. For economic values, nothing distinguishes the Hispanic Democratic from the Hispanic Non vote, and while the Hispanic Reagan vote does differ from both, this is only because it escapes *any* policy relationship. Hispanic Reagan voters are equally distributed across all but the extremes of the economic continuum (Figure 6.9.B). For cultural values, strong liberals in the Hispanic group do diverge clearly from both Republican and Non voters by swinging strongly Democratic—it is just that there are very few such individuals in this population (Figure 6.9.E).

The picture that results, when these individual portraits are put back together in the same fashion used in density maps for social groups by family income or educational attainment, is of three racial and ethnic groups with not only radically different policy profiles but also radically different ways of *linking* policy preferences to presidential voting. Figure 6.10.A, in its background distribution, confirms that the Black population is heavily concentrated among economic liberals. Yet within this liberal population, the high ground of overrepresentation (by our 50 percent standard) is effectively coterminous for Republicans and Democrats. Among Black Americans, policy preferences just do not distinguish between Democratic and (the handful of) Republican voters. There is a small terrain that overproduces for the Democrats only, among economic liberals who are also cultural liberals. But the dominant point is just that the

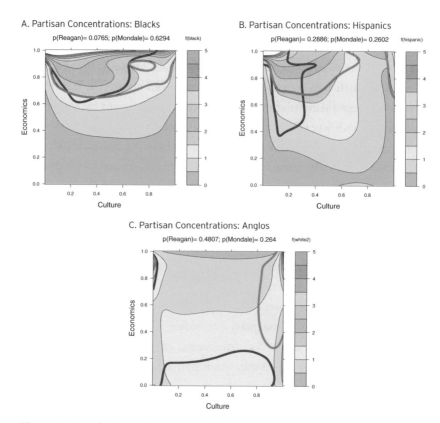

Figure 6.10 Ideological Density and Voting Behavior: Racial and Ethnic Groups, 1984

Republican vote is effectively *inside* the Democratic vote, not in opposition to it.

What this picture also suggests is a vote that is overwhelmingly generated by an underlying group identification, a social identity—by the simple fact of whether an individual is or is not a member of this racial group. In strategic terms, this is an ideological landscape offering little hope that the partisan choices of group members can be altered through policy shifts by presidential candidates. Instead, for those who fall within group boundaries, the question revolves much more around whether the individual actually votes. These facts nevertheless translate into some further, explicitly partisan, strategic propositions.

For Republicans, there are two of these, one pointless and the other discouraging. In the first, there is nearly no current Republican vote among

Black Americans, and no apparent policy-related way of generating one. On economics, a Republican presidential candidate would have to move so far away from the Republican high ground among Anglos (Figure 6.10.C) as to make such a move patently implausible. On culture, a Republican presidential candidate might secure some marginal benefit by having the *Democratic* candidate move farther off to the cultural left, but that is not an option under direct Republican control. Otherwise, a Republican candidate has little to do, except to avoid antagonizing group members. For such a Republican, low voter turnout must suffice in a world where policy promises are irrelevant.

For Democrats, the background situation is much sunnier, with strategic implications that are nevertheless almost equally discouraging. There is already a huge Democratic vote among Black Americans, to the point where the crucial intragroup difference is between voting Democratic or not voting at all. The density map suggests that this trade-off is maximized by Democratic presidential candidates who are strong economic liberals and moderate cultural conservatives. Yet here, as with the situation among Republicans, an emphasis on economic liberalism coupled with a move to the cultural right is so far away from the Democratic high ground among Anglos (Figure 6.10.C) as to make such a move, likewise, patently implausible. What such a candidate is left with is efforts to ramp up the power of social identity, by way of group attachment.

Figure 6.9.B, in its background distribution, confirms that the Hispanic population is more dispersed than the Black population on economics and more concentrated than the Black population on culture. This leaves it solidly liberal on economics and impressively conservative on culture. Unlike the Black population, however, this generates a distinctive Democratic high ground, a distinctive Republican high ground, and an overlapping high ground among Hispanics. The distinctively Democratic Hispanics are economic liberals who are cultural moderates. The distinctively Republican Hispanics are cultural conservatives who are economic moderates. And those living in the territory that can generate disproportionate Hispanic support for both parties are strong economic liberals who are also strong cultural conservatives.

Unlike the situation among Blacks, this is a world allowing strategic competition by way of policy promises among Hispanics. This remains a competition sharply constrained by a concentrated group preference for a particular set of public policies: liberal on economics and conservative on culture. Moreover, the Anglo picture (Figure 6.10.C) suggests that neither party is likely to be able to offer that combination as a national program. Yet both parties have something—something major—that they can offer to this ethnic group: economic liberalism from the Democrats, cultural conservatism from the Republicans. And very much unlike the story for Black Americans, these emphases do carve out distinguishable territory among Hispanic Americans. For Hispanics, policy does show a relationship, albeit constrained, to the vote.

Yet it is still ultimately this constraint, rather than that relationship, that appears more impressive by comparison with the situation among the Anglos, the other grand social group carved out by racial and ethnic principles. Figure 6.10.C confirms that economic and cultural preferences among these Anglos are distributed in roughly even fashion, as the statistical setup would suggest. What must be said about the partisan high ground within this distribution, on the other hand, is that the overrepresented areas for Democrats versus Republicans are not just nonoverlapping. Their partisan high grounds are actually organized around different policy principles.

Among these Anglos, overrepresented Democrats are strong *cultural* liberals, varying from strong liberalism through moderate conservatism on economics, while overrepresented Republicans are strong *economic* conservatives, who vary from moderate conservatism through moderate liberalism on culture. This was the story of national politics, at Figure 6.3, before Blacks and Hispanics were removed from that picture. Because it is still the story after they have been removed, it seems clear that the central strategic dilemmas characterizing the nation as a whole, set out in the first section of this chapter, remain alive and well within the Anglo population.

Religious Background and the Vote

Denominational Attachment

The main indicators of religious background, namely denominational attachment and generic religiosity, differ as well when the focus is their relationship to political values and voting behavior. They differ from race and ethnicity in that religious background, measured either way, is reliably linked by political values to the presidential vote. They differ from social class, also reliably linked by values to the vote, in that religious background (again measured either way) contributes relatively little added group-based anchoring to these voting relationships. Yet these two indicators of religious background then differ powerfully *from each other* when the focus shifts to the distribution of political values and partisan choices underneath those voting relationships, while they lend a sharply increased complexity to the ideological landscape for electoral conflict—a complexity that is masked by attention to voting relationships as opposed to density maps.

For both economic and cultural values, among Reagan, Mondale, and Non voters, voting relationships by denominational group track very closely with national patterns (Figure 6.11). For economics, conservatism is strongly associated with a Reagan vote; liberalism is clearly if less strongly associated with a Mondale vote; and liberalism is much more weakly associated with a Non vote. For culture, neither liberal nor conservative values are associated with either a Reagan or a Mondale vote, except among strong cultural liberals, who are attracted by Mondale and repelled by Reagan. There is a slight further tendency for liberals to turn out more than conservatives, with the additional twist that both cultural extremes are more likely to vote than is the ideological center. By itself, all this is roughly the same story that could be told by either indictor of social class.

Yet unlike the story as told by class indicators, the closeness of these patterns to the national template in the case of denominational attachment leaves little room for additional group-based distinctions. There is a modest further ordering to these great religious families when the focus is economic values. Reagan does best among Evangelicals, then Mainstreams, then Catholics, then Non-Christians, while Mondale does the reverse—at any given point on the ideological spectrum (Figures 6.11.A and 6.11.B). There are some idiosyncratic blips when the focus shifts to cultural values, in a modest but clear propensity for the two Protestant groups, Evangelicals and Mainstreams, to oppose the two others, Catholics and Non-Christians, in voting for Reagan, along with a modest propensity for Catholics to give an extra increment to Mondale (Figures 6.11.D and 6.11.E). And there is a general propensity for Non-Christians

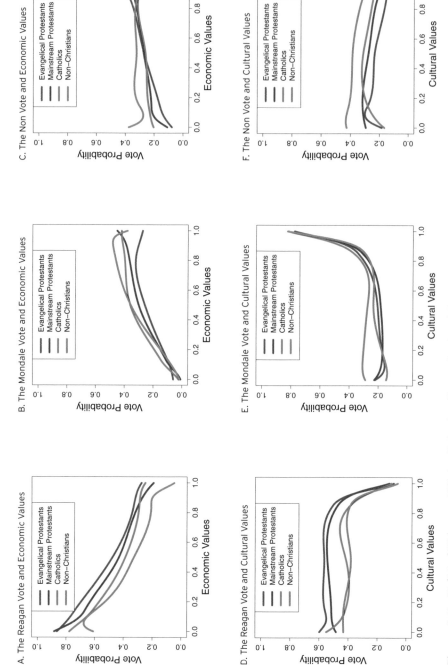

Figure 6.11 Political Values and Voting Behavior: Denominational Groups, 1984

to vote less than the three other denominational groups, whether examined by economics or culture (Figures 6.11.C and 6.11.F).[8]

Those are much more modest twists on national patterns than were contributed by social groups delineated by family income or educational attainment, and this same story of limited room for additional group-based distinctions continues when the two individual domains, economics and culture, are considered for their joint relationship to the vote. What results is just a weaker copy of the patterning associated with social class (tables not shown). Social groups delineated by religious denomination do feature a closer relationship between economic values and the Reagan vote among each of the four great religious families, and a closer relationship between cultural values and the Mondale vote among these same four families. Beyond that, the power of economics rises as one moves from Non-Christians to Mainstreams to Catholics to Evangelicals, while the power of culture rises in the opposite direction.

Where the story becomes consequentially different is with consideration of the density maps, that is, with the coming of a concern for the actual location of denominational groups on the ideological landscape and with the nature of the partisan concentrations associated with these groups in those locations. And here, the comparative simplicity of voting relationships masks extreme diversity not just in the actual distribution of economic and cultural values among these groups but now in associated partisan behavior. This was an important aspect of the strategic landscape for social groups delineated by income or education. Yet the story of intragroup divisions among denominational groups is so different from that same story among class groups that it contributes a different *kind* of further complexity to the strategic landscape.

The background distributions of political values within denominational groups—their density maps—provide an immediate signal that voting relationships, seen in isolation, may obscure as much as they clarify about the strategic landscape when shaped by denominational attachment (Figure 6.12). What distinguishes the Evangelical Protestants is their concentration on the far right of the cultural spectrum, along with a further concentration on the right of the economic spectrum. Their opposites are then the Non-Christians, concentrated on the far left of the cultural spectrum, with a much more modest concentration on the economic left. Both the

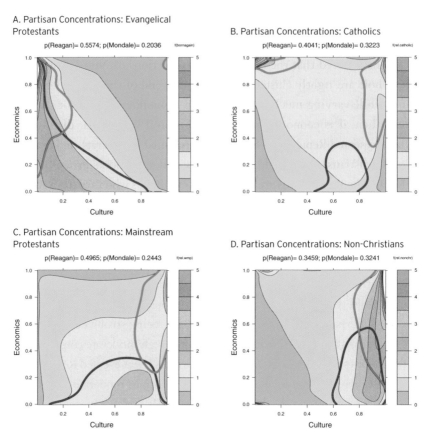

Figure 6.12 Ideological Density and Voting Behavior: Denominational Groups, 1984

Catholics and the Mainstream Protestants are far less concentrated on either dimension. In particular, and unlike the Evangelicals or Non-Christians, they encompass a wide swath of cultural values. What distinguishes them from each other—Catholics from Mainstreams—is the way the former lean toward the liberal end of the economic continuum while the latter lean toward the conservative end.

Yet within that setup, density maps confirm that the dominant further fact about this ideological landscape, when viewed through the lens of denominational attachment, is the great divide between partisan factions characterizing the Evangelical Protestants versus partisan factions within the three other groups, though the latter do show modest further intra-group distinctions. To see this most clearly, it helps to begin the exposition with the Non-Christians rather than the Evangelicals, and to work backward toward the latter by way of the Mainstream Protestants and Catholics.

We have noted that the overrepresented sections of Non-Christianity as a whole are tightly clustered at the liberal end of the cultural continuum, while varying much more widely in economic values. Not surprisingly, then, it is economic rather than cultural values that distinguish overrepresented Republicans from overrepresented Democrats among these Non-Christians—as they do among every denominational group (Figure 6.12.D). The Republicans are strong cultural liberals who vary from strong conservatism through true centrism on economics, while the Democrats are strong cultural liberals who reach all the way from strong liberalism through moderate conservatism on economics.

The overrepresented sections of Mainstream Protestantism feature a clear but modest lean toward the cultural left and the economic right. Within this, the overrepresented Democrats look very similar to their partisan counterparts among the Non-Christians, being strong cultural liberals who again vary from strong liberalism through moderate conservatism on economics (Figure 6.12.C). By contrast, the overrepresented Republicans are both more conservative on economics and more moderate on culture than they were among the Non-Christians. This is also a more populated region of the Mainstream landscape overall, suggesting that the Republican faction is more advantageously placed than the Democratic faction within it, and the Republican share of the vote is indeed larger among Mainstream Protestants than among Non-Christians.

The overrepresented sections of Catholicism are less liberal on culture but more liberal on economics than their Mainstream counterparts. Yet their overrepresented partisan factions actually look very similar to those of the Mainstream Protestants, for both political parties (Figure 6.12.B). The dominant faction of overrepresented Democrats again features strong cultural liberals who vary from strong liberalism through true centrism on economics, though there is a secondary concentration of Catholic Democrats who are strong economic liberals and strong cultural conservatives. Neither the Non-Christians nor the Mainstream Protestants possess any counterpart to this secondary concentration. The overrepresented Republicans are tightly focused on moderate cultural liberalism, while varying only from strong to moderate conservatism on economics. This time, however, it is the Democratic faction that lives in the more populated region of the Catholic landscape, albeit only modestly so.

Which brings the analysis back to the great denominational family that, as a whole, is farthest away from the Non-Christians, the Mainstream Protestants, and the Catholics: these are the Evangelical Protestants, and their ideological homeland is concentrated among cultural conservatives—and here, even more so among Democratic than among Republican voters (Figure 6.12.A). The Evangelical Republican vote contains a significant minority of cultural moderates and even moderate liberals; the Evangelical Democratic vote does not. The overrepresented Democratic faction within this great religious family is composed of strong cultural conservatives who vary from strong economic liberalism to moderate economic conservatism, with moderate liberalism as their modal preference. The overrepresented Republican faction is powerfully concentrated at the combination of strong cultural and strong economic conservatism, and tails away in both directions.

As a result, partisan competition among the Evangelical Protestants is similar to that inside the other three great denominational families, in the sense of pitting economic liberals against economic conservatives. Yet it is different from the other three in taking place largely within the territory of cultural conservatism. When the focus is purely the Evangelical Protestants, this is an unequivocal advantage to the Republican Party. The overrepresented Republican faction among these Evangelicals tracks almost perfectly with the distribution of policy preferences within the group as a whole. When the focus is instead the *four* denominational families, however, as structuring devices on the national landscape, what results is a sharp increase in potential strategic complexity.

Seen this second way, all four denominational groups are characterized by internal economic conflict of a similar sort, pitting the more-conservative Republicans against the more-liberal Democrats. Three of the four denominational groups are further characterized by internal cultural conflict, though this is a much more complicated matter. Three of the four groups pit more-conservative Republicans against more-liberal Democrats (apart from that secondary Catholic cluster). Otherwise, there is not really much cultural difference between Republicans and Democrats among the Non-Christians, while the overrepresented Evangelical

Republicans actually include much more liberal territory on culture than do the overrepresented Evangelical Democrats.

As a result, three of these denominational groups might reasonably prefer electoral appeals that at least lean toward cultural liberalism. Yet the one group that would not, the Evangelical Protestants, is also the group that provides the largest disproportionate advantage to Republicans. In practical terms, this means that it is the Republicans who are most stressed internally by the voting behavior of social groups as defined by denominational background. Yet it is also the Republicans who have most to gain by successfully managing this stress, leaving them with the more operationally difficult—but also more potentially rewarding—strategic challenge.

Generic Religiosity

Different from denomination, at least in theory, is religiosity. The former is a matter of attachment to a specific faith, with its particular theology, its particular liturgy, and its particular history. The latter is instead the *intensity* with which that faith is held, regardless of its specifics, most especially as measured by the regularity with which it is practiced. As principles of group stratification, these two major aspects of religious background are entirely separable, and each proved to have an independent influence on political values in the presence of the other. At the same time, some religious families are reliably more observant than others—the Evangelical Protestants at one end of the continuum, the Non-Christians at the other—so that the actual degree to which denomination and religiosity are separable influences when it comes to voting behavior is, as ever, an empirical question.

Figure 6.13 begins to seek an answer by arraying the voting behavior of the generically religious and the generically irreligious, according to their economic and then their cultural values. Recall that the *religious* group is constituted from those who (claim to) attend church weekly or more, and the *irreligious* group from those who (claim to) attend rarely or never.[9] The result is like the story of denominational attachment in strongly reflecting national patterns within religious groups. Yet it is more like the story of social class in leaving room for an evident secondary role for religious groups in anchoring these overall relationships. And it makes a striking contribution to the ideological landscape, one that is unlike any other.

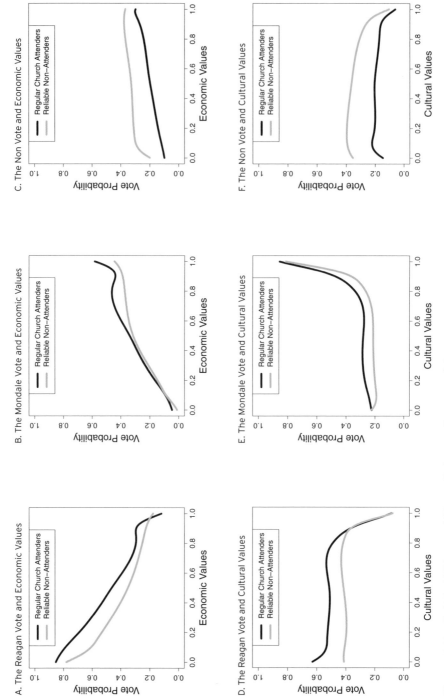

Figure 6.13 Political Values and Voting Behavior: Devotional Groups, 1984

National effects are now so familiar as to require little further exposition when the two valuational dimensions, economics and culture, are considered individually. For economic values, the Reagan vote shows a strong negative relationship, the Mondale vote shows a clear but weaker positive relationship, and the Non vote shows a highly attenuated version of the Mondale pattern. For cultural values, both the Reagan and the Mondale votes show no relationship across most of the ideological spectrum, before plunging for Reagan and surging for Mondale among strong liberals, while the Non vote is a highly attenuated version of the Reagan pattern. Yet like the situation for social class and unlike that for religious denomination, generic religiosity as a basis for group membership retains three further relationships—three anchoring effects—all its own.

The largest effect on voting relationships for social groups stratified by generic religiosity actually occurs among the Non voters. The religious are more likely to vote than the irreligious whether economics or culture is the focus, at every point on either ideological continuum (Figures 6.13.C and 6.13.F). Economic conservatives are then more likely to vote than economic liberals, while cultural liberals are more likely to vote than cultural conservatives. This effect is sufficiently strong that the religious make a greater contribution to *both* the Reagan and the Mondale vote than do the irreligious, again whether the focus is economics (Figures 6.13.A and 6.13.B) or culture (Figures 6.13.D and 6.13.E). Though note that the difference between the two groups is additionally greater among Reagan than among Mondale voters: higher vote turnout among the religious is inevitably harvested by the candidate whom this group prefers, and for 1984 that was Ronald Reagan.

Generic religiosity is also very good at recapitulating a set of joint voting relationships that characterized not only both aspects of social class but also denominational attachment when economic and cultural values were considered simultaneously (Figure 6.14). Once again and very clearly, the Reagan vote in each social group is more aligned with economic values, the Mondale vote with cultural values. This is done for the religious and for the irreligious as well. At the same time, it is the high-attenders among the generically religious whose vote is more aligned with economic values and the low-attenders whose vote is more aligned with cultural values. This is true for Reagan voters and for Mondale voters as well.

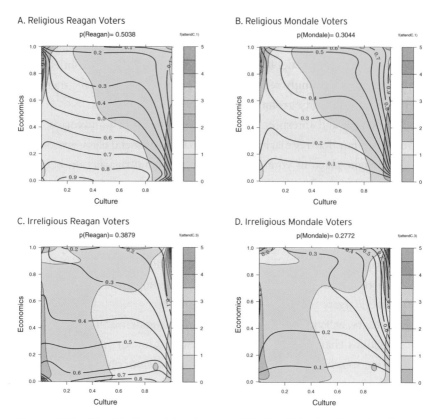

Figure 6.14   The Ideological Landscape and Voting Behavior: Devotional Groups, 1984

These relationships are so clear and clean for generic religiosity, so stereotypically present, that they provide an excellent opportunity for a reminder about what these joint relationships do—and do not—imply. One further and obvious extrapolation from these joint relationships—one further thing that they do imply—is that economic values are most strongly registered within the Reagan vote among the religious while, conversely, cultural values are most strongly registered within the Mondale vote among the irreligious. This follows logically from the preceding analysis, and these are indeed the extreme voting categories which it generates.

Yet recall what this analysis of extreme voting categories does *not* imply. It handily says that the highly religious who voted for Reagan were most moved by economics and the minimally religious who voted for Mondale were most moved by culture. We have already seen quite the reverse. For example, high religiosity took the Reagan vote to its peak among religious groups, at 50.4 percent, a full twenty percentage points ahead of Walter Mondale. It is just that, having done so, economic values were then more strongly registered than cultural values *among* members of this high-religiosity group who voted for Ronald Reagan.

The display and interpretation of this regularity in joint voting relationships, a familiar regularity after the analysis of social class, is probably also the right place to comment on a fundamental distinction between religion and class that lies beneath this very regularity. Both family income and educational attainment give an order to the social groups that they create, an order that might be described as inherent, running from high to low or low to high, and this order appears to have obvious implications for partisan choice. The more economically conservative party at a point in time should appeal to high-income groups, the more economically liberal party to low-income groups.

Religiosity, at least as measured by church attendance, likewise creates social groups that can be ranked from high to low or low to high, and this order, too, has obvious implications for partisan choice.[10] Religious practice is a central element of cultural traditionalism, so that the more culturally conservative party at a point in time should appeal to highly religious groups, the more culturally progressive party to minimally religious groups. The logic of alignment is thus the same for both indicators of social class and for one indicator of religious background. Yet that inherent logic is not the same—it is effectively missing—in the case of the other main religious indicator, namely denominational attachment. It is not at all obvious how the great religious families should be ordered. It is clear that they *are* ordered differently between economics and culture. It is just that the objective denominational characteristic that produces these orders is not intrinsically obvious.

In any case, with voting behavior, there is additional value added by a focus on religiosity when the analytic focus shifts away from voting relationships and onto density maps. This is true not only for religiosity in its own right. It is also true because the two aspects of religious background, denominational attachment and generic religiosity, show further differentiation in their density maps, along with further differentiation in the partisan concentration of group members when their vote is arrayed jointly

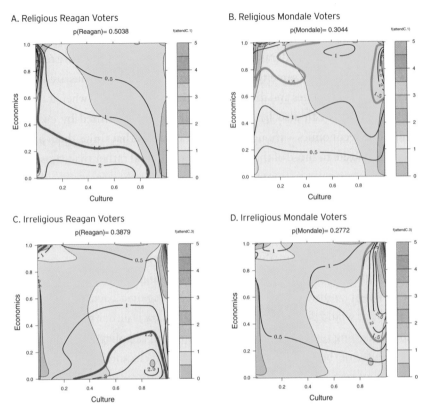

Figure 6.15   Ideological Density and Voting Behavior: Devotional Groups, 1984

by economic and cultural values (Figure 6.15). Indeed, the density maps for generic religiosity may be the most striking array of such maps associated with any of our major demographic variables, since the four main categories—the religious and the irreligious who vote disproportionately Democratic or Republican—live at the four extremes of the ideological landscape, in realms that do not overlap, for any of the four, with any of the others.

The religious who vote Republican are disproportionately strong economic conservatives who range from strong conservatism through moderate liberalism on culture (Figure 6.15.A). The religious who vote Democratic are disproportionately strong economic liberals who are strong cultural conservatives as well, though they do have a small secondary outlier that looks more like the Democratic irreligious (Figure 6.15.B). The irreligious who vote Republican are disproportionately strong economic conservatives but cultural liberals, whose modal position is actually strong cultural liberalism (Figure 6.15.C). And the irreligious who vote Democratic are disproportionately strong cultural liberals, who range from strong liberalism to moderate conservatism on economics (Figure 6.15.D).

One way to say the same thing differently is that the religious are united by their cultural values and divided by their economic values when it comes to voting. This can also be said of the irreligious—united by culture, divided by economics—though the cultural values that unite them are of course opposite to those of the religious, being liberal rather than conservative. A different way to summarize this relationship, however, comes much closer to the strategic world of electoral politics. When stratified by generic religiosity, Republican voters are united by their economic conservatism, divided by their cultural values. Just as Democratic voters are united by their economic liberalism, divided by *their* cultural values.

Strategically, under those conditions, campaigns waged on economic issues ought to unite the two political parties against each other. Potentially, what would determine a winner in this case is either the state of the economy going into the campaign (the campaign as policy referendum) or the balance of these united parties in the overall electorate (the campaign as partisan register). Any candidate who was not happy with these policy implications, or with those likely outcomes, would then need to shift the emphasis onto cultural issues. Such a move should stress both party coalitions, by pulling culturally conservative Democrats (especially those regular church-attenders) toward the Republicans and culturally liberal Republicans (especially those reliable non-attenders) toward the Democrats. The winner should then be the candidate who holds onto the most partisans while shedding the fewest.

Domestic Roles and the Vote

Sex

The last of our major demographic divisions, the ones that create social groups for this analysis, involves what can be called "domestic roles." Many distinctions might be grouped under this heading, but two leading examples are sexual identity and family structure. The Pew Values surveys permit the simple categorization of all individuals as men or women and as parents or

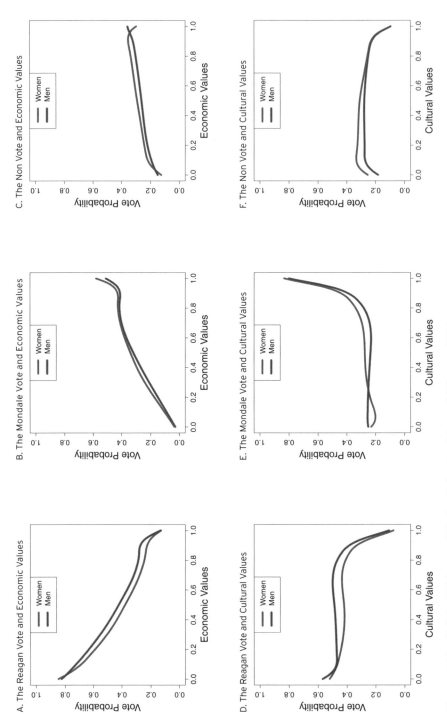

Figure 6.16 Political Values and Voting Behavior: Men and Women, 1984

non-parents,[11] and these serve as the major indicators of domestic roles here. By comparison to social class, race and ethnicity, or religious background, these are comparatively minor contributors to the ideological landscape of American politics, when the links among social groups, political values, and voting behavior become the focus. Yet they do complete the picture of this landscape, and they do add nuances to it as a strategic environment.

Figure 6.16 begins this analysis with voting relationships that compare men with women, by way of economic and then cultural values. The picture that emerges is one of minimal difference. Voting relationships for men versus women are nearly identical, so that both groups track national patterns closely. Two nuanced differences may nevertheless merit a mention. In one, women are slightly less likely to vote than men (Figures 6.16.C and 6.16.F). In the other, there is a tiny but consistent tendency for men to vote Republican and women to vote Democratic (Figures 6.16.A, 6.16.B, 6.16.D and 6.16.E).

That those are tiny twists on an overall similarity should probably not come as much of a surprise, since differences in political values by sex were smaller than those by social class, race and ethnicity, or religious background, whether the focus was sex as a separate principle of social division in Chapter 3 or sex as the distinguishing basis for social groups in Chapter 4. Regardless, the strength of these group-based similarities in individual voting relationships leaves little room for expanded differences between the two groups when economics and culture are considered together (figures not shown). What remains are only traces of a familiar pattern that characterized both social class and religious background.

In this, the votes of those who went with Reagan are clearly more aligned with their economic preferences, while the votes of those who went with Mondale are clearly more aligned with their cultural preferences, for both men and women. Conversely, the votes of men are modestly more aligned with their economic preferences, while the votes of women are modestly more aligned with their cultural preferences, for both Reagan and Mondale voters. As a result, the comparative power of economic values in summarizing a voter alignment is maximized among male Reaganites, while the comparative power of cultural values is maximized among female Mondalites.

As ever, none of this implies that disproportionate concentrations of men and women who chose a Reagan, a Mondale, or a Non vote would therefore be indistinguishable. What the preceding does imply is that residual differences are not likely to have major strategic implications when policy promises are the instrument for pursuing electoral strategies, since men and women at any given point on the policy landscape are likely to respond in roughly similar fashion. Figure 6.17 shifts to the relevant density maps for men and women in order to address any residual strategic implications and finds one clear exception, with some potential for strategic exploitation.

This one sex-based aspect of the political landscape that does seem worth noting involves ideological concentrations among Republican voters. Both male and female concentrations of those who voted disproportionately for Ronald Reagan were characterized by strong economic conservatism. There was no real difference between them on economics. Yet they differed noticeably on culture. The male high ground was concentrated among moderate cultural liberals, while the female high ground was not only more evenly distributed, but also featured an uptick that was entirely missing for their male counterparts among those who were strong cultural conservatives (Figures 6.17.A and 6.17.B).

There is no such division among those who voted disproportionately for Walter Mondale. Both male and female concentrations within this Democratic vote were strong cultural liberals. Yet there was no real economic division among these Mondale voters either: both male and female concentrations range from strong liberalism through true centrism on

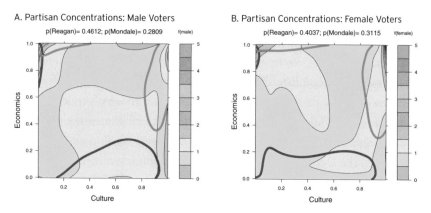

Figure 6.17 Ideological Density and Voting Behavior: Men and Women, 1984

economics, in roughly even proportions. This is the same description that would summarize a national picture of the Democratic vote, absent any distinction based on sex. It is only among Republican voters that a further cultural division by sex appears, a division that would not be inherent from the national picture.

Even then—to jump ahead of the story—this is one of the few group-based distinctions in partisan behavior that was actually to disappear as time passed. In its earlier years, the pattern found in 1984 retained strategic implications: since there were cultural concentrations of potential Republican supporters at very difference ideological locations between men and women, a Republican candidate was additionally encouraged to emphasize economics and de-emphasize culture. While a Democratic candidate might feel encouraged to move in the opposite direction by overrepresented individuals within the Democratic Party, emphasizing culture and de-emphasizing economics, there were no male/female distinctions reinforcing this advice. In any case, as Chapter 8 will affirm, this is a set of strategic incentives that would essentially be gone a quarter-century later.

Parenthood

The overall story of parenthood, the other category of domestic roles available here, is sufficiently similar to that of sex that it mainly reinforces a sense of domestic roles as the least consequential of our grand social cleavages when analyzed through their impact on the electoral landscape. Nevertheless, there are distinctions between sex and parenthood in their linkage to the vote, such that an investigation of the role of parenthood not only completes our comprehensive group-based portrait of the ideological landscape for political conflict but simultaneously adds nuances to it.

Figure 6.18 offers voting relationships for parents and non-parents, by way of economic and then cultural values. These are impressively similar between the two groups, and thus between the two group portraits and the national picture. For parents and non-parents, like all Americans together, the Republican vote shows a strong negative relationship to economic liberalism; the Democratic vote shows a clear but less strong positive relationship to economic liberalism; and the Non vote is a weak copy of the Democratic vote, with its main ideological relationship concentrated among parents. For parents and non-parents, like all Americans, the Republican

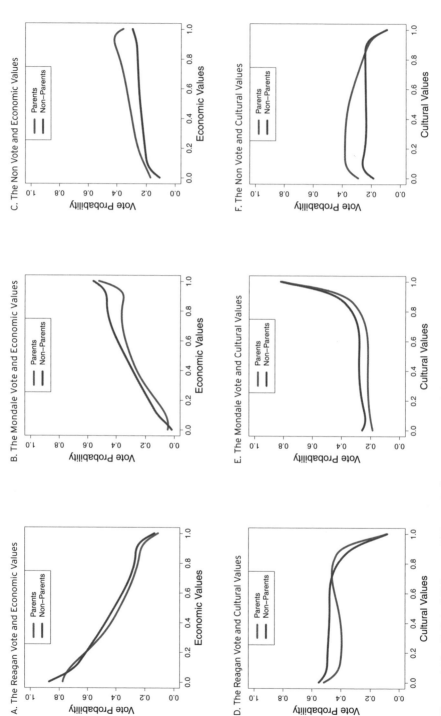

Figure 6.18 Political Values and Voting Behavior: Parents and Non-Parents, 1984

vote is essentially unrelated to cultural values before dipping among strong cultural liberals; the Democratic vote is essentially unrelated before rising among strong cultural liberals; and the Non vote is a pale copy of the Republican vote this time, with its main ideological relationship again concentrated among parents.

The biggest residual intergroup distinction, as with men and women, involves voter turnout (Figures 6.18.C and 6.18.F). Economic liberals and cultural conservatives among parents are less likely to vote, not only in comparison with economic conservatives and cultural liberals within their own group, but even in comparison with economic liberals and cultural conservatives among the non-parents. With sex, an intergroup difference on voter turnout coincided with a tiny but consistent partisan difference: men who voted were more Republican, while women who voted were more Democratic. With parenthood, however, non-parents contribute slightly more to both the Reagan and the Mondale vote at most points on the economic and cultural continuums. Because economic liberals are less likely to vote than economic conservatives, Mondale loses an extra decrement in his vote among parents who are liberals. Because cultural conservatives are less likely to vote than cultural liberals, Reagan loses an extra decrement in his vote among parents who are conservative.

The Reagan vote remains more aligned with economics and the Mondale vote with culture in both the parental and the non-parental population when these voting relationships are considered jointly, as the national picture would suggest that they almost must (figures not shown). Likewise the parental vote remains more aligned with economics and the non-parental vote with culture among both Reagan and Mondale voters. These are small effects, though they do mean that the parental Reagan vote is most aligned with economic values and the non-parental Mondale vote most aligned with cultural values instead.

Density maps then rebalance these small intergroup differences in ways that distinguish parents and non-parents modestly but additionally (Figure 6.19). Moreover, as with men and women, this distinction between parents and non-parents is principally confined to Republican ranks. The Republican high ground is once more concentrated among economic conservatives for both parents and non-parents, as it was for both men and women. Within this economically conservative terrain, however, parents

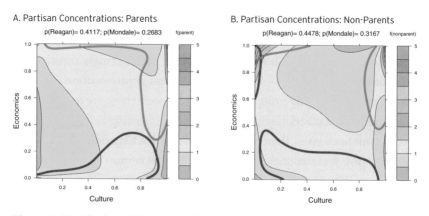

Figure 6.19 Ideological Density and Voting Behavior: Parents and Non-Parents, 1984

are tilted strongly toward moderate cultural liberalism, while non-parents are not just much more broadly dispersed across the entire cultural continuum but actually have their modal member in the territory of strong cultural conservatism. This is a sharper difference between parents and non-parents than the counterpart distinction between men and women. As such, it acquires augmented strategic implications.

From one side, this parental difference represents an even stronger incentive for Republicans to emphasize economics, which unites, rather than culture, which divides. Yet even just within the Republican Party, the share of those who have an apparent stake in either moderate liberalism or strong conservatism on culture is greater with parenthood than with sex—which is to say, the group cleavage is more divisive—suggesting that it should be more difficult for the Republican Party to follow this strategic advice when parenthood is a major stratifying influence on the vote. From the other side, Democrats seem well positioned to capitalize on this Republican tension, if they can manage their own smaller divides on both culture and economics, divides that for them are concentrated among non-parents.

The Baseline and Its Evolution

What emerges from this attempt to create a baseline for the evolution of the strategic environment for a presidential vote over the last quarter-century is, in its specifics, a national picture with group components. The national picture is additionally differentiated by economic *versus* cultural values. Each valuational dimension is additionally differentiated among Reagan, Mondale, or Non voters. Most of the social groups constituting this national picture then offer their own rough approximation of it, anchored differentially by group membership, though there are demographic cleavages whose categories do not do much to distinguish the national picture further, just as there are social groups that actually do something different from the national picture within their confines.

In any case, by the time a national picture has been teased out—with voting relationships to economic and cultural values individually, with voting relationships to economics and culture jointly, and with density maps for the partisan concentrations beneath these voting relationships—it is already clear that the tripartite focus on voting behavior, as well as the repeated insistence that campaign strategies can be influenced as much by ideological densities as by voting relationships, have come into their own. Seen this way, there is a voting relationship to the Reagan vote, the Mondale vote, and the Non vote across the full economic continuum, but it is different for each voter category: strongest among Reagan voters, clear though less strong and in the opposite direction among Mondale voters, and weakest but more like the Mondale than the Reagan vote among Non voters.

The voting relationship to cultural values is different from this economic relationship, making it immediately clear that culture is not some epiphenomenon of economics, while once again validating the need to investigate three voting categories separately. The cultural relationship to a Reagan or a Mondale vote does contribute a pair of mirror images this time. Yet this parallelism is additionally unlike the situation with economics because a cultural relationship is effectively nonexistent—flat—across most of the ideological spectrum. It comes to life only among (and is thereby confined to) strong cultural liberals, who split radically: against Reagan and in favor of Mondale.[12] Non voters are, however, different in kind, showing a modest tendency for turnout to fall with rising cultural conservatism across the broad middle of the cultural spectrum, coupled with a clear tendency for turnout to rise at the extremes, both liberal and conservative.

By contrast, it is the shift from a focus on voting relationships to a focus on the density maps inherently associated with them that creates the set of pictures that are most unfamiliar. In these, the partisan high ground for Republicans, the ideological territory where Republican voters are most strongly represented, is organized almost entirely by economic values. This is an ideological terrain of strong economic conservatism. Yet the partisan high ground for Democrats, the ideological territory where Democratic voters are most strongly represented, is organized almost entirely by cultural values instead: this is an ideological terrain of strong cultural liberalism. Accordingly, not only are the two parties not mirror images when examined for their ideological composition, they are not even organized by the same substantive concerns. And just to complicate the picture further, the high ground for Non voters is located about as far away from the dominant positions within either of the two major parties as it is possible to get: in the territory where strong economic liberalism is coupled with strong cultural conservatism.

Every bit of this national story will change—evolve—between 1984 and 2008 (in Chapter 7). Individual voting relations to economic and cultural values will change. Joint voting relationships to economic *plus* cultural values will change. And the ideological densities associated with both will change as well. As a result, a benchmark is exactly what it claims to be: a means to organize the search for stability and change. Even in isolation, however, 1984 confirms the extent of the difference between voting relationships and density maps. Moreover, and more to the practical point, these density maps—the actual distribution of value-holders beneath those voting relationships—can be as influential, or more so, with campaign strategists than are the associated relationships, though real-world strategists are likely to have learned about ideological density by way of repeated experience, rather than through any familiarity with the contour maps of high social science.

In any case, when the focus shifts to what *social groups* are actually contributing to the national picture, the story of this benchmark year becomes only more complex. Social groups differ widely among themselves in the economic and cultural values that their members hold, as well as in the combinations thereof. These groups differ additionally in the way they link those values (and combinations) to voting behavior. And after all that, roughly similar voting relationships can mask radically different ideological concentrations within these groups, when that great tool of the campaign strategist, the density map, is allowed into the story. Inevitably, then, social groups make widely varying contributions—different kinds of contributions, actually—to the structure of the ideological landscape, and hence to its strategic implications.

The grand cleavages of social class and religious background—as embodied most stereotypically in family income and denominational attachment—generate social groups that can be described abstractly in parallel fashion, when the focus is the way they link political values to voting behavior.[13] Yet the strategic implications for electoral politics that result from these two descriptions are not just inconsistent but actively in tension. That is to say: practical expectations that derive from one set of social groups are explicitly contradicted—directly violated—by expectations that derive from the other. For some elections, the question of the relative balance of these group effects must thus be the dominant influence on the actual outcome.

In abstract terms, all four social groups within each of these two grand cleavages do reflect national patterns for economic and cultural values among Reagan, Mondale, and Non voters. Each set of four groups goes on to anchor their membership at different levels of support within the three voting categories, though income actually has a slightly stronger effect than denomination in this regard. Moreover, the two sets of social groups share a common pattern to the voting relationship of economic and cultural values jointly. In this, the Reagan vote is comparatively more related to economics, the Mondale vote comparatively more related to culture, for every one of these eight social groups. Beyond that, the two sets of groups can be given a clear ordering of economic and cultural effects *within* each set: from low- to middle- to upper-middle to high-income (or vice versa) for social class, and from Evangelical to Mainstream to Catholic to Non-Christian (or again vice versa) for denominational attachment.

Yet this comparative ordering immediately hints at the different contributions that family income and denominational attachment make to the strategic landscape for electoral politics. For while the ordering from income is in some sense inherent, following logically from income level, the ordering from denomination is an empirical finding, following from no inescapable ranking principle. Moreover, the alignments that the analyst might expect from one set of social groups, from groups delineated by social class or groups delineated by religious background, are sharply at variance from—indeed, inconsistent with—the alignments that this same analyst might expect from the other. Thus family income would lead to an expectation that the wealthiest denominational family, the Non-Christians, would vote most Republican, while the poorest denominational family, the Evangelical Protestants, would vote most Democratic. Exactly the opposite is in fact the case.

By contrast, race and ethnicity as a grand social cleavage generate key social groups, of Black and Hispanic Americans respectively, that are radically different in the very nature of their voting relationships. That is, they differ from the national picture not only in the specific strengths of the way they link political values to voting behavior but also in the very manner in which they do (or do not) do so. In the process, they allow treating the residual category, the Anglos, as a racial/ethnic group as well:

- For Black Americans, political values are essentially unrelated to the vote. Blacks are thus the classic social group for whom group identifications, not policy preferences, are the key to voting behavior. Unlike class or religious groups, whose members are moved in parallel ways by political values but anchored differently by group membership, Black Americans give no evidence of being moved by policy options at all.

- For Hispanic Americans, voting relationships to political values fall between those of Blacks and Anglos, looking more like Blacks in the distribution of their policy preferences, more like Anglos in the voting relationships associated with those preferences, yet like neither—uniquely themselves—in the density maps that determine what Hispanics contribute to the political landscape. As a result, it should be possible to appeal to this social group through policy promises, but the appeal is constrained by a substantial homogeneity of values and by weaker links from values to voting behavior than those that characterize the Anglos.

- Anglo Americans, a category containing 85 percent of the total sample, can hardly function as a "social group" in either a statistical or a behavioral sense. They cannot get very far from the overall national story; they cannot meaningfully be said to interact with each other. What these Anglos can do is to confirm that the two most distinctive racial and ethnic groups, Blacks and Hispanics, do indeed make race and ethnicity first among the four great demographic divisions in their ability to structure the political landscape and elicit alternatives strategies among their members.

Domestic roles as a grand social cleavage, finally, generate social groups that differ only minimally from each other when the focus shifts to voting behavior. The resulting groups thus differ only minimally from national patterns as well, for both economics and culture, among Reagan, Mondale, and Non voters. Voting relationships do feature a partisan connection to social groups by sexual identity (men versus women) that is missing among social groups by family structure (parents versus non-parents) in their comparative strengths. Density maps do privilege social groups by family structure over social groups by sexual identity in their comparative internal partisan concentrations, and hence in their potential strategic consequence. Yet these distinctions are painfully nuanced, so that social groups defined by domestic roles remain fourth among the four great demographic divisions in their ability to structure the political landscape and elicit alternatives strategies.

Or at least, that is the story for 1984, where the Pew Values surveys are at their earliest, their largest, and arguably their administrative best. But could 1984 be viewed as idiosyncratic? In other words, is this a particularly bad year to use in establishing a baseline, perhaps because it was a solid reelection year and not a close contest, or just because it featured a Republican and not a Democratic victory? Alternatively, are there no "good" years, because each one is idiosyncratic, shaped by the personalities and strategies—but especially the issues and events—of a given point in time? We think that a focus on voting relationships and density maps goes some way toward mitigating this concern from the start. The preceding analysis is, after all, focused not on the specific level of any vote or cluster of political values but on linkages and associations.

Yet the simplest way to demonstrate the value of this baseline, while allaying abstract concerns about idiosyncrasy, is just to follow the evolution of all such associations across time. No one seeking to understand the linkages between social backgrounds, political values, and voting behavior would want to assert that any given baseline, intended to set up the strategic context for subsequent electoral politics, could or should remain static. What has to be said is that the reliability of a putative baseline—the course of its evolution over time along with questions about the things that move it—can only be unpacked by extending the analysis over a period sufficient to allow any or all of these effects to surface. Chapter 7 thus follows the national pattern from 1984 through 2008. Chapter 8 will return and follow the evolution of subgroup contributions over that same period.

7
The Evolution of the Strategic Landscape
1984-2008

Chapter 6 offered a comprehensive picture—a benchmark—for the relationship among social backgrounds, political values, and voting behavior, both as a national composite and in its group components. Nothing guarantees that this is anything more than a single (if already complex) snapshot of the ideological landscape for electoral politics. Indeed, it surely must be a picture that is shaped by elements—candidates, tactics, and events—that are idiosyncratic to 1984. On the other hand, rooting responses to these elements in relationships that involve long-recognized social characteristics, along with the policy preferences that are regularly tied to them, should put limits on any such idiosyncrasy. This suggests that evolution, rather than stasis or change, is the more likely fate of these benchmark patterns across time.

Note immediately, however, that even if these comprehensive voting relationships were to prove essentially static, the overall stability of this composite structure would not promise a static character for the associated politics. To begin with, the strategic landscape created by this structure is impressively complex. Different groups do not just hold different values; they attach them to the vote in different ways. This means that a national composite of the ideological landscape for electoral politics may obscure as much as it clarifies about the behavior of the group pieces that go to constitute this picture. Even more conditionally, it means that there may be some elections where the national composite is critical, others where group combinations are more important. Or, of course, some mix of both.

Accordingly, Chapters 7 and 8 must attend to the temporal evolution of benchmark patterns isolated in Chapter 6. Chapter 7 is concerned with the overall picture—the comprehensive strategic landscape for American electoral politics. This is our version of the more usual focus on elections as singular events, though ours is much less singular than many.[1] Chapter 8 is then concerned with specific social groups, in their contributions to the composite picture. This allows different groups to deviate from, approximate, or overstate national patterns. Only when the two are put back together will it be possible to address questions about the extent to which these patterns permeate most social groups, as well as the extent to which changes in particular social groups are what drive national patterns.

Such a focus inevitably captures some elements of what might be called the ephemera of electoral politicking, which is not thereby to label them inconsequential. Things like candidate personalities, campaign tactics, and, most especially, events of the day are included here. Each election after 1984 will provide some of these. Any given example might prove decisive in a particular contest. Yet the focus here is mainly on capturing fundamentals, structural characteristics of politics that are temporally enduring, in effect disciplining the ephemera. For us, these include enduring incarnations of social background, lasting dimensions of public preference, and recurrent translations of both into voting behavior. These structural characteristics thus provide the means for organizing an examination of presidential contests from 1984 to 2008.

From one side, if social backgrounds and policy preferences as they relate to voting behavior are indeed the fundamentals of electoral politics, they should impose patterns on candidate personalities, campaigns tactics, and events of the day. This is not a matter of *preventing* these ephemeral elements from appearing in a partially idiosyncratic fashion. Rather, it is a matter of providing the continuing framework through which even they are expressed. From the other side, isolating some relationships as fundamental cannot mean that they themselves do not change, especially if a long enough time period is available. The elections from 1984 through 2008, at a quarter-century and counting, will in fact prove sufficient to isolate some important shifts in these fundamentals. Yet those elections can only be suggestive of other shifts that offer only traces in this time period, having begun well before there were Pew Values surveys. No doubt there are still others that are so long-running that we cannot recognize them in our data at all.

In any case, Chapter 7 begins with the relationship to the national vote for economic and cultural values, considered individually and proceeding election by election. This is a familiar and orthodox form of election analysis. In this opening section, we pursue it from 1984 through 2000, as a means to set up the later analysis of the structure of the contemporary world. Despite the orthodoxy of this approach, three themes stand out—and contend with each other. The first is continuity. It is possible to see the electoral structure of our benchmark year in everything that follows. The second is idiosyncrasy. The years from 1984 through 2000 are sufficient to allow recognition of elections that deviate from the benchmark template in lesser respects, and then move back toward it. And the third such theme is true evolution. Some deviations do not snap back.

The chapter then switches to considering the relationship to the national vote of economics and culture *jointly*, in order to illuminate the strategic landscape for electoral politics. This second section, too, proceeds chronologically from 1984 through 2000. But this time, each election analysis has two parts. The first merely considers the *joint* relationship of economics and culture to the vote. Much of this joint relationship is constrained, even prefigured, by the preceding examination of individual relationships. Nevertheless, there are major aspects of the evolution of the joint relationship between public values and voting behavior that can only be unpacked when both valuational dimensions are simultaneously in the analysis.

The second part of each analysis moves to density maps rather than voting relationships, and hence to the question of where the Republican voters, Democratic voters, Non voters, and the occasional third-party or independent voting blocs within these relationships actually reside. Again, joint voting relationships constrain possibilities for these underlying distributions. Yet in Chapter 7, as in Chapter 6, the policy landscape for electoral politicking can look noticeably different when actual densities reenter the analysis. It is this combined product of voting relationships and density maps that is in some abstract sense the ideological landscape for political conflict. As such, it is simultaneously the practical structure to which campaign strategists must respond.

This leads more or less ineluctably to the third major section of this chapter, which returns to the theme of electoral evolution as a way to introduce the contemporary ideological landscape, its structural lineaments, and thus the strategic world for contemporary electoral politicking. This section is mainly focused on the implications of this landscape for major-party strategies, but takes a side look at the independent and third-party sphere as well. Most of the time, major-party politics is and must be the center of this story. Moreover, the full picture of voting relationships and density maps suggests that both political parties face major and ongoing strategic dilemmas. Yet the prospects for independent or third-party candidacies within this strategic landscape also prove to have more implications for major-party strategy than is commonly recognized.

Economic Values, Cultural Values, and the Evolving Vote

The Presidential Contest of 1988

The presidential election of 1984 had been in many ways a classic incarnation of partisan conflict in modern American politics. The two nominees were archetypal embodiments of contemporary ideology. Ronald Reagan was a conservative Republican, and Walter Mondale was a liberal Democrat. Both presented stereotypical positions on the great dimensions of policy combat. Reagan was a clear-cut economic conservative, while Mondale was a clear-cut economic liberal, just as Reagan was an obvious cultural traditionalist, while Mondale was a conscious cultural progressive. Accordingly, the two candidates offered an almost archetypal incarnation of the ideological character of the partisan conflict of their time.

The presidential election of 1988, on its surface, blurred these distinctions. The candidates effectively denied them in their intended personas. George H. W. Bush promised to be a "kinder, gentler" extension of his predecessor, Ronald Reagan. Michael Dukakis presented himself as a technocrat, not an ideologue like his predecessor, Walter Mondale. The policies that gave life to these presentations went on to pull both candidates toward the ideological center. Bush spoke of his concern for education and the environment. Dukakis emphasized fiscal management and generic problem-solving. What resulted was, on its face, the classic centrist contest, with both presidential nominees moving clearly and consciously toward the ideological middle in their general election campaigns.

What was not necessarily different was the structure of policy preferences within which both pairs of candidates, Reagan and Mondale or Bush and Dukakis, had to pursue their electoral goals. Indeed, what makes it worth underlining the comprehensive surface distinctions between pairs of candidates in successor years is the further fact that, when the ballots were finally cast, the underlying structural relationships among social backgrounds, political values, and voting behavior were essentially identical, at least when examined for the nation as a whole. In presentational terms, this parallelism—a kind of structural recapitulation—means that little needs to be said about the associated patterns in 1988. They essentially recapitulate counterpart patterns from the benchmark contest of 1984. All that needs to be presented instead is evidence sufficient to confirm the parallel underlying structure of these superficially distinctive contests.

To that end, Figure 7.1 offers the relationships between policy preferences on economics and then culture among Republican, Democratic, and Non voters in both years. The parallels are overwhelming. When economic values are the focus, there remains, first, a strong negative relationship between economics and a Republican vote, in the person of George H. W. Bush this time, with conservatives preferring him strongly and liberals avoiding him (Figure 7.1.A). With this same economic focus, there remains, second, a weaker positive relationship between economic values and a Democratic vote, by way of Michael Dukakis this time, with liberals preferring him and conservatives avoiding him (Figure 7.1.B). And there remains, third, a still-weaker positive relationship to the Non vote, with economic conservatives more inclined to vote and economic liberals more inclined not to do so in both years (Figure 7.1.C).

What is most striking about these economic relationships overall—surely their signature characteristic in 1988—is the degree to which they are effectively overlaid. It is not just that all three relationships are parallel

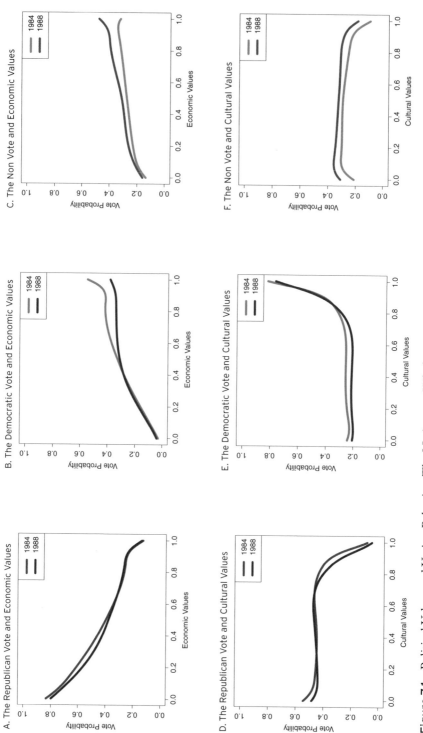

Figure 7.1 Political Values and Voting Behavior: The Nation as a Whole, 1984–1988

between these two presidential elections; they are close to indistinguishable. In the case of the Republican vote, there is truly nothing further to say: 1984 and 1988 *are* indistinguishable (Figure 7.1.A). In the case of the Democratic vote, economic liberals appear to have been a trifle less enthused by Dukakis than by Mondale, causing the Democratic vote to sag slightly in this ideological population while the Non vote ticked up in the same area (Figures 7.1.B versus 7.1.C). Yet that was still a minor distinction, and it was really all there was.

Much the same can be said for the three voting categories when the focus shifts to cultural values. There remains an essentially flat relationship to the Republican vote along most of the cultural continuum, for George Bush this time, before plunging among strong cultural liberals (Figure 7.1.D). There remains an equally flat relationship to the Democratic vote along most of the same continuum, by way of Michael Dukakis, before surging among strong cultural liberals (Figure 7.1.E). And there remains a very slight tendency across most of the cultural continuum for liberals to vote more than conservatives, along with a more pronounced tendency for the cultural extremes, both liberal and conservative, to turn out more (Figure 7.1.F).

Again, the dominant characteristic of all three relationships, between cultural values and voting behavior this time, is that they are not just parallel but close to indistinguishable. Despite the presence of *two* more-centrist candidates in a non-incumbent year, 1988 generates individual voting relationships that are nearly overlaid on those of 1984. The Non vote was up modestly all along the cultural continuum, and this fact was reflected in both the Bush and the Dukakis vote. Yet these were, once again, small twists on an essentially constant larger story.

The Presidential Contest of 1992

The same cannot be said of 1992. Just on its surface, the presidential contest looked inescapably different from that of either 1984 or 1988, in two critical regards. In the first, it was the challenging Democrat, Arkansas Governor William J. "Bill" Clinton, not the incumbent Republican, President George H. W. Bush, who was to emerge victorious. That alone was a change from the two preceding elections, raising the inherent possibility that social backgrounds, political values, and voting behavior were related in a different fashion in years of Democratic rather than Republican victory.

Yet it was the second critical difference from preceding elections that appeared almost to require substantial disturbances in previous links among backgrounds, values, and behavior. For 1992 featured a serious third candidate for president, in the person of billionaire businessman H. Ross Perot. Perot was to achieve both the largest vote and the largest vote *share* of any independent candidate since former President Theodore Roosevelt in 1912. This vote had to come from somewhere, so his success raised the prospect not only that his own patterns of support would be idiosyncratic, as they almost had to be, but also that these would cause both Democratic and Republican voting patterns to look different as well.

Whether either of these developments would reflect additional changes in the strategic landscape for electoral politics, fundamental or otherwise, was an additionally open question in 1992. Recall, however, that 1988 could be argued to have been different from 1984 in the character of its elite politics, yet proved overwhelmingly similar beneath this elite surface, among rank and file voters. In continuing pursuit of an understanding of their behavior, Figure 7.2 sets up the individual relationships between political values and the vote for 1984, 1988, and 1992 in the usual manner: first economics, then culture. Inevitably, the picture for 1992 includes a further voting category, to capture the political behavior of those who went with independent candidate Perot; thus, four categories arrayed in this order: Republican, Democratic, Independent, and Non voters.

There remained a strongly negative relationship between economic values and voting for the Republican, sitting President George H. W. Bush, who was seeking reelection. Yet while the Republican vote retained its overall contours in 1992, it was also immediately different—clearly distinguishable—from the two preceding presidential elections. The larger part of this was simple aggregate decline, directly captured in Figure 7.2.A. The two previous elections were much happier Republican affairs than the election of 1992. Yet there was a modest further shift within this aggregate drop, as the decline proved to be modestly greater among economic conservatives than among economic liberals.

The reason for both effects was also immediately clear. In achieving the largest vote for an independent candidate for president in eighty years, Ross

Perot, too, generated a clearly negative relationship to economic values (Figure 7.2.C). In aping the classic Republican voting relationship, Perot almost inevitably contributed to lowering the Republican voting line. In appealing more to economic conservatives than to economic liberals, he appeared to provide an easy explanation for why the economically conservative Republican vote should decline a bit more. The patterned weaknesses of the Republican candidate in 1992 thus looked very much like the patterned strengths of Ross Perot.

By contrast, it was the Democratic vote among the four voting categories that remained most like its baseline pattern (Figure 7.2.B). As previously, there was a clear and positive relationship between economic values and voting for the Democrat, in this case Arkansas Governor Bill Clinton, the Democratic challenger to sitting President Bush. Liberals were attracted, conservatives repelled (Figure 7.2.C). Beyond that, the economic voting line for Democrats in 1992 essentially returned to the pattern of 1984, as Clinton resecured those strong economic liberals who had supported Walter Mondale but had been less enthusiastic about Michael Dukakis. As a self-described "New Democrat," Clinton was not nearly as liberal as Mondale. Yet he was running in a year of economic downturn; he talked about the economy incessantly; and he managed to restore the Democratic vote from economics in the process.

This does not guarantee that the same individuals, or even the same social groups, were doing in 1992 what they had done in 1984 or 1988 when they voted Democratic. That is a separate empirical question, addressed more systematically in Chapter 8. At a minimum, though, this Democratic patterning makes it hard to argue that the Perot candidacy was having much effect on the overall Democratic vote. Beyond that, what it confirms is the theoretical possibility—now realized—that Clinton's party could win the presidency (and not just lose it) with the *exact same* voting relationships as those of 1984. Or at least, these relationships were obviously sufficient to deliver victory in a year with a serious three-way voting split. Whether they could deliver victory in a year without such a split remained an open question.

The movement of strong economic liberals back into the Democratic column should simultaneously have reduced the Non vote within this ideological faction, as indeed it did (Figure 7.2.D). Voter turnout among

A. The Republican Vote and Economic Values

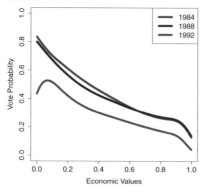

B. The Democratic Vote and the Economic Values

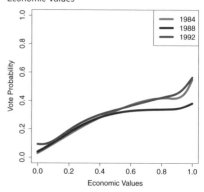

C. The Perot Vote and the Economic Values

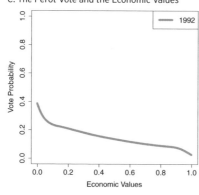

D. The Non Vote and the Economic Values

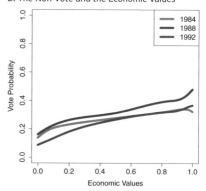

E. The Republican Vote and Cultural Values

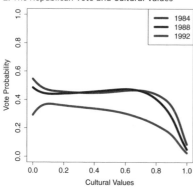

F. The Democratic Vote and Cultural Values

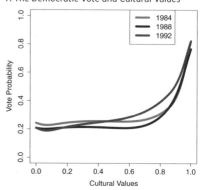

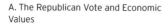

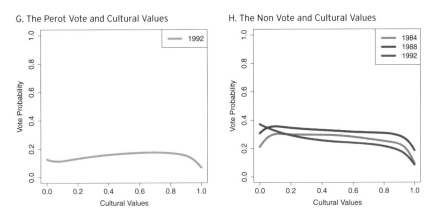

Figure 7.2 Political Values and Voting Behavior: The Nation as a Whole, 1984, 1988, 1992

economic liberals was back to its 1984 levels. The propensity of strong economic conservatives to back Perot, in a year when Perot gave this faction an additional voting option, simultaneously augmented voter turnout at the conservative end of the ideological spectrum. This was the best turnout among economic conservatives of the three elections. The Non vote thus remained related in a positive way to economic values, in the manner that it had been in 1988, but at a level more like that of 1984.

When the focus shifts to cultural values, the Republican vote in 1992 was even more clearly distinguishable from the Republican vote of previous years. Whether stratified by economics or culture, this vote of course fell in comparison with both preceding elections, and Figure 7.2.E captures this fall. Yet its *form* was clearly different this time as well. What had previously been an essentially flat relationship along most of the cultural continuum, before falling sharply among strong liberals, was now a relationship that reached more or less across the full continuum. Its fall was additionally augmented among moderate liberals in 1992, yet the decline began on the far right and reached all the way to the far left.

What was harder to judge from the vantage point of 1992 was the degree to which this change was like the one associated with economic values, in being principally a response to the presence of Ross Perot. Perot did secure his best vote among moderate cultural liberals, precisely the individuals who deserted President Bush disproportionately (Figure 7.2.G). Yet as Figure 7.2.F attests, these individuals also swelled the Democratic vote in

1992, while the more important fact about the Perot vote as arrayed by culture was that its overall relationship was modest. So, Perot may have served as a modest "parking place" for moderate liberals who were attracted neither to Bush nor to Clinton, though this attraction, if such it was, did not extend to strong liberals.

In fact, the Democratic vote was up most in this same terrain, that of the moderate cultural liberals, suggesting that there might be something more under way than a "Perot interruption" (Figure 7.2.F). On the one hand, this Democratic vote as stratified by culture was still the one most like the previous two elections among the four voting groups: Republican, Democratic, Perot, and Non voters. On the other hand, this vote, like the Republican vote though more modestly so, was related to cultural values across a broader ideological spectrum in 1992 than it had been in 1984 or 1988. That suggested as much a response to the Republican candidate as to a major independent.

Regardless, Perot probably did contribute to the one distinctive twist in the Non vote in 1992 when the focus is cultural values (Figure 7.2.H). In the aggregate, voter turnout was up, and Perot surely deserved some credit for this, by providing an additional generic option. For economics, that option consisted of strong conservatism, and strong economic conservatives responded by giving Perot his best vote showing. For culture, it was less clear that Perot *meant* to represent moderate liberalism. But in a year when moderate liberals nevertheless found him, strong cultural conservatives could reasonably have seen themselves as possessing no obvious champion: the sitting president was, at best, a born-again conservative. In any case, it was strong cultural conservatives who showed the only increase in the Non vote of any ideological faction.

The Presidential Contest of 1996

The presidential contest of 1984 had ended in the reelection of a sitting Republican. The presidential contest of 1988 had produced the initial election of a Republican successor. The presidential contest of 1992 had brought the initial election of a Democratic counterpart. And the presidential contest of 1996 in some sense completed the cycle by ending in the reelection of that sitting Democrat. These four elections thus covered the apparent range of available outcomes. The 1992 election had been additionally different in providing a serious independent candidate, unattached to any political party, in the person of Ross Perot. In continuing this Perot difference, the 1996 election made it possible to look not only at continuity or change in the Perot vote, but also at continuity or change in the way it interacted with Republican and Democratic voting.

In pursuit of these partisan and independent stories, Figure 7.3 offers the standard setup. Four populations are again isolated, for Republican, Democratic, Independent, and Non voters. Each is examined for the relationship between voting behavior and economic or cultural values. Comparison is with the benchmark election of 1984, to which the election of 1988 had proved quite similar, and with the predecessor election of 1992, rattled distinctively by the initial appearance of Perot. For most commentators, the Perot effect in 1992 that had drawn most attention was his impressive aggregate showing. For the analysis here, that showing is trumped by the direct interaction of this Perot effect with the Republican vote on economics and by the indirect interaction of this Perot effect with each of the cultural votes.

Two central aspects of voting behavior in the presidential contest of 1992 were left unclear, or at least open-ended, in its aftermath. The first was the nature of the Perot vote in isolation: Was it distinctive to the program of the candidate himself, that is, to his policy attractions? Or was it more a response to a particular context, involving candidates and policies over which Perot had only the most marginal control? The second question involves the nature of the interaction of this Perot vote with Republican, Democratic, and Non voting. To cut directly to the chase: for most commentators, the Perot effect in 1996 that drew the most attention was the aggregate collapse of the Perot vote, from 19 percent of the total to just 8 percent. Yet for this analysis, the critical fact about the "Perot effect" on voting relationships in 1996 was instead that there was *close to none*.

As importantly, the effect that did exist, the residual, was noticeably different from that of 1992. The most impressive relationship between public values and a Perot vote in that prior year had been the negative one with economic values: conservatives had been clearly attracted, while liberals had not. This relationship largely disappeared in 1996, becoming essentially flat across the broad middle of the economic continuum (Figure 7.3.C). Moreover, to the extent that there was any relationship left, it

A. The Republican Vote and Economic
Values

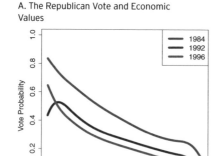

B. The Democratic Vote and the
Economic Values

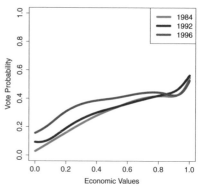

C. The Perot Vote and the Economic Values

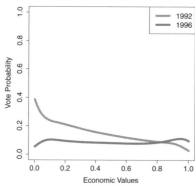
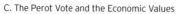

D. The Non Vote and the Economic Values

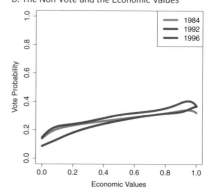

E. The Republican Vote and Cultural Values

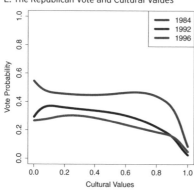

F. The Democratic Vote and Cultural Values

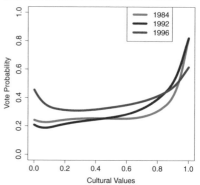

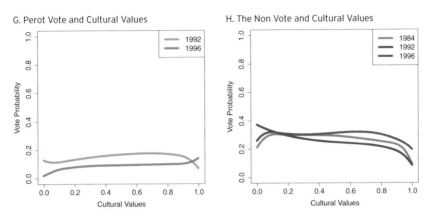

Figure 7.3 Political Values and Voting Behavior: The Nation as a Whole, 1984, 1992, 1996

was now strong liberals who were attracted to Perot and strong conservatives who were repelled.

The presidential contest of 1992 had featured a secondary tendency for moderate cultural liberals to support Perot, though this effect was so mild—and nonlinear, since it fell away in both directions—that it was hard to be sure that it was a cultural effect at all (Figure 7.2.G). Either way, this relationship, too, was gone in 1996 (Figure 7.3.G). Once more, its replacement was essentially flat across the broad middle of the ideological continuum. Once more, any relationship that remained was confined to the ideological extremes, with strong liberals attracted and strong conservatives repelled.

This pattern of change from 1992 to 1996 goes a long way toward answering the question of whether the Perot candidacy responded to a distinctive set of policy preferences welling up from the general public or was more of a parking place for elements of this public that were themselves in transition. To believe in Perot as a policy register, one has to believe that the Perot of 1992 was an extremely stiff economic conservative with some moderate cultural proclivities, while the Perot of 1996 was morphing into an incipient champion of the far left on both economics and culture. More plausible, we think, is the view that the Perot vote was defined more by voters looking for some alternative to the two major-party candidates than by anything the independent candidate did or did not promise. Note that this parking-place interpretation leaves very open the question of whether the result was a response to specific alternative candidacies—Bush versus Clinton, then Clinton versus Dole—or was instead a product of nascent and evolving changes on the larger ideological landscape for American politics.

Beyond that, the aggregate collapse of the Perot vote, as well as the flattening out of any relationships to economics or culture that remained, left room for only reduced impacts on the Republican, the Democratic, or the Non vote. For economics, this meant that the main conflicts in the 1996 election were once more (and despite the presence of Perot) about voting Republican, voting Democratic, or not voting at all:

- For economics and the Republican vote, there was, as ever, a strong negative association with policy preferences (Figure 7.3.A). Because Perot was no longer attracting strong economic conservatives, their defections from 1992 were erased, with the result that the overall relationship looked very much like that of 1984. On the other hand, because Robert Dole was losing solidly rather than winning solidly, the *location* of that relationship was still much more like 1992 than 1984.
- For economics and the Democratic vote, there was once again a weaker but positive association with policy preferences (Figure 7.3.B). Because Ross Perot had now switched to attracting some strong economic liberals, Bill Clinton in his reelection campaign did not manage to increase his margin among them. Everywhere else on the economic continuum, however, the Clinton vote of 1996 was up over the Clinton vote of 1992.
- For economics and the Non vote, finally, there was, once more and as ever, a clear but weak association between economic liberalism and Non voting (Figure 7.3.D). For 1996, this looked like a cross between 1984 and 1992, though the larger point is just that there was less distinction among the Non voter lines from all three years than there was among Republican, Democratic, or indeed Perot voters.

On the other hand, the story of culture in the 1996 election was different. It was different in its individual pieces, for Republican, Democratic, or Non voters. It was different in its collective implications, hinting at some larger and thus potentially enduring change in the relationship between cultural values and voting behavior. It was thus different as an indicator of the structural evolution of American politics, though the nature, strength, and destination of any such change could not be deduced from one election:

- For culture and the Republican vote, the key fact was that the voting relationship for 1996 did not revert to that of the benchmark year of 1984 (Figure 7.3.D). Instead, it was closer to the pattern of 1992, despite the fact that Perot was no longer contributing to this pattern. As a result, it was the Republican vote of 1992 that looked more like an interim, with Perot as a way station on the road to 1996, rather than as a deviation from 1984/88.
- For culture and the Democratic vote, by contrast, Perot was still having a marginal but clear effect (Figure 7.3.E). Because he was attracting some strong liberals and even more powerfully repelling strong conservatives, the Democratic candidate, Bill Clinton in his reelection campaign, did not secure the usual Democratic increment among strong liberals but did secure just such an increment among cultural moderates and, especially, strong conservatives.
- Different yet again was the situation among Non voters (Figure 7.3.H). Gone was the distinctive story of 1992, when strong conservatives had dropped out of the electorate disproportionately. Back was more of the benchmark story of 1984, with its tendency for cultural extremists, both liberals and conservatives, to turn out more than moderates. The larger point was again, however, that there was less distinction among the Non voter lines from all three years than there was among Republican, Democratic, or even Perot voters.

The Presidential Contest of 2000

In their time, the presidential contests of 1984, 1988, 1992, and 1996 must have appeared to cover the gamut of available partisan outcomes: Republican reelection, initial Republican election, initial Democratic election, and Democratic reelection, respectively. If those outcomes contribute no patterned variation of their own to the linkage among social backgrounds, political values, and voting behavior—no variation that goes with Republican versus Democratic victories, no variation that goes with initial winners versus the reelected—then the search for such variation needs naturally to go elsewhere. Here, this would mean turning to simultaneous relationships with economics and culture, to density maps for the ideological locations associated with those relationships, or, of course, to differences between group behaviors and the nation as a whole.

Yet the presidential contest of 2000 was to remind everyone that, in practice, there is one other possible outcome, even when partisanship and incumbency define the available possibilities. For 2000 was to provide, in effect, a dead heat. The nationwide vote was to be so close that the actual outcome became dependent on the application of rules-of-the-game by a nested set of courts. Texas Governor George W. Bush, the Republican, or Vice President Albert "Al" Gore, the Democrat, would still have to qualify as the winner, but the vote by itself would not determine this choice. On the other hand, in analytic terms, the 2000 outcome allowed investigation of the possibility that an effective dead heat might do something notably different either to the opening relationships derived from the Pew surveys of 1984 and 1988 or to the evolution of those relationships in 1992 and 1996.

In the abstract, a result as close as that in 2000 might have produced any number of distinct but presumably moderate deviations from bench-marked norms. At the very least, such an outcome promised to squeeze out any potentially distorting effects from large wins by either party, while 2000 was also a return to electoral normality in the sense that there was no independent candidate with a substantial vote, not even as substantial as that created by Ross Perot in the year (1996) of his precipitous decline.[2] In practice, what 2000 actually did, more than any preceding election, was feature a perverse and tricky combination of outcomes that requires care in exposition. From one side, *individual* voting relationships looked like nothing so much as a reversion to older patterns. From the other side, as we shall see later in this chapter, *joint* relationships to economic plus cultural values—and then their associated density maps—were to look much more like the incipient arrival of the modern world.

In the process, the 2000 election was to provide a powerful reminder of the way that individual and joint voting relationships could differ in their analytic implications. Indeed, the presidential contest of 2000 ultimately stands out as the lead example from the entire period between 1984 and 2008 of an election where individual relationships were at their most misleading about the nature of joint relationships. Nevertheless, in the interests of consistent exposition and on the way to those joint relationships and their density maps, Figure 7.4 offers individual relationships to the vote for economic and then cultural values. It returns to embedding these individual relationships in three voting populations: voters for Bush the Republican, voters for Gore the Democrat, or Non voters. As before, the figure compares the result in three diagnostic years: 1984 as our ongoing benchmark, 1996 as the predecessor election, and 2000 itself.

Among Republican voters, what emerges from such a picture is a powerful repeat of the relationship between economic values and Republican support, not only from the predecessor election of 1996 but also from the benchmark contest of 1984 (Figure 7.4.A). George W. Bush in 2000 ran noticeably better than Bob Dole in 1996, so the line for this relationship is pitched at a higher and happier place for Republicans. Yet the line itself is minimally different from either 1996 or 1984. Clearly, it was the first Perot election of 1992 that had been the deviant case for Republican voting and economic values.

Among Democratic voters, what emerges is likewise an apparent repeat of the relationship between economic values and Democratic support from the benchmark election of 1984, though *not* from the predecessor election of 1996 (Figure 7.4.B). Al Gore in 2000 ran noticeably worse than Bill Clinton in 1996, so the line for this relationship is inevitably pitched at a lower and sadder place for Democrats. Yet that line also differs in form from 1996, being instead nearly identical to—effectively overlaid with—its counterpart in 1984. Apparently, it was the contest of 1996 that had been the deviant case for Democratic voting and economic values.

Among Non voters, lastly, what emerges is just a powerful repetition of previous voting relationships, for both economics and culture. Economic conservatives had been and remained modestly more likely to turn out and economic liberals modestly less likely to do so (Figure 7.4.C), just as cultural liberals had been and remained modestly more likely to turn out and cultural conservatives modestly less likely to do so (Figure 7.4.F). Relationships between both economic and cultural values had always been more stable among those who took the nonvoting option, rather than choosing the Republican or the Democrat, and 2000 offered no apparent exception.

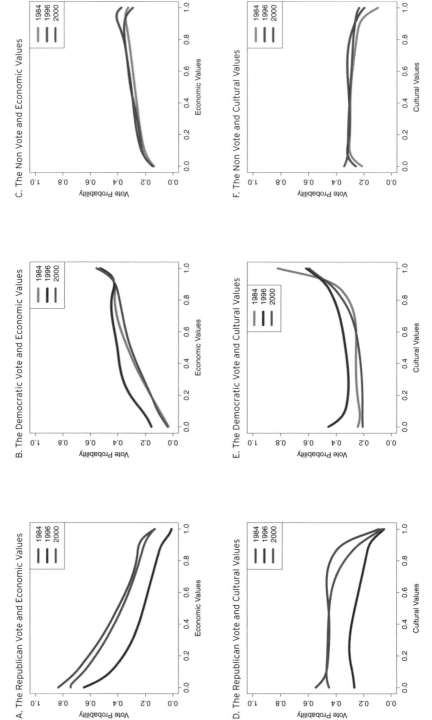

Figure 7.4 Political Values and Voting Behavior: The Nation as a Whole, 1984, 1996, 2000

The remainder of the story of cultural values and the presidential vote in 2000 could be told in roughly the same way, as one of reversion to earlier patterns, with parallel relationships pitched in a slightly different place from their most recent incarnations. Yet this cultural story had just enough further twists in the retelling to hint at the potential for something prospectively different, depending not on the contest of 2000 but on where these twists went in subsequent elections. At a minimum, if the individual relationships between economic or cultural values and the vote contained any harbingers of electoral evolution, these had to be found in the realm of culture rather than economics.

Even the Republican story of cultural values and voting behavior in 2000 could be characterized, overall, as a reversion toward the benchmark pattern of 1984 (Figure 7.4.D). That original voting relationship had featured Republican support as largely invariant from strong conservatives through moderate liberals, before dropping sharply among strong liberals. The contest of 1996 had suggested that cultural conflict had extended much farther along the ideological continuum. The contest of 2000 suggested instead—the main twist on a story of continuing stability—that the guaranteed fall in Republican support had expanded to include only the range from true centrists to strong liberals but remained flat on the cultural right.

If the Democratic story of cultural values in 2000 also looked more like a simple reversion to the benchmark pattern of 1984, however, this was still more of a restoration than a diminution of cultural influence (Figure 7.4.E). The original relationship had been the obverse of its Republican counterpart: largely invariant from strong conservatives through moderate liberals before jumping up sharply among strong liberals. Yet where the Republican story for 1996 had shown an *extension* of cultural relationships to the vote, its Democratic counterpart had shown a *moderation* of these relationships. What 2000 did for the Democrats, then, was to recapitulate the cultural voting line of 1984, making 1996 look, for Democrats, like the obvious anomaly.

The Missing Presidential Contest of 2004

On the one hand, then, the largest single story of voting relationships in the contest of 2000 was their reversion toward the (increasingly far-off) benchmark pattern of 1984, as replicated in 1988. In that light, it was the two contests involving Ross Perot as a third voting possibility, those of 1992 and 1996, that stood out as aberrant. On the other hand, if the reversion story was neatly accurate for economic values and voting behavior in 2000, cultural values allowed for just enough further difference, both from its immediate predecessor and from the more-distant benchmark, to gainsay the presence of a uniform *and lasting* voter reversion, at least without consideration of one or more successor elections.

The presidential contest of 2004 was, alas, not to provide this key comparative successor. For 2004 was to be the one election year from 1984 through 2008 for which there were no Pew Values surveys that asked about a vote in the preceding presidential contest. Familiar policy questions were still asked, so that the evolving role of both demographic cleavages (as in Chapter 3) and social groups (as in Chapter 4) could be monitored. Yet in the absence of a voting item, there was a disappointing and stark methodological choice. We could move to a different survey and its dataset for 2004, or we could stay with a fully consistent instrument at the cost of lacking 2004 in the overall analysis. Having experimented extensively with the former solution, we settled ultimately on the latter.

The most attractive alternative dataset was the General Social Survey (GSS), which offered some policy items on both of our major policy domains and was particularly rich for cultural values. It was possible to operate mechanically with these items in the same fashion, generating our two main dimensions to investigate voting relationships and density maps. Yet this operation produced only further dilemmas. Results from the 2004 GSS looked roughly similar to—indeed, fell roughly in between—results from the 2000 and 2008 Pew Values surveys. This was basically reassuring. On the other hand, this very similarity intensified the underlying problem, for it was precisely the year-specific differences that justified including 2004 from a different dataset. Yet these lesser differences were simultaneously the place where different items, rather than different behaviors, had the most scope to explain what were otherwise apparent but lesser shifts.

In the end, we judged that possessing a set of policy items that had the same wording across our entire time period was superior to adding individual years with idiosyncratic content, most especially in a sequence where the main evolutionary moves were gradual but where there were numerous single-year deviations that were *not* evolutionary.[3] We did retain the analyses conducted for 2004 through the GSS, and we consulted these while drafting the section of this chapter on the coming of the contemporary era. Nothing that we shall say about the general drift to this era from 2000 to 2008 is inconsistent with these experimental results for 2004 derived from the GSS. Yet, in the end, we thought that the ambiguities inherent in presenting a detailed analysis of that year with different items from a different survey did not justify merely having "something" that brought the presidential contest of 2004 into the overall sequence.

Economic Values, Cultural Values, and the Strategic Landscape

As in the benchmark year of 1984, so in all the years to follow: these individual relationships to the vote, for economic or cultural values, remained central to their joint relationships. At a minimum, they set limits on how different any joint picture could be. On the other hand, individual relationships, again for either economics or culture, never required proportionate associations with the alternative dimension. So it remains essential to go on and examine actual joint relationships to the vote, since these are the crucial intermediary step on the way to understanding the strategic landscape for electoral politics. As we shall see, these began to change in ways not evidently prefigured by the individual relationships.

Moreover, these joint relationships, by themselves, impose specific limits on the potential contours of the ideological landscape for American politics. When these are unpacked, some electoral strategies are obviously encouraged, while others look increasingly implausible. Yet once again, what such joint relationships actually do is to constrain the possible distributions of voters on the ideological landscape. That is, they constrain but do not determine these distributions. So it is ultimately the translation of joint voting relationships into associated density maps that produces the ideological landscape for electoral politics, a theoretical landscape to which very practical strategists must respond. Together, it is these joint ideological contours, as captured by the density maps associated with them, that determine whether any given strategic adjustment—any given alteration of policy promises—does or does not make sense.[4]

Year-on-year comparisons will show pairs of successor contests that varied only modestly for these joint relationships, as with 1984 and 1988, just as year-on-year comparisons will feature noteworthy but one-time deviations, as with 1992 and, to a lesser extent, 1996. These paired sets of earlier comparisons then combine to make the results in 2000 additionally provocative, intriguing more for their differences than for their similarities to earlier years. So that in the end, what all these year-on-year comparisons ultimately accomplish is to set up the picture of a substantial evolution of the American electoral landscape.

The Presidential Contest of 1988

Accordingly, Figure 7.5 moves on from individual to joint relationships with the vote for economic and cultural values among Republican, Democratic, and Non voting groups, with 1988 as the opening point of comparison to the benchmark year of 1984. Individual analyses for 1984 and 1988 (at Figure 7.1) testify to remarkable continuity. The two years come close to being a simple overlay. Joint analyses make the same central point: a powerful—in most ways remarkable—continuity between these two superficially very different years.

Recall that the Republican vote in 1984, for Ronald Reagan the incumbent president, was as pure an economic vote as would be registered for any candidate in any election from 1984 through 2008. What stands out immediately is the degree to which this voting pattern is recapitulated in 1988, with George H. W. Bush as the Republican candidate instead (Figure 7.5.A; compare with Figure 6.2.A). In both years, the Republican vote increases regularly and relentlessly from liberal to conservative on the economic continuum. In both years, this vote moves up in such a dominating fashion as to be unaffected by cultural preferences across most of the cultural continuum. There is that same modest uptick among extreme cultural conservatives, while the decline in Republican voting among strong cultural liberals begins a bit earlier in 1988 than it did in 1984, and the drop is a bit larger where it does occur. But that is really all there is to add.

Much work on elite politics emphasizes Ronald Reagan's role in expanding the partisan gap on cultural issues within the two political parties, and analyses of major-party platforms would confirm the widening of this gap during his administration.[5] But at the polls, among the general public, the

A. The Republican Vote

B. The Democratic Vote

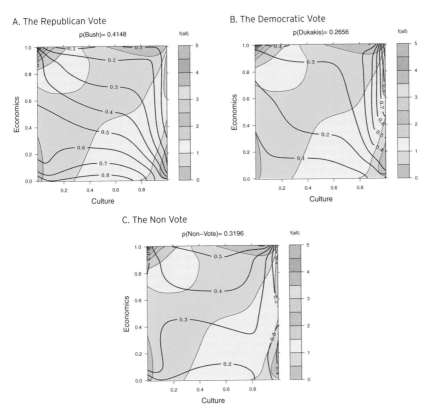

C. The Non Vote

Figure 7.5 The Ideological Landscape and Voting Behavior: The Nation as a Whole, 1988

Reagan vote was the purest picture the Pew surveys can provide of an *economic* vote. Most work on the Reagan and Bush campaigns, and indeed on the Reagan and Bush presidencies, would likewise agree that the two presidents came out of very different wings—not to mention career paths—within the Republican Party. Yet at the mass public level, their votes remained nearly interchangeable. Indeed, to the degree that they could be distinguished at all, the Bush vote was an intensification, not a moderation, of patterns characterizing the Reagan vote.

In turn, recall that the Democratic vote in 1984, for Walter Mondale the former vice president, was also related predominantly to economic values, albeit inversely, rising with economic liberalism and falling with economic conservatism. This, too, is quite literally the closest to a pure economic ballot among Democratic voters for any election in the Pew

Values era. On the other hand, it was already showing more of a role for cultural values among Democratic as opposed to Republican voters. Once more, what stands out is the degree to which this voting pattern is essentially recapitulated in 1988, with Michael Dukakis as the Democratic candidate this time (Figure 7.5.B; compare with Figure 6.2.B). Dukakis does garner added support somewhat earlier on the cultural continuum, among moderate liberals. But again, similarities within the Democratic vote across these successor years overwhelm this marginal difference.

Across the broad middle of the cultural continuum, then, economic preferences still tell most of the story in 1988, as they did in 1984, for Democrats as they did for Republicans. Where there is a difference between the two parties is in the more advanced role for cultural values within the Democratic vote, a Democratic edge that will continue for a generation before converging at last in the 2000s. Much work on elite politics traces the origins of an expanding cultural gap between the two parties not to the Reagan nomination of 1980 but to the McGovern nomination of 1972. Analyses of party platforms would affirm this impression, too, at the level of the active Democratic Party (as with Layman 2001), and this certainly leaves room for the voting public to have picked up some of these elite cues during the succeeding dozen years. While the Pew data cannot reach back to 1972, they can confirm, in parallel with the situation inside the Republican Party, that while Michael Dukakis was more moderate than Walter Mondale culturally, the Dukakis vote was still an intensification, not a moderation, of the Mondale pattern.

Perhaps surprisingly, the clearest shift in joint voting relationships between 1984 and 1988, albeit not very great even then, arrives with the Non voters, those who fell outside the active electorate. In 1984, the Non vote was a powerfully economic phenomenon, rising regularly with economic liberalism while being tweaked by culture in two places. Among strong economic liberals, strong cultural conservatism augmented the propensity not to vote, yet strong cultural liberals voted so overwhelmingly that economics added little further relationship to their electoral behavior. In 1988, the Non vote was still a powerfully economic phenomenon (Figure 7.5.C; compare with Figure 6.2.C). Yet in this successor year, it was cultural moderates who appeared additionally disinclined to vote. Strong cultural liberals still voted overwhelmingly, but strong cultural conservatives had improved their voting performance over 1988, such that it was the moderates who lagged both cultural extremes.

The presidential contests of 1984 and 1988 remain impressively similar when the focus moves on from joint relationships with the vote to the actual distribution of individuals whose vote operationalizes those relationships. Such distributions are best captured through density maps for the two elections, in figures that feature not the likelihood of voting one way or another at any given point of economic and cultural preference, but rather the share of voters who are actually concentrated (and voting) at that point. While these density maps, too, are similar for both elections, for 1984 and 1988, they immediately remind the analyst of how different the implications of a picture of voting relationships can look when transformed this way.

For both years, the dominant fact about these density maps among Republican voters is that they are concentrated among strong economic conservatives, who are otherwise dispersed across a broad range of cultural values (Figure 7.6.A; compare with Figure 6.3.A). Moreover, in both years, the modal Republican voter is strongly conservative on economics, moderately liberal on culture. Such results are not inconsistent with joint voting relationships that show a strong relationship to economic values and little relationship to cultural values except at the far liberal end, where the Republican vote plunges. Those are entirely accurate as relationships. Yet those individual (even joint) relationships might—they probably would not—produce an expectation that the modal Republican voter was a strong economic conservative who was a moderate cultural *liberal*.

While parallelism is thus the dominant theme in comparing density maps for the Republican votes of 1984 and 1988, there are two clear but related, lesser differences in the high ground of Republican voting—the area on the ideological landscape that was more than 50 percent more likely than the nation as a whole to vote Republican. In the first, this Republican high ground was notably reduced among strong cultural conservatives in 1988 compared with 1984. In the second, this high ground was increased among true cultural centrists, who simultaneously pulled the modal Republican voter into more moderate territory on economics. In moving ever so slightly left on both economics and culture, then, this modal Republican might reasonably have been reflecting the shift from Ronald Reagan to George H. W. Bush.

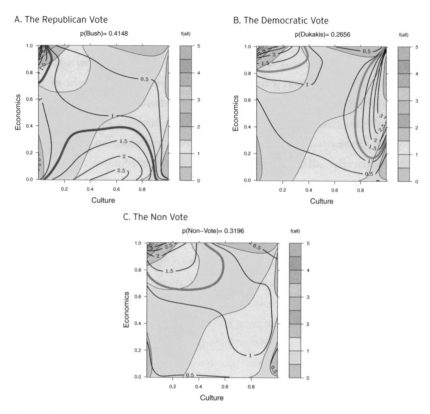

Figure 7.6 Ideological Density and Voting Behavior: The Nation as a Whole, 1988

By contrast, the dominant fact about these density maps among Democratic voters for both years is that they are concentrated among strong cultural liberals who are otherwise dispersed across a broad range of economic values, while featuring a small secondary concentration among strong economic liberals who are strong cultural conservatives (Figure 7.6.B; compare with Figure 6.3.B).[6] In both years, the modal Democratic voter is strongly liberal on culture, in an essentially unchanging fashion. In 1988, this overrepresented Democratic electorate actually extends into the terrain of moderate economic conservatism, and the modal Democrat is arguably a true economic centrist rather than a moderate liberal. If Michael Dukakis intended to moderate his self-presentation on both dimensions, it was working on economics but not on culture.

These results, too, are obviously not inconsistent with individual voting relationships that are simultaneously derived from the same underlying data. Both individual and joint voting relationships show a clear link to economic values and a weak link to culture until the point of strong cultural liberalism—which is, of course, where the Democratic high ground is located. But again, those joint relationships, examined in isolation, might not—again probably would not—produce an expectation of the comparative power of culture and weakness of economics in structuring this disproportionately Democratic turf.

The Non voters of 1984 are, as ever, a different story from their voting brethren. Where individual voting relationships had suggested a modest shift in Non voting between 1984 and 1988, density maps warn against treating this as any sort of shift in strategic incentives for either the Republican or the Democratic candidate (Figure 7.6.C; compare with Figure 6.3.C). Examined through voting relationships, there appeared to be less consequence to strong cultural conservatism and more consequence to cultural moderation in producing Non voters between the two years. But translated into density maps, these joint relationships no longer offer anything in the way of serious difference. A candidate who expected cultural adjustments in 1988 to produce increased voter turnout, much less an increase for the Republican or Democratic candidate specifically, would have been chasing a shadow.

The Presidential Contest of 1992

The comparable story for joint relationships and density maps almost had to be different for the presidential contest of 1992. This was the contest, after all, in which an independent candidate, Ross Perot, gained almost one in five of the votes cast. Individual voting relationships suggest that this Perot vote was structured differently by economics as opposed to culture, and was clearly associated with strong economic conservatism and weakly associated with moderate cultural liberalism (Figures 7.2.C and 7.2.F). These relationships also suggest that this vote shuffled relationships with both economics and culture more strongly among Republican (Figures 7.2.A and 7.2.B) than among Democratic (Figures 7.2.D and 7.2.E) voters.

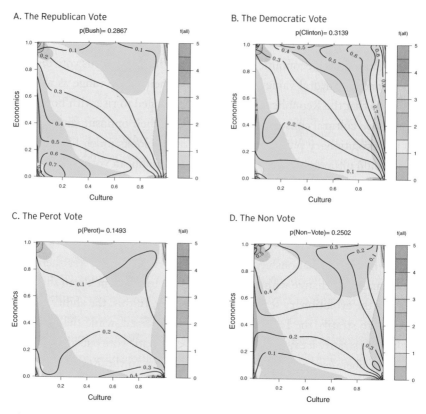

Figure 7.7 The Ideological Landscape and Voting Behavior: The Nation as a Whole, 1992

Joint voting relationships with economic and cultural values tickle these understandings in important ways. Seen through these joint relationships, the Perot vote looks even more clearly like an embodiment of economic rather than cultural values (Figure 7.7.C). Its joint pattern is fundamentally economic, rising with conservatism and falling with liberalism at every point on the cultural continuum. Cultural values play a role only at the extremes, where support from strong cultural conservatives declines sharply and support from strong cultural liberals absolutely craters. In other words, the Perot defection is a strongly economic vote, where strong cultural conservatives stay with the Republican and strong cultural liberals stay with the Democrat.

The Republican vote, seen this way, remains the major-party vote that is most different from 1988. Yet the lens of joint voting relationships magnifies this difference (Figure 7.7.A). It is not that economic values did not continue to shape this vote across their entire range; they certainly did. But now, with economic conservatives pulled out of this vote disproportionately, cultural values shape it across their entire range as well, so much so that the Republican vote in 1992 managed to rise with both economic *and* cultural conservatism, and fall with their opposite states. More to the evolutionary point, because this pattern looks much like the one that would ultimately come to characterize Republican voting in general, it raises the possibility that 1992 was an actual harbinger of later results, quite apart from the idiosyncrasies of Ross Perot.

The Democratic vote changed far less between 1988 and 1992, when surveyed through individual voting relationships, and the same remains true when joint relationships are the focus (Figure 7.7.B). Yet there was some marginal change within it, too—parallel to the Republican shift and teasing the evolutionary search in the same way. In this, the ability of economics to stratify the Democratic vote also declined, while the ability of culture to stratify it expanded. Now, the Democratic vote outside of strong cultural liberalism assumed the opposite pattern to the Republican vote, rising with *both* economic and cultural liberalism and falling with their opposite states. Economics remained even more powerful among Republicans and culture among Democrats, but in 1992, both dimensions were powerful in both voter categories.

The Non vote, finally, just reflected the joint pattern of 1984, rising toward strong economic liberalism coupled with strong cultural conservatism and falling away in all directions from there (Figure 7.7.D). Non voters thus remained the only voting category apparently unaffected by the Perot performance, returning in 1992 to what had been their joint relationship in 1984 (Figure 6.2.C of Chapter 6). Joint voting relationships for 1988 had suggested a modest ideological shift within the Non voter population, a shift already belied by the density maps for that year. Joint voting relationships for 1992 did not even hint at any similar shift.

Once again, density maps take the strategic implications of these voting relationships in somewhat different directions. The Perot vote remains distinctive, almost by definition. But where the territory for a disproportionate Republican vote looks noticeably different from previous years,

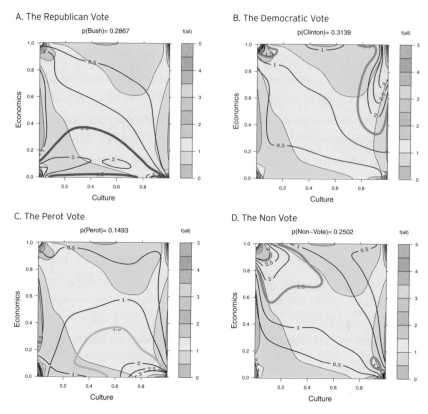

Figure 7.8 Ideological Density and Voting Behavior: The Nation as a Whole, 1992

the Democratic *and* Non voter high grounds look much the same as they did previously. This is yet another indication of the way in which the Perot vote shaped—and in this sense, injured—the Republican much more than the Democratic (or the Non) votes in 1992. In its time, it would have been quite reasonable to believe that this was a "Perot effect," due to recede when the man himself left the scene. Once we have added 1996 to the analysis, this will seem much less obvious.

   In any case, the modal Perot voter was a strong to moderate conservative on economics who ranged from being truly centrist to moderately liberal on culture (Figure 7.8.C). Seen comparatively, the Bush vote was likewise concentrated among strong to moderate economic conservatives, who ranged from being truly centrist to moderately conservative on culture (Figure 7.8.A). This represented a clear shift toward the cultural right among Republican voters, though the explanation is simple enough. Remarkably, it was the previously modal Republican voter, a strong economic conservative but moderate cultural liberal, who was most attracted to an alternative candidate, Ross Perot, in 1992. Again, the question insistently arises: Was this harbinger or idiosyncrasy? Again, the answer can only come from analysis of subsequent elections.

In the meantime, note that both the modal Democratic and the modal Non voter looked similar to their incarnations in the two preceding elections. The modal Democrat was, as ever, a strong cultural liberal, ranging from strong liberalism through true centrism on economics (Figure 7.8.B). This was marginally more like the picture of 1984 than of 1988, having shed some moderate economic conservatives, but the more impressive fact about all three years was their overarching similarity. This remained even more true for the modal Non voter, whose high ground remained the territory of strong economic liberalism coupled with strong cultural conservatism, for the third time in three elections (Figure 7.8.D). This, too, looked marginally more like the story of 1984 than of 1988, though similarities again far outweighed differences.

To say the same thing differently, the four paired comparisons of overrepresented voters in the electoral conflict of 1992 were each united by one great ideological dimension and divided by the other, in four distinct ways:

- The Republican and Perot votes were both concentrated among moderate to strong *economic conservatives*. They were then divided by culture, where the modal Republican leaned conservative while the modal Perotista leaned liberal (Figures 7.8.A and 7.8.C).
- The Perot and Democratic votes were concentrated instead among *cultural liberals*—strongly for the Democrats, moderately for the Perotistas. Yet they were divided by economics, where the modal Democrat leaned liberal and the modal Perot voter was clearly conservative (Figures 7.8.B and 7.8.C).
- The Democratic and Non votes were in turn concentrated among *economic liberals*—strongly for the Nons, moderately for the Democrats. They were then massively divided by culture, where the modal

Democrat was a strong liberal, the modal Non a strong to moderate conservative (Figures 7.8.B and 7.8.D).

- The Republican and Non votes, last but not least, were both concentrated among *cultural conservatives*. Yet they were massively divided by economics, where the modal Republican was a strong to moderate conservative, and the modal Non was a strong to moderate liberal (Figure 7.8.A and 7.8.D).

The Presidential Contest of 1996

The leading major-party story of the presidential contest of 1996 was the solid—indeed, easy—reelection of Bill Clinton, sitting Democratic president. Unsympathetic analysts had attributed his victory in 1992 to the vote-splitting capabilities of Ross Perot. Perot was still around in 1996, yet no one attributed a thumping reelection for Clinton to his influence this time. The leading third-candidate story was rather the *collapse* of the Perot vote, and this in two senses. First, Perot's aggregate tally fell by more than half, from 19 percent to 8 percent. Beyond that, the vote that remained showed little relationship to either economic or cultural values individually. The story of their joint relationship in 1996, however, was to feature (a) a strikingly different combined profile for the Perot vote, (b) a partial return to established patterns for both the Republican and the Democratic tally, and (c) a return to one of two recurrent patterns within the Non vote.

Despite the comparative collapse of the Perot vote, it makes sense to begin the 1996 analysis with his tally, since it retained the potential to color Democratic and Republican relationships, but most especially since it was so different *from itself* only one election before. In the predecessor year of 1992, the Perot vote had risen strongly toward economic conservatism, while peaking simultaneously among true centrists and moderate liberals on culture (Figure 7.7.C). In 1996, by contrast, it rose and fell in peaks and valleys scattered all across the ideological landscape (Figure 7.9.C). This was a vote pattern unlike any other for any candidate in any election for which there are Pew Values surveys. It was very hard to attribute any comprehensive ideological rationale to it.

By comparison, the 1996 Republican vote, for Bob Dole as the standard-bearer this time, showed a modest regression from the pattern of 1992 (Figure 7.7.A), because this Republican vote was a bit less colored by a

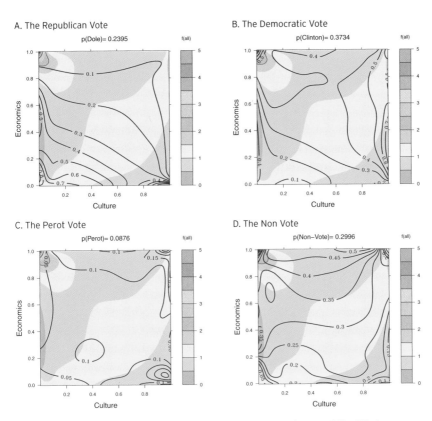

A. The Republican Vote

B. The Democratic Vote

C. The Perot Vote

D. The Non Vote

Figure 7.9   The Ideological Landscape and Voting Behavior: The Nation as a Whole, 1996

simultaneous relationship to both economic and cultural conservatism (Figure 7.9.A). On the other hand, this regression was nowhere near the economic dominance of these joint voting relationships in 1984 or 1988. The resultant patterning thus raised the incipient possibility that the next presidential election, in 2000, would merely feature a further regression toward established relationships. Yet it also raised the contrary possibility that 1996 was in effect consolidating an evolving change that had first been registered in 1992.

In its time, this theme of incipient change might have received reinforcement—had analysts been able to see the future—from a newly chaotic patterning to the Democratic vote of 1996 (Figure 7.9.B). In 1992, Democratic voters had offered the same full-spectrum effect that characterized the Republicans, featuring simultaneous effects from both economics and culture (Figure 7.7.B). Indeed, to say the same thing more accurately, it was actually the Democrats who had foreshadowed this effect in 1984 and 1988. Yet for 1996, this effect was instead chopped into three distinct pieces. The dominant Democratic cluster of strong cultural liberals showed almost no influence from economics. The secondary Democratic cluster of strong economic liberals who were strong cultural conservatives showed little influence from culture. And the residual showed both economics and culture in play.

If both Republican and Democratic voters were receding from their voting patterns in 1992, it should probably not be surprising that the joint relationship to the Non voter in 1996 reverted as well. In 1984, this Non vote had risen toward economic liberals who were cultural conservatives (Figure 6.2.D in Chapter 6). In 1988, it had instead risen toward economic liberals who were cultural moderates (Figure 7.5.D). For 1992, the Non vote had again risen toward economic liberals who were strong cultural conservatives (Figure 7.7.D). For 1996, it was back to rising toward economic liberals who were cultural moderates (Figure 7.9.D). The difference thus appeared to revolve around the strong cultural conservatives within their ranks. When their turnout was up, as in 1988 and 1996, the Non vote was associated with cultural moderation. When their turnout was down, as in 1984 and 1992, the Non vote was associated with cultural conservatism instead. It was, however, always associated with economic liberalism.

The idiosyncrasy of the Perot vote, already evident in its joint relationship to economic and cultural values, becomes screamingly evident when the focus shifts to the density map underlying that relationship (Figure 7.10.C). For 1996, the high ground of Perot support, the ideological terrain that was more than 50 percent more likely to vote for the independent candidate than was the nation as a whole, was actually split into three clusters, each remarkably distant from the others. One featured strong cultural liberals who were moderate to strong economic liberals. Another featured strong economic liberals who were strong cultural conservatives. And a third featured strong economic conservatives who were strong cultural liberals!

On the other hand, the second key point in interpreting the Perot density map for 1996 is that none of these areas was of any serious size. In other words, the Perot vote really was flatter—more evenly distributed—not only

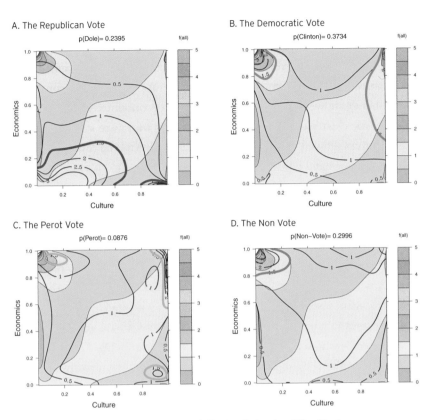

Figure 7.10 Ideological Density and Voting Behavior: The Nation as a Whole, 1996

by comparison to itself in 1992, but also by comparison to the other three voting categories in 1996. The difficulty in interpreting this Perot vote through its joint voting relationships had been a difficulty in creating any policy rationale to fit its pattern of support, and this becomes impossible with a focus on its density map. Instead, this is the classic picture of a vote that is a parking place rather than a policy preference. Note, however, one other feature that will become important later in this chapter: although the voters who parked with Perot in 1996 were found in wildly divergent places on the ideological map, these were all *extreme* places. It was extremists, of otherwise wildly varied stripes, who were looking for an electoral alternative, not moderates.

Seen through its density map as well as its voting relationships, the Republican vote of 1996 looked instead to be an example of further and ongoing electoral evolution (Figure 7.10.A). What had been economically conservative terrain for this high ground of Republicanism in 1984, 1988, and 1992 remained economically conservative terrain in 1996. That had not changed. But having found its modal voter in moderately liberal territory on culture in 1984 and 1988, shifting to moderately conservative territory in 1992, it settled onto culturally centrist terrain for 1996. Seen one way, this was more a consolidation of the previous rightward drift on culture, rather than any further movement. Looked at the other way, the modal Republican voter of 1984 and 1988, a moderate cultural liberal, was actually absent from the Republican high ground by 1996.

By contrast, the main Democratic high ground looked impressively stable (Figure 7.10.B). It was concentrated among strong cultural liberals who ranged from strong liberalism through true centrism on economics. The signature characteristic of this disproportionate Democratic vote had been strong cultural liberalism in every preceding election, and 1996 was no exception. What varied was only the reach of its economic preferences, which were always more varied. The main secondary Democratic cluster, among strong economic liberals who were strong cultural conservatives, likewise remained remarkably stable. This cluster had resided in that location in 1984, 1988, and 1992, and it still did so in 1996.

As did the disproportionate cluster of Non voters (Figure 7.10.D). A population that had been headquartered in the land of strong economic liberalism and strong cultural conservatism in 1984, 1988, and 1992 continued to reside there in 1996. Once again, this meant that the modest ideological fluctuation that voting relationships suggested for this population from election to election—sometimes more closely associated with cultural conservatism, other times with cultural moderation—had little potential for altering electoral strategies. Republicans who featured strong economic conservatism, as well as Democrats who featured strong cultural liberalism, would be hard-pressed to offer policy concessions that could even potentially move the Non voters into the electorate.

The Presidential Contest of 2000

The presidential contest of 2000 featured a sitting vice president, Al Gore, attempting to succeed his president. Distinguishing himself from his predecessor (Bill Clinton) was an obvious task for such a campaign, but so was a simultaneous emphasis on continuity and stability. The presidential contest of 2000 pitted Gore against a sitting governor of Texas, George W. Bush, who was attempting to derail the succession. Bush was even more concerned than Gore with sketching a moderate, problem-solving persona, gathered under his theme of "compassionate conservatism." Beyond Gore and Bush, the presidential contest of 2000 was distinguished by the absence not just of Ross Perot but of a substantial independent vote. Ralph Nader would run as the Green Party candidate for president, and his vote would have a huge impact on the ultimate outcome. But the vote itself would be tiny.

Under those conditions, it was more than a little surprising that voting patterns in 2000 did not revert to the established template that characterized presidential politics in 1984 and 1988, before the Perot intrusion. Instead, these patterns looked much more like those for the major-party candidates in 1992, the great year of the Perot ascendancy. Perot had been in decline by 1996, and he was missing in 2000. So voting patterns that looked more like 1992 than any other preceding year inevitably raised the question of change versus idiosyncrasy. With Perot out of the way, was the pattern of major-party support indeed undergoing change? Or was 2000 merely one more wobble in a system whose fundamentals endured? Only a subsequent election or two could answers these questions, but the year 2000 certainly raised them.

Thus the Republican vote for president in 2000, for George W. Bush, resurrected a powerful joint relationship to both economic and cultural values (Figure 7.11.A). Economics was present, as ever, and in the classical fashion. Economic conservatives were more inclined to vote for Bush and economic liberals less inclined at every level of cultural values. Yet cultural conservatives were now likewise more inclined to vote for Bush and cultural liberals even less so at almost every level of economic values. The strongest economic conservatives were unlikely to vote for Gore, regardless of their cultural preferences. The strongest cultural liberals were unlikely to vote for Bush, regardless of their economics. But otherwise, both economics and culture were in play across most of the ideological continuum. As a result, the Bush vote of 2000 looked more like the Bush vote of 1992, for George H. W. Bush that time, than it did like the Dole vote of 1996.

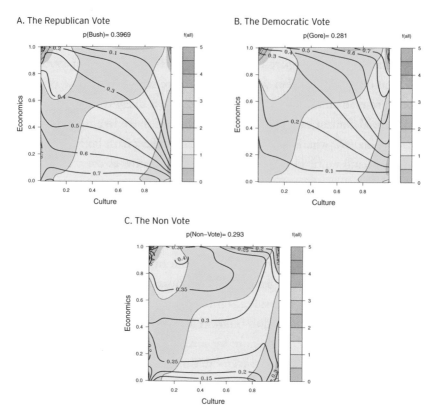

Figure 7.11 The Ideological Landscape and Voting Behavior: The Nation as a Whole, 2000

The Democratic vote for president in 2000, for Al Gore, likewise testified to a powerful joint relationship with both economic and cultural values (Figure 7.11.B). As ever, economics was more neatly related to the Republican than to the Democratic vote. That said, economic liberals were still more inclined to vote for Gore and economic conservatives less inclined at every level of cultural values. Extreme economic conservatives just did not vote for Gore, almost regardless of their cultural values, and strong cultural liberals did vote for him, regardless of their economics. Otherwise, cultural liberals were more inclined to vote for him and cultural conservatives against him in an orderly gradient in between. As a result, the Gore vote of 2000 looked more like the Clinton vote of 1992 than like the Clinton vote of 1996. In the process, the bizarrely trifurcated pattern of Democratic voting in 1996 had disappeared.

This left the Non vote of 2000 to attest to stability rather than change for the longer run, as indeed it did, though even this vote looked more like 1992 than like 1996 (Figure 7.11.C). The presidential contest of 1996 had featured one of those Non vote patterns where strong economic liberals who were true cultural moderates had been least likely to turn out. The presidential contest of 2000, by contrast, looked more like the Non vote patterns of 1992 where the Non vote rose regularly with both economic liberalism and cultural conservatism. Though again, as ever, not much should be made of this difference in a population that was heavily concentrated among strong economic liberals who were strong cultural conservatives regardless of the details of their voting relationships.

Inside those voting relationships, density maps continued to unearth well-established differences among Republican, Democratic, and Non voters, along with evidence for modest evolutionary change, at least among the partisan voting categories (Figure 7.12). As aspects of continuity, Republican voters continued to be concentrated among strong economic conservatives, while varying more by cultural preference, just as Democratic voters continued to be concentrated among strong cultural liberals, while varying more by economic preference. And Non voters, as ever, continued to be concentrated among strong economic liberals who were strong cultural conservatives.

Within those general outlines, the modal Republican voter of 2000 was a strong economic conservative who was a true cultural centrist (Figure 7.12.A). On the one hand, this drew some of the Republican high ground back into the territory of moderate cultural liberalism, where it had been largely absent in 1996. On the other hand, this was still nothing like the old world of 1984 and 1988, when it was these moderate cultural liberals who had actually contributed the modal Republican voter. By contrast, the modal Democratic voter of 2000 was a strong cultural liberal, who once again ranged from strong liberalism through true centrism on economics.

The small secondary high ground for Democratic voters remained far distant, in the land of strong economic liberals who were strong cultural conservatives, as it had been for every election of the Pew Values era. That was a picture of true stability, though it was outdone by the Non vote, still even more powerfully concentrated among those same strong economic liberals who were strong cultural conservatives (Figure 7.12.C).

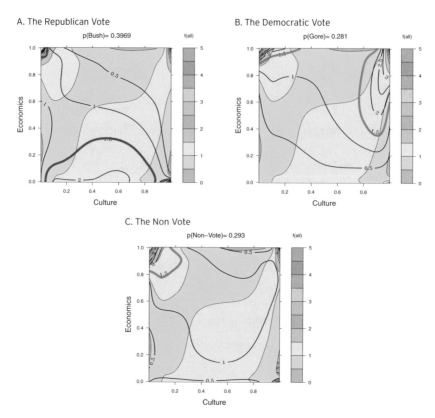

Figure 7.12   Ideological Density and Voting Behavior: The Nation as a Whole, 2000

Non voters had lived disproportionately in this territory since the advent of the Pew Values surveys. They still sat overwhelmingly in that same place. As such, they continued to overlap the main secondary cluster of Democratic voters, but to have little to do with any serious Republican voting population.

The Evolution of the Strategic Landscape

Economic Values, Cultural Values, and the Evolving Vote

On its surface, there were two great story lines to the presidential contest of 2008, one involving major-party nominations and one involving the general election. In the first, commentators emphasized that this would be the only election since 1952 (and the only one for which there is Pew survey data) with neither a sitting president seeking reelection nor a sitting vice president trying to succeed his president. The argument was that this fact maximized possible variety in the nature of the individuals who might end up as presidential nominees and hence, for us, possible influences on the ongoing relationships among social backgrounds, political values, and voting behavior.

The successor story line, involving the general election, was very different. The nation was already in recession when nominating politics began in earnest, and as the months passed, the economy only declined further. When a comprehensive bank meltdown threatened in mid-September, the central theme of the general election campaign, and the apparent priority of economics as an issue, seemed established. Commentators dubbed the presidential contest of 2008 as the greatest economic election since the Great Depression and hence, for this analysis, as *the* great economic election of the survey-research era.

On their face, both story lines seem inherently plausible. What they did not offer, even on their own terms, was any systematic link between this elite narrative and mass political behavior. The former was usually just allowed to imply the latter. What they did not offer, on our terms, was any interaction between these story lines and the ongoing ideological landscape for electoral conflict in American politics. To that end, Figure 7.13 sets up the now-standard arrangement: voting relationships with first economic and then cultural values; for Republican, Democratic, and Non voting groups; comparing the presidential contest of 2008 with the transitional election of 2000 and the benchmark contest of 1984.

For economics, what results in 2008 is largely the classic picture of the relationship between economic values and the vote in modern American politics, tickled in a manner consistent with the elite narrative about presidential politicking in a year of expanded economic concern. Voter turnout remained weakly associated with economic values, being highest among conservatives and lowest among liberals (Figure 7.13.C). Turnout was otherwise up modestly over both comparison elections at almost every point on the economic continuum, though this increase was perhaps over-celebrated by commentators, given the way the lines of relationship for all three comparison years were effectively clustered.

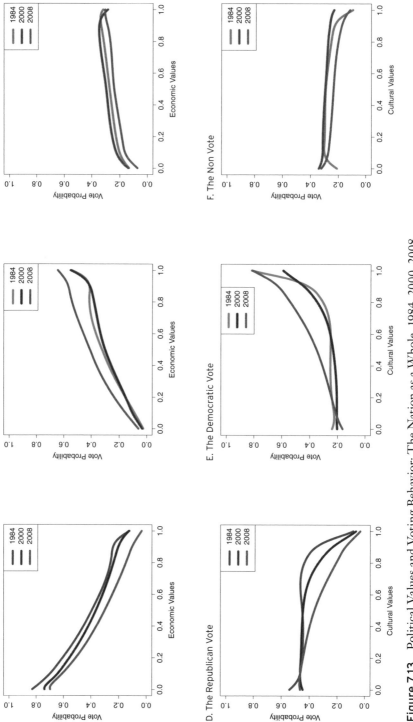

Figure 7.13 Political Values and Voting Behavior: The Nation as a Whole, 1984, 2000, 2008

The Republican vote was then, classically and as ever, strongly associated with economic values in the negative direction, such that conservatives were attracted and liberals repelled (Figure 7.13.A). What was different in 2008 in contrast to either 2000 or 1984 was, first, that this Republican vote was comparatively down at every point on the economic continuum and, second, that it was down the most among strong economic liberals. Both twists were presumably appropriate for an election of heightened economic concern where the in-party was being punished for economic conditions.

And the Democratic vote was, also classically and as ever, clearly if less strongly associated with economic values in the opposite direction, such that liberals were attracted and conservatives repelled (Figure 7.13.C). What was different in 2008 was just the obverse of the Republican story. Overall, the Democratic vote was up over either comparison year at every point on the economic continuum. Yet it was up most among strong economic liberals, presumably the ideological faction in which it ought to be up most in an "economic year."

That was basically a story of continuity, one consistent with descriptions that could have been offered for every presidential contest from 1984 through 2000, with the partial exception of 1992. In its adjustments to that continuing picture, the story of 2008 was also consistent with the elite narrative about economic conditions and economic values. On the other hand, both of those facts, an underlying continuity plus adjustments consistent with contemporary commentary, served to mask the degree of change in relationships between cultural values and the vote, and thus to make these look even larger when they are isolated and unpacked.

The Republican vote of 2008, when stratified by culture and contrasted with 2000 and 1984, looked like a story of ongoing evolution—and within this, looked as if it might even have reached a kind of ultimate terminus (Figure 7.13.D). In 1984, this Republican vote had been unrelated to cultural values across most of the ideological continuum, before plunging sharply among strong liberals. By 2000, there was more of a relationship, in that the same drop began earlier, among moderate liberals. For 2008, the drop now ran across the entire cultural continuum, from strong cultural conservatives through strong liberals.

The Democratic vote was then its obverse (Figure 7.13.E). In 1984, this Democratic vote, too, had been unrelated to cultural values across most of the ideological continuum, before jumping up sharply among strong liberals. For 2000, it showed only hints of an augmented relationship. Yet by 2008, this relationship not only ran across the entire cultural continuum, from strong conservatives through strong liberals, in the opposite direction to its Republican counterpart; it also managed to look even more impressive than this counterpart, in the sense that it featured an even sharper jump since 2000.

It was with the Non vote, finally and once again, that change was smallest (Figure 7.13.F). Cultural liberals were again more likely to vote than cultural conservatives all along the ideological continuum, albeit weakly so, with a special turnout bonus among strong liberals and a special turnout decrement among strong conservatives. Voter turnout was also up overall in 2008, so that the line of this relationship was improved everywhere except the conservative and liberal extremes. Yet it was otherwise basically the same line.

This combination of individual economic and cultural relationships did contribute an ironic shading to the main journalistic lines of commentary on the presidential contest of 2008. The actual course of nominating politics had certainly affirmed the prospect that the specific nominees might be different in this non-incumbent year, in the persons of maverick Republican nominee, Arizona Senator John McCain, and of first-ever Black Democratic nominee, Illinois Senator Barack Obama.

The actual course of electoral politics was not thereafter inconsistent with an elite narrative that made the general election campaign of 2008, in the midst of the Great Recession, one in which economic values mattered strongly. Even more than usual, they did. It was just that the other great story of this most recent contest, one that actually represented a larger change, remained nearly invisible in this elite narrative. This alternative story was the confirmation of the power not of economics but of culture in the strength of its association with a partisan vote.

Two additional things need to be said about this evolutionary story before it is immersed in joint relationships to the vote for the two valuational dimensions, and well before considering the distribution of voters on the ideological landscape implied by those joint relationships. The first is the increasing relationship to voting behavior of political values generally. Both economics and culture acquired a stronger relationship between

1984 and 2008 to the two main voting categories, that is, among Republican *and* Democratic voters. Yet the second further story is that culture had caught up with economics across this same quarter-century. In this, culture was on the rise in both main voting categories, not only in comparison with itself but also in comparison with economics.

Economic and Cultural Values Jointly with the Evolving Vote

When these voting relationships are then considered jointly rather than singly, as they do in fact appear in the actual world of practical politics, change over time only grows in impressiveness. The Republican vote of 1984, for sitting President Ronald Reagan, had been the archetypal economic vote for any candidate in any year of this voting series (Figure 7.14.A). Beyond economics, there was only that major drop-off among strong cultural liberals, along with a modest uptick among strong cultural conservatives, though this latter was as much prospective hint as established reality. Otherwise, the Reagan vote had moved more or less regularly up and down the ideological scale in sync with economic values: the lines of Republican voting were overwhelmingly horizontal.

By contrast, the Republican vote of 2008, for Arizona Senator John McCain, was neatly related to both economics and culture across the full range of both (Figure 7.14.B). Symmetry across the board made both dimensions impressive. Economics was still inescapably in evidence. Yet it had been joined on an equal footing by culture. And the overall distance from the Reagan vote of 1984 was striking indeed. In a parallel display a quarter-century later, the McCain vote actually carved out one of the ideological diagonals on these joint relationships, rising toward economic and cultural conservatism, falling toward economic and cultural liberalism.

The support lines that most closely approximated McCain's overall vote (from 0.2 to 0.4) were in fact nearly perfect diagonals between the two ideological end points. His best performance remained among strong economic conservatives, where there was only a lesser role for culture. His worst performance remained among strong cultural liberals, where there was hardly any role for economics. But these best and worst performances were all that was left of the earliest joint relationships. What characterized those relationships now was the parallel mutual behavior of both economic and cultural values.

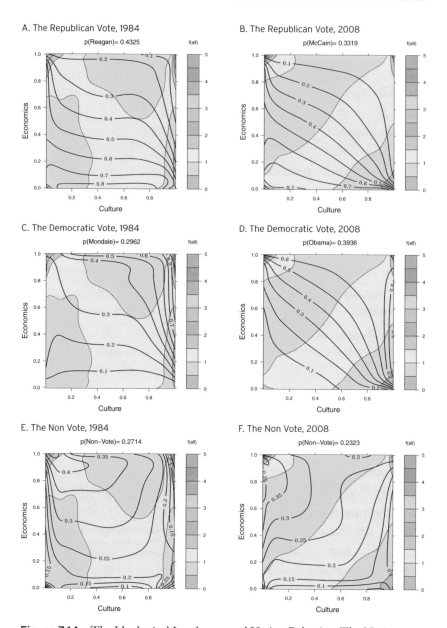

Figure 7.14 The Ideological Landscape and Voting Behavior: The Nation as a Whole, 1984, 2008

The Democratic vote of 1984, for former Vice President Walter Mondale, had likewise been archetypically economic among Democratic tallies, though it already showed a bit more cultural relationship among strong economic conservatives and a substantial cultural role among strong economic liberals (Figure 7.14.C). Nevertheless, in a display of joint relationships to economics and culture, the Mondale vote had still privileged economics over culture, moving more or less regularly up and down the ideological scale with economic values. As with the Republican vote, this line of relationship for the Democratic vote had still been principally horizontal.

By contrast, the Democratic vote of 2008, for Illinois Senator Barack Obama, was neatly related to both economics and culture across the full range of values on both (Figure 7.14.D). Symmetry across the board made both dimensions impressive. Economics had hardly disappeared. But it had been joined on an equal footing by culture. As a result, it was nearly as hard to recognize the Mondale vote within the Obama vote as it was to see the Reagan vote inside the McCain tally. Like the McCain vote, the Obama vote now hewed closely to the same great ideological diagonal for these joint relationships, albeit rising toward economic and cultural liberalism while falling toward economic and cultural conservatism.

As with McCain, so with Obama: the support lines that most closely approximated Obama's total vote (from 0.3 to 0.5) were nearly perfect diagonals between the two ideological end points. His vote did retain a clear reflection of the old and ongoing Democratic advantage among strong cultural liberals. For those with cultural values greater than 0.8, economics was effectively irrelevant, and this remained a significant population. Yet this was also the only population not characterized by the parallel mutual behavior of economics and culture among Democratic voters.

As ever, the Non vote showed the smallest change between 1984 and 2008, featuring parallel overall relationships to economics and culture jointly. The dominant fact remained that the Non vote in both years was concentrated in the same small corner of the ideological landscape, joining economic liberalism with cultural conservatism and falling away in every direction. Yet even this picture of joint (Non)voting relationships implicitly acknowledged the increasing role of culture. In 1984, the Non vote had been concentrated among strong economic liberals who were strong or moderate cultural conservatives (Figure 7.14.E). For 2008, the Non vote was concentrated instead among strong cultural conservatives who were strong or moderate economic liberals (Figure 7.14.F).

Note, finally, that there had been a further evolution of political values during this quarter-century. Within the general public in 1984, there had been little relationship between economic and cultural values (compare the yellow underlays with the orange underlays in Figures 7.14.A, 7.14.C, or 7.14.E). Yet to the extent that there was a relationship, it was inverse, featuring a clear tendency for economic liberals to be cultural conservatives along with a weak and wobbly tendency for economic conservatives to be cultural liberals. By 2008, this underlying relationship had not only become regular, it had in fact changed direction (compare the yellow underlays with the orange underlays in Figures 7.14.B, 7.14.D, or 7.14.F). Now, there was a clear if loose tendency for economic liberals to be cultural liberals and economic conservatives to be cultural conservatives, along with that unrelated ideological island of strong economic liberals who remained strong cultural conservatives.

Whether this resulted from the direct evolution of political values within the general public, from the evolution of these values among political elites and their gradual transmission to the general public, or from simple replacement of individuals holding one mix of values by individuals holding a different mix cannot be deduced from Figure 7.14. Regardless, note that the modern cluster that did not share in this overall evolution, that modest overrepresentation of strong economic liberals who were strong cultural conservatives, was now much farther out of the ideological mainstream than it had been in 1984.

Yet that is not the end of the evolutionary story, not nearly, since joint relationships to voting behavior, however they were changing, did not imply even a roughly uniform distribution of voters *within* those relationships. Moreover, the evolutionary story of the density of these voters on the ideological landscape has shown that this distribution can be every bit as important for campaign strategy as the voting relationships associated with it. Yet here, there are three different stories. There is a story of change among Republican voters. There is a story of adjustment among Democratic voters. And there is a story of stasis among Non voters. Though in the end, these stories collectively make the strategic dilemmas explored in the benchmark year of 1984 look more intense, not more relaxed, by 2008.

In 1984, with Ronald Reagan as the candidate, the Republican vote was disproportionately found among strong economic conservatives (Figure 7.15.A). Yet within their ranks, there was a mild further tendency for this Republican vote to be concentrated among moderate cultural liberals. These were not strong liberals, a sector where the Republican vote plunged. But neither were they strong conservatives, at all. They were, to repeat, moderate liberals on culture. This does not reflect some hidden tendency for cultural liberalism in its own right to foster Republican voting. Figure 6.2.A has explicitly dismissed that possibility. Rather, Figure 7.15.A here reflects the simple fact that Republican voters, in the opening Pew survey in our benchmark year, were just disproportionately located at this point on the cultural landscape.

In 2008, with John McCain as the candidate, the Republican picture had changed strikingly (Figure 7.15.B). The lesser part of this change was an expansion of overrepresented sectors of the Republican electorate from strongly conservative into moderately conservative territory on economics. Whether this was a moderation of the Republican coalition or evidence of increasing polarization between the two parties is a question that we shall address below. Regardless, the far larger part of the change was not just a continuation of the general rise of culture but of a specifically Republican variant thereof, involving the simultaneous shift from liberal to conservative along the cultural dimension. Where once the modal Republican voter had been a moderate cultural liberal, this same modal Republican was now a strong cultural conservative.

There was a certain irony in this evolution, in that its register for 2008, John McCain, had actually represented the old faction of moderate cultural *liberals* as recently as 2000, in his first run for a presidential nomination. Yet their support had been insufficient to nominate him even in that earlier year, and by 2008, the peak of Republican overrepresentation on the cultural dimension stood unequivocally among cultural conservatives— who, even if they remembered McCain as an erstwhile apostate, supported him disproportionately against Barack Obama.

In 1984, with Walter Mondale as the candidate, the Democratic vote was different from its Republican opposition in being found disproportionately

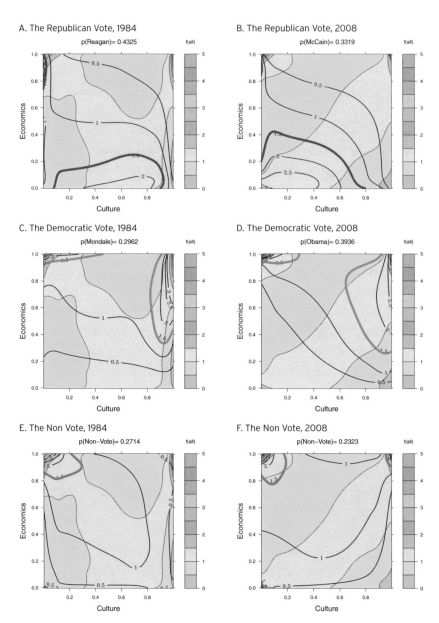

Figure 7.15   Ideological Density and Voting Behavior: The Nation as a Whole, 1984, 2008

on the opposite valuational dimension, on culture rather than on economics, where the overrepresented voters within the Democratic coalition were strong cultural liberals (Figure 7.15.C). Among them, there was substantial variation in economic preferences, ranging from strong economic liberals into the territory of moderate economic conservatives. It was not that culture organized the bulk of the ideological landscape among Democratic voters; Figure 6.2.B has confirmed that this was still done by economics. But it was already the case that cultural values created the largest ideological *faction* within the Democratic coalition in 1984.

By 2008, with Barack Obama as the Democratic candidate, this main area of disproportionately Democratic terrain had expanded to include moderate as well as strong cultural liberals (Figure 7.15.D). In that sense, it was a direct counterpart to the Republican situation. Economic conservatism principally organized the Republican coalition, and it had expanded from strong to moderate conservatism over time. Cultural liberalism principally organized the Democratic coalition, and it had expanded from strong to moderate liberalism over time. Yet where the main secondary characteristic of this overrepresented population had shifted dramatically among Republicans, from moderate cultural liberalism to strong cultural conservatism, the main secondary characteristic of the overrepresented Democrats remained where it had long been, among moderate economic liberals.

For the Republicans, then, this was a story of ideological change, even ideological migration. For the Democrats, it was more a story of ideological adjustment. For both, it would be possible to argue formalistically that they contained simultaneous elements, albeit lesser elements, of moderation. Thus overrepresented Republicans were now moderate and not just strong conservatives, just as overrepresented Democrats were now moderate and not just strong cultural liberals. Yet the density maps at Figure 7.15 argue differently, especially when the two partisan high grounds are considered together. For what was occurring here were really two mutual and related trends.

In the first, each party had become additionally headquartered in one joint extreme of the ideological landscape. Republicans shifts had been more central to this, yet the Democratic version contributed to the same mutual outcome. In the second, the increasing size of these joint extremes was thus additionally polarizing. And this time, the Democrats contributed every bit as much to the same mutual outcome. Republicans fanned out from the land of strong economic and cultural conservatism. Democrats fanned out from the land of strong economic and cultural liberalism. Economics contributed more to the Republican homeland, while culture contributed more to its Democratic counterpart. But that was all that was left of the old world.

For Non voters, finally, there was just no further story at all. They had been headquartered among those who were strong economic liberals and strong cultural conservatives in 1984 (Figure 7.15.E). They remained headquartered among strong economic liberals who were strong cultural conservatives twenty-five years later (Figure 7.15.F). By comparison to the change among overrepresented Republican voters in particular, the nearly perfect overlay among overrepresented Non voters between 1984 and 2008 was genuinely remarkable.

The Strategic Landscape for Challengers to Major-Party Nominees

In the end, this evolution of the electoral landscape may sharpen, rather than resolve, the strategic dilemmas inherent in the picture provided in Chapter 6. There, the simple distribution of votes on this electoral landscape had certain inherent incentives for presidential candidates from the major parties. For Republicans, there was an especial anchoring in the realm of economic conservatism. For Democrats, there was a counterpart anchoring in the realm of cultural liberalism. It was not just that the two party coalitions were disproportionately present in those two locations. It was more that those residing in these disproportionate policy realms could be expected to *want* to see their respective parties situated there, and probably to have the numerical muscle to see their wishes honored.

Nothing in this examination of the evolution of that landscape in Chapter 7 has suggested that any of this is wrong. The major-party landscape for electoral politics as it evolved from 1984 through 2008, the elections covered by the Pew Values surveys to date, possessed a certain internal logic—and an evident ideological trajectory. In this, the role of economic values did not decline, and that was an important point about the ideological landscape for major-party politics. Reports of a displacement of economics by culture were obviously misplaced. Yet the role of cultural values did expand enormously, and this was the other consequential two-party point. What was once an influence at the margins of economics had become a counterpart influence across the full ideological spectrum.

In the process, the overrepresented sections of both major-party coalitions remained far apart while also shifting, more so for the Republicans than for the Democrats, though perhaps only because the Democratic shift had begun earlier, before its inception could be captured by these Pew surveys. In any case, in moving from moderate cultural liberalism to moderate cultural conservatism, the modal Republican had actually moved across the ideological center and back away from it in the opposite direction. What could already be portrayed as a strategic dilemma—pleasing the overrepresented sections of both major-party coalitions, the partisan base, versus reaching out to the necessary increment for victory, the potential "swing vote"—was thus made only more intense by this activation of *both* major policy dimensions across the entire ideological spectrum. In the process, both major-party coalitions had moved away from the joint ideological center.

Yet this period also encompassed three presidential candidacies, with evident electoral consequences, that did not emerge from either of the two major parties. First was the independent candidacy of Ross Perot, with its electoral surge in 1992. Second was a return of the Perot candidacy, with an electoral decline in 1996. And last was the third-party candidacy of Ralph Nader, based in the Green Party in 2000. We have attended to the Perot surge both for its overall scale and for its distinctive ideological mix. We have attended to the Perot collapse both for its overall scale, shedding more than half of the Perot total in one electoral cycle, and even more for the disappearance of any ideological attachments. We now attend additionally to the third-party vote of 2000 because it was so central to the ultimate outcome, even though this Nader vote was comparatively modest at under 3 percent of the national total. By moving Florida from Al Gore to George Bush, Nader voters nevertheless made the latter president—and thereby justify a quick look at a small-N sample.

The biggest of these votes—big by any standard—was the Perot vote of 1992. Joint voting relationships reveal that this vote rose diagnostically with strong economic conservatism, while achieving a secondary peak among true cultural centrists more or less by subtraction (Figure 7.16.A). By failing to draw strong economic conservatives on the far cultural left or the far cultural right, Perot was in effect left with the broad cultural middle. The ideological terrain overrepresented *within* this vote, as captured by its density map, tells roughly the same story, with the high ground of Perot voting located among strong to moderate economic conservatives who were disproportionately true centrists and moderate liberals on culture (Figure 7.16.B). This was an impressively—ideologically—concentrated vote.

That makes the disjunction between the Perot vote of 1992 and the Perot vote of 1996 even more striking. Joint voting relationships show this vote drifting, in a very choppy fashion, toward strong cultural liberalism and especially strong economic liberalism this time (Figure 7.16.C). Yet what the density map beneath these voting relationships emphasizes is not so much a striking ideological shift, from one coherent profile to another, but rather a shift into ideological incoherence (Figure 7.16.D). Now, in 1996, the Perot vote was undifferentiated across the vast bulk of the ideological terrain, while being otherwise concentrated at three disconnected ideological extremes: among strong economic liberals who were strong cultural liberals, among strong economic liberals who were strong cultural conservatives, and among strong cultural liberals who were strong economic conservatives.

Several larger implications follow from this peculiar structural evolution. Most concretely, Perot in 1992 was drawing disproportionate support from voters normally found inside the Republican coalition. It would be hard to argue that he did not damage the reelection prospects of President George H. W. Bush in the process. Yet by 1996, Perot was drawing his much-reduced support from diverse areas that were all within or closer to the Democratic than the Republican heartland. Though in decline, his vote was small enough to pose no threat to the reelection of President Bill Clinton.

More systemically, notice that even in the process of shifting his electoral high ground sharply, Perot did not move to the ideological center. On the one hand, his actual vote in the ideological center was sharply reduced. On the other hand, he managed to abandon strong economic conservatives who were cultural moderates in favor of three alternative clusters,

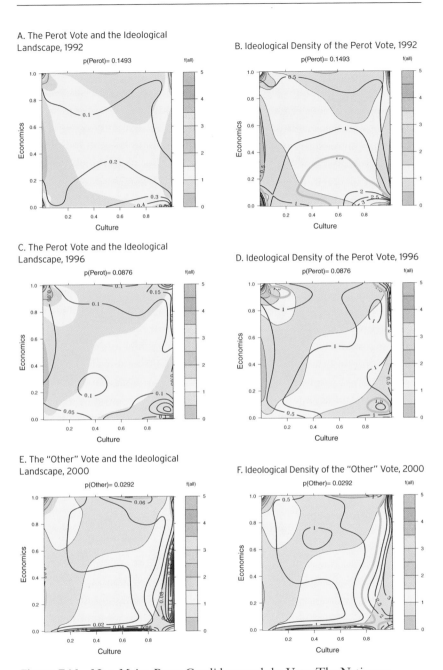

Figure 7.16   Non-Major-Party Candidates and the Vote: The Nation as a Whole, 1992, 1996, 2000

none of which was more central than his previous electoral high ground. This shift, and the comparison between 1992 and 1996, does make Perot himself look more like a parking place in both years—a choice for the disaffected, whoever they might be and whatever they might want—rather than a clearly drawn ideological influence. Yet the shift also suggests that those who constitute the greatest threat of abandonment to the major parties, that is, those with the greatest potential to vote for independent candidates, reside at the ideological extremes and not in the center.

The Pew Values survey for 2000 has two drawbacks for addressing valuational relationships and their associated density maps in connection with the Nader vote. In the first, that vote was just very small, so that third-party Ns are small as well. Worse yet, the Pew survey asks not for the Nader vote, but only for Democratic, Republican, or Other, thus lumping a small Nader tally with a tiny Buchanan vote, where Patrick Buchanan was the presidential candidate of the Reform Party, which had been the presidential vehicle for Ross Perot in 1996. On the other hand, when the focus is not the composite specifics of the Nader (much less the Buchanan) vote, but only the role of third parties on the electoral landscape, there remains much that can still be said.

Figure 7.16.E makes the principal drivers clear for both the Nader and the Buchanan vote: rising cultural liberalism for Nader, rising economic conservatism for Buchanan. Idiosyncratically, this is an obvious irony for both men. While Nader did run as the presidential candidate of the Green Party, whose central concern was essentially a cultural value, the candidate himself spoke overwhelmingly about economics, styling himself as the enemy of corporate America. The density map suggests strongly that the cultural side of this presentation registered, while the economic side did not (Figure 7.16.F). The Nader supporters of 2000 were tightly concentrated among strong cultural liberals, while varying across the full economic spectrum.

Conversely but with equal irony, Buchanan, as the presidential candidate of the Reform Party, identified himself mainly as a soldier in the culture war that he saw engulfing America, though he did also style himself as an economic protectionist. At a minimum, the density map again suggests strongly that the cultural side of this presentation failed to register, while the economic side made him the champion not of "peasants with pitchforks"—one of his favorite phrases—but of extreme economic conservatives of all cultural stripes (Figure 7.16.F).

Systemically, however, these concentrations have two further implications. The first is direct and concrete, involving votes lost by the major-party nominees. In this, Buchanan represented a marginal numerical injury to George W. Bush, the Republican nominee for president. His voters would normally have been stereotypical Republican voters. By contrast, Nader represented a larger but still-limited numerical injury to Al Gore, the Democratic nominee—though a fatal wound, courtesy of his impact on the electoral vote of Florida. His voters would normally have been stereotypical Democratic voters instead.

The second of these further implications is indirect and abstract, involving the incentives for electoral strategy both among third-party challengers and among major-party nominees. To repeat the dominant point: these challengers found their high ground—the terrain where they could achieve disproportionate support—at the extremes and not in the center. Ross Perot had initially found this high ground among strong economic conservatives. Ross Perot had subsequently found it in no less than three extreme alternative locations. And the year 2000 then resurrected two of these four (extreme) terrains for challengers outside the major parties: strong economic conservatives for Patrick Buchanan, strong cultural liberals for Ralph Nader.

To say the same thing differently: a look at the ideological landscape for a polarizing major-party politics, and at the overrepresented factions within it, might suggest abstractly that the ideological center was the obvious home for independent candidates and third parties. Republican, Democratic, and Non voters were concentrated respectively among strong economic conservatives, strong cultural liberals, and strong economic liberals who were also strong cultural conservatives. The big, hypothetically attractive, available territory was the center. Yet what all three of these elections and all four of these non-major-party candidacies suggest is that this ostensible advice to autonomous candidates looking for "spare" voters—move to the ideological center—had little attraction.

Or perhaps it should be said the other way around: that those voters looking for someone outside the two-party framework, like those voters disproportionately supporting one or the other of the two major parties, were to be found at the ideological extremes, if they were to be found at all. In passing, the result for presidential 2000 additionally refined the notion of the two Perot candidacies as parking places for disaffected voters, rather than as ideological homes for new electoral alignments. For it was the Perot vote of 1992 and the Buchanan vote of 2000 that occupied common ground, just as it was the Perot vote of 1996 and the Nader vote of 2000 that likewise shared a common overrepresented terrain.

Which fact should not deny candidate Perot one further, substantial, historical footnote. For the two Perot elections of 1992 and 1996 did occur during—and in their time, did effectively mask—the transition between an older electoral world of apparently stable patterns, those characterizing 1984 and 1988, and a newer electoral world of apparently stable patterns, those characterizing 2000 and 2008. That older world featured economic preferences as the key to voting behavior, with cultural preferences as twists around the edges. The newer world featured both policy domains and their interaction as the key to voting behavior across the full ideological spectrum. Ross Perot does not appear to have directly shaped either. But he certainly obscured—and served as an interim parking place for—the transition between them.

8

Social Groups and Electoral Evolution

1984-2008

Chapter 6 introduced a comprehensive picture of the strategic landscape for electoral politics in the United States, both as a national composite and in its group components, by way of the opening survey in the Pew Values series. Chapter 7 then traced the modern evolution of the composite national picture, with particular attention to the benchmark patterns of 1984 and their most recent incarnation in 2008. Accordingly, the function of Chapter 8, almost inevitably, is to ask about the interaction among social groups, political values, and voting behavior underneath that national picture, as this group story itself evolved.

One grand and gross question for this group evolution must be whether different social groups evolved in different ways, or whether the evolution of the composite national picture reached into most groups and informed their movement in a roughly similar fashion. Note, however, that even if this second option is more the case, it allows for two quite different scenarios. In one, parallel evolution implies that group differences in the benchmark year of 1984 were still largely visible in 2008, having moved in roughly identical ways during the intervening years. In the other, most social groups had effectively converged on the national pattern by 2008, which implies that different groups with their different starting points had evolved in substantially different ways in order to arrive at a common locus.

Yet interactions among group membership, political values, and voting behavior *were* extremely diverse in 1984. This complexity suggests that neither lagged reflection of a national evolution nor simple convergence to a common pattern were automatic. Rather, social groups could contribute quite differentially to change over time, with the result that the central analytic questions change. Was group membership largely an accelerant or a brake on the impact of a national evolution? Did some groups accelerate and others impede this national patterning among their members? At the extreme, did some move toward the national pattern, while others actually moved away? Regardless, was group evolution tied to something inherent in the social cleavages by which sets of groups were themselves defined? Or was there instead a kind of "learning effect," in which different groups picked up the changing structure of national politics more rapidly than others, though the passage of time would presumably inform even the laggards?

To say the same thing more concretely, what happened to individual relationships to the vote for economic and cultural values within disparate social groups? We know what happened to joint relationships for the nation as a whole: the aligning power of economics increased, while the aligning power of culture increased hugely. But was this effect uniform across groups? Was it consistent across them but uneven and mottled by individual group characteristics? Or was the national picture ultimately just a net result of different group movements? Finally, what happened to the ideological distribution of voters underneath these relationships, recognizing that the density maps capturing these distributions can be more important to electoral strategy than voting relationships themselves? Were these essentially stable? Did they change in tandem with national trends? Or did party factions restructure these density maps *within* social groups? Along the way, did inevitable change from the simple growth and decline of various groups itself alter the strategic landscape?

Social Class

Family Income

It is the four great demographic cleavages of Chapter 6, producing the same four sets of social groups, that must show the way to some answers in Chapter 8. To that end, Figure 8.1 returns to social class as measured by family income. This is otherwise the standard setup for individual relationships among social groups, political values, and voting behavior. Recall that social groups here are low-income, middle-income, upper-middle, and upper-income; political values are first economics and then culture; voting options, for 2008 as in 1984, are Republican (John McCain rather than Ronald Reagan), Democratic (Barack Obama rather than Walter Mondale), and Non (perennially the same).

The main story of income groups, economic values, and voting behavior is one of continuity. Among voters, once again and as ever, there is a strong negative relationship between economic preferences and a Republican vote within all groups stratified by family income (Figure 8.1.A), with conservatives attracted and liberals repelled, and a clear if weaker positive relationship between economic preferences and a Democratic vote (Figure 8.1.B), with liberals attracted and conservatives repelled. The Democratic version of these relationships has gotten stronger over time (compare with Figures 6.4.A and 6.4.B). Otherwise, group distinctions within both partisan voting categories remain limited and look much the same.[1] Political values as embodied in economics thus continue to trump group membership when delineated by family income.

By contrast, it is the Non vote that looks most different across time (Figure 8.1.C). In 1984, the four income groups had possessed a rough ordering, from highest to lowest income and from highest to lowest turnout. By 2008, the only remaining divide was between the poorest group and all others. Now, members of the low-income group voted much less than members of all other income groups at every point on the economic continuum, while the three other groups showed no further distinctions. A clear group-based anchoring effect for the Non vote had thus disappeared in the modern world.

A focus on cultural values, however, generates a picture of change rather than continuity. In 1984, the Republican and Democratic votes

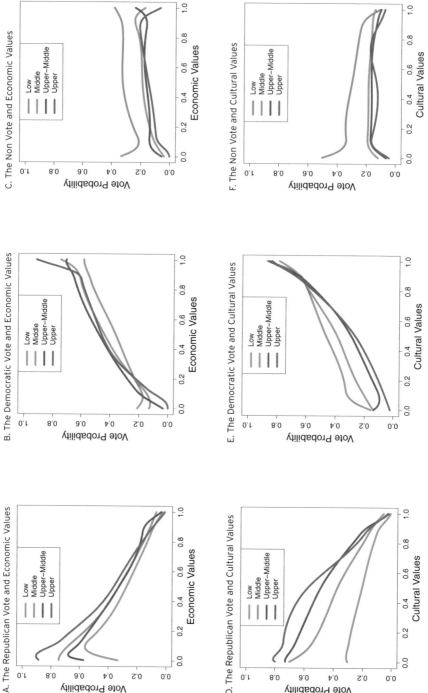

Figure 8.1 Political Values and Voting Behavior: Income Groups, 2008

were essentially flat across most of the ideological spectrum, before plunging and surging, respectively, among strong liberals (Figures 6.4.D and 6.4.E). By 2008, both sets of partisan votes were related to cultural values across the full ideological spectrum within every income group, with the Republican vote rising with cultural conservatism and the Democratic vote rising with cultural liberalism (Figures 8.1.D and 8.1.E). Nevertheless, group membership continued to contribute a further internal organization to these relationships, with Republican support falling from richer to poorer and Democratic support rising in the opposite fashion—before all groups converged among the strongest cultural liberals.

Finally, approached by way of culture rather than economics, what had been a world of Non voting differentiated by income groups in 1984, with a relatively neat gradation from high-income through low-income, now featured a group array merely distinguishing the low-income group from all others (Figures 8.1.C and 8.1.F; compare with Figures 6.4.C and 6.4.F). Said the other way around, cultural values continued to distinguish this Non vote within the low-income group in 2008, with the more culturally conservative being less likely to vote. But the other three income groups now featured nearly identical—and essentially flat—relationships between cultural values and voter turnout.

Between Democratic and Republican voters, two further summary points are worth making. When the focus is political values, the benchmark voting patterns of 1984 remained for economics but shifted for culture. With economic values, the old benchmark patterns remained fully evident, indeed slightly augmented, in 2008. Yet for cultural values, the benchmark patterns of 1984 simply no longer existed. They had been displaced. When the focus is, instead, social groups, the benchmark contributions of group membership in 1984 likewise remained for economics but shifted for culture. With economic values, ideology had trumped group membership solidly in 1984. It still did in 2008. With cultural values, group membership had solidly trumped ideology in 1984, but the anchoring effect of income groups now interacted with ideological position. And both mattered.

Voting behavior for social groups stratified by family income in relation to economic and cultural values *jointly* had been easily described in 1984 (Figure 6.5). Four generalizations tell this story. The influence of economic issues rose with declining income and fell with rising income

A. Low-Income Republican Voters

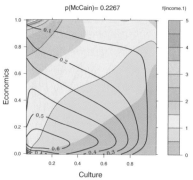

B. Low-Income Democratic Voters

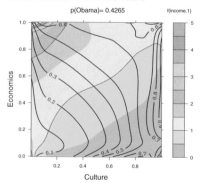

C. Middle-Income Republican Voters

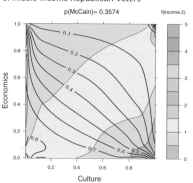

D. Middle-Income Democratic Voters

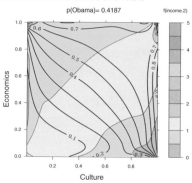

E. Upper-Middle Republican Voters

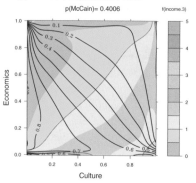

F. Upper-Middle Democratic Voters

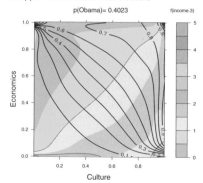

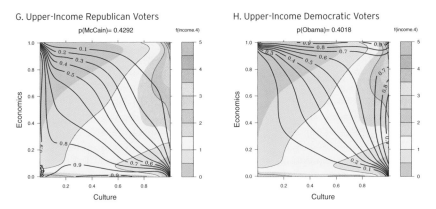

Figure 8.2 The Ideological Landscape and Voting Behavior: Income Groups, 2008

among both Republican and Democratic voters. The influence of cultural issues rose with rising income and fell with declining income, again among both Republican and Democratic voters. Economic issues were more aligned with voting behavior among Republican than among Democratic voters for every income group. Cultural issues were more aligned with voting behavior among Democratic than among Republican voters, again for every income group.

With that as context, the main point of Figure 8.2 is that every one of these four relationships had been largely obliterated by 2008. In their place, all four groups had come to reflect the new national pattern within their confines, whereby economic and cultural values were aligned with the vote simultaneously and regularly across the full ideological spectrum. Members of the low-income group who voted Republican retained the most influence for economic values among their members, just as members of the high-income group who voted Democratic retained the most influence for cultural values among theirs. Yet the overwhelming point is the increased similarity in these joint relationships across all income groups, and hence the sharply decreased power of group membership to structure joint voting relationships.

Do not fail to note, however, that the members of different groups had to accomplish different things—they had to change differentially—in order for this to happen. Most especially, cultural values had to invade the voting decisions of groups lower down the income scale much more than they did in 1984, while economic values had to inform the voting decisions of the higher-income groups more than they previously did. Both developments did occur, which meant that it was the low-income group, among both Republican and Democratic voters, that made the greatest contribution to the national shift in the power of cultural values for organizing the vote, just as it was the upper-income group, likewise among both Republican and Democratic voters, that made the greatest contribution to the simultaneous and more modest strengthening of economic relationships nationwide.

All of which makes the density maps underlying these joint voting relationships, and hence the distribution of actual voters within them, look even more strategically consequential. Here, a general convergence of joint voting relationships across income groups *did not* imply convergence among concentrations of Republican and Democratic factions within them (Figure 8.3). What had actually occurred was partisan distancing, not convergence, within each income group. This distancing, in turn, was driven more by Republican voters in every case, who moved in notably parallel ways—although, if it was shifts within the Republican coalition that were mainly driving partisan change, it was not clear that these promised an unequivocal benefit to the Republican Party.

Within the low-income group, overrepresented Republicans continued to be strong cultural conservatives of all economic stripes, though they had lost some appeal to strong economic liberals, while overrepresented Democrats remained strong economic liberals who were now of all cultural stripes, having gained a population of strong cultural liberals that they had not previously possessed (Figure 8.3.A; compare with Figure 6.6.A). In both cases, these low-income factions were the ones most out of step with their larger political parties. The Republican high ground included the only economically liberal cluster in their coalition. The Democratic high ground included the only culturally conservative cluster in theirs, though this mismatched Democratic territory was considerably larger than its Republican counterpart.

A bigger change was evident within the middle-income group. In 1984, economic conservatism had distinguished the overrepresented middle-income Republicans, while cultural liberalism had distinguished the overrepresented middle-income Democrats. By 2008, the two groups had moved into the polar-opposite corners of the joint ideological landscape

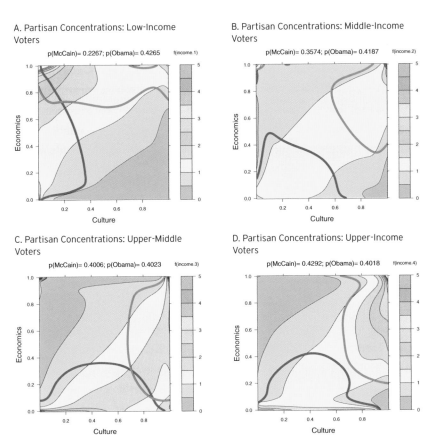

Figure 8.3 Ideological Density and Voting Behavior: Income Groups, 2008

(Figure 8.3.B; compare with Figure 6.6.B). Republicans were clustered on the territory of economic *and cultural* conservatism. Democrats were clustered on the territory of cultural *and economic* liberalism, though there were still some cultural centrists among these Republicans and substantial economic centrists among these middle-income Democrats. In any case, the two internal partisan groupings were now headquartered at the two joint extremes: strong economic and cultural conservatism for the Republicans and strong economic and cultural liberalism for the Democrats.

The upper-middle group likewise featured a move to the right on culture among its overrepresented Republicans, albeit in this case from a concentration among moderate liberals to one in the broad cultural center. They were otherwise economically unchanged, remaining moderate to strong conservatives (Figure 8.3.C; compare with Figure 6.6.C). Overrepresented Democrats in this upper-middle group remained impressively stable across time, being defined by a strong cultural liberalism that otherwise ranged all the way from strong liberalism to strong conservatism on economics. Very much unlike their middle-income counterparts, this made the upper-middle group the one that was still most characterized by a single policy dimension: economics for the Republicans, culture for the Democrats.

Lastly, the high-income group featured its own group-specific version of the general story. Here too, the signature shift was the way that over-represented Republican territory had moved to the right on culture, from strong liberalism all the way to genuine moderation (Figure 8.3.D; compare with Figure 6.6.D). Their high ground had thus moved the most of any income group, even as this still made them a moderate Republican cluster. Overrepresented Democrats were again largely unchanged, being strong cultural liberals who retained a great array of economic prefer-ences, from strong liberalism through moderate conservatism. This in-come group as a whole had featured some noteworthy partisan overlap in 1984, among strong cultural liberals who were moderate economic con-servatives. By 2008, this overlap had entirely disappeared, being effec-tively absorbed into the Democratic high ground.

If membership in income groups had been sufficiently determinative for voting behavior, these changes should have constituted a mild but consis-tent advantage to the Democrats. This was not so much because the two parties had pulled farther apart within each income group. By itself, such a shift was neutral in partisan terms. It was more that the overall distribu-tion of preferences within each group had simultaneously shifted in ways that were more consistent with the new Democratic than the new Repub-lican high grounds. To see this, compare the underlying color-coded areas that are "yellow and up" with the "orange and down" in Figure 8.3:

- Within the low-income group, the growth area from 1984 to 2008 was among strong economic liberals who were strong cultural liber-als, and this was Democratic high ground (again, compare Figure 8.3.A with Figure 6.6.A).

- Within the middle-income group, the growth area was likewise among strong economic liberals who were strong cultural liberals, again an overpopulated Democratic territory (compare Figure 8.3.B with Figure 6.6.B).
- Among upper-middle groups, the new pattern was in one sense a wash, as both Republican and Democratic factions captured large parts of dominant group opinion. Yet in 1984, this dominant opinion had been concentrated almost entirely within the Republican high ground, so that even this new neutrality was a potential Democratic gain (compare Figure 8.3.C with Figure 6.6.C).
- Lastly, where concentrated opinion in the upper-income group had been neatly split between the two parties in 1984, this concentration in 2008—strong cultural liberals with widely varied economic values— was now fully inside the Democratic high ground (compare Figure 8.3.D with Figure 6.6.D).

On the one hand, then, shifts of opinion within these four income groups were all in directions that should, ceteris paribus, have benefitted the Democrats. On the other hand, it is important to recall that this benefit is actually conferred only if other group influences—that is, only if the behavior of groups classified by something other than family income—did not produce countervailing influences. Race and ethnicity, religious background, and domestic roles all had the potential to generate just such countervailing influences. Though as we are about to see, the analyst does not have to wait that long: educational attainment, the other main measure of social class here, itself modifies this patterning of partisan advantage in ambiguous but potentially consequential ways.

Educational Attainment

The interactions among educational attainment, political values, and voting behavior in 1984 paralleled those involving family income in most regards, and the same can be said about this comparison in 2008. Yet here, what was undeniably different by 2008 was the nature of the educational continuum itself. In the old world, high school graduates were the modal group, with college graduates an increasing but still secondary population.

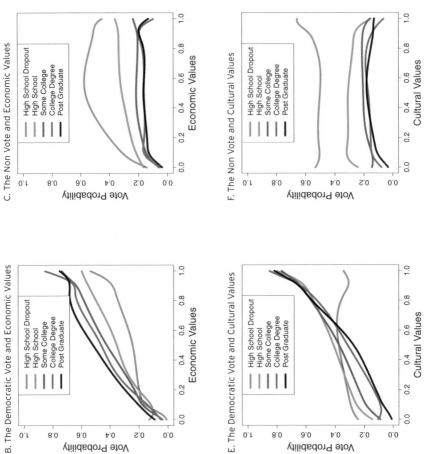

Figure 8.4 Political Values and Voting Behavior: Contemporary Education Groups, 2008

In the modern world, keeping the same categories, college graduates had become the modal group, while high school dropouts had declined precipitously. Yet what was even more different formally—though the practical difference remains to be confirmed—is the expanded presence of (and thus the statistical possibility for studying) the postgraduates, those who attained an advanced degree beyond the baccalaureate.

Investigation of the political values associated with postgraduate education turned up contradictory evidence about the possibility that these values would sustain distinctive voting behavior. As a demographic cleavage (in Chapter 3), postgraduate education appeared to contribute additional liberalism on culture and actual moderation on economics. Converted into a social group (in Chapter 4), however, postgraduates appeared only marginally different from college graduates. In 1984, it had been impossible to check for behavioral consequences from this demographic cleavage or this group membership: the postgraduate population was so small that a question about advanced degrees was not asked. But from 1992 onward it was asked, and by 2008, the postgraduates were actually a larger educational group than the high school dropouts. It therefore seems essential to inquire.

As it turns out, the major fresh distinction among individual voting relationships by educational group involves not these growing postgraduates, but the declining group at the other end of the educational continuum, the high school dropouts. There is in fact little to distinguish the two high-education groups, the college graduates and the postgraduates, and not much to distinguish either from the some-colleges, whether the focus is economic or cultural values, whether the voting category is Republican, Democratic, or Non. As with family income, so with educational attainment: it is instead the bottom group, the high school dropouts, who stand out, with the high school graduates contributing a modest further echo of the same effects.

Like the low-income group but even more so, the low-eds, these high school dropouts, are distinguished by very low voter turnout (Figures 8.4.C and 8.4.F). For economics, this results in their lagging all other educational groups in their contribution to the Democratic as well as the Republican vote (Figures 8.4.A and 8.4.B). For culture, the high school dropouts prove instead to be the sole educational group that shows no relationship to either the Republican or the Democratic vote (Figures 8.4.D and 8.4.E). In the process, these high school dropouts constitute the only group in our entire pantheon to show an actual decline in individual relationships between a political value and the vote.

Beyond that, the linkages between economic or cultural values and the vote are roughly the same for both family income and educational attainment. The high school graduates do vote somewhat less than the three higher educational groups at every point on the economic or cultural spectrum, placing them between the high school dropouts and the rest (Figures 8.4.C and 8.4.F). Very much unlike the dropouts, however, these high school graduates otherwise reflect national voting patterns, just more weakly. The three remaining groups—some-colleges, college graduates, and postgraduates—then reflect these national patterns directly and strongly, in more or less identical fashion.

This group array is shuffled a bit by a focus on joint voting relationships among educational groups, in a manner that elides the three largest groups but restores some modest, group-specific differences to the postgraduates:

- The three largest groups—the high school graduates, the some-colleges, and the college graduates—conform neatly and overwhelmingly to the dominant national pattern (Figures 8.5.C, D, E, F, G, and H). For them, economic and cultural values influence voting behavior across the entire ideological spectrum, and in impressively symmetric fashion. As a result, the three groups are largely showing the same joint relationships to the vote.[2]

- The postgraduates can be distinguished from these three educational groups, including most crucially the college graduates, by the greater power of cultural values to align their vote (Figures 8.5.I and 8.5.J). Joint voting relationships are not qualitatively different, and economics hardly disappears among their members, but culture clearly predominates. The postgraduates are the lone educational group for which this can be said.

- The high school dropouts, lastly, offer the only partisan faction, their Republicans, that retains a nearly pure economic patterning to its ballot, along with another faction, their Democrats, in which these relationships are at their most chaotic and least patterned (Figures 8.5.A and 8.5.B). Whatever else can be said about the high school dropouts, they are the other educational group that differs from the three largest (and essentially parallel) groups.

Note that this has an additional interpretive implication. When the focus was individual voting relationships at Figure 8.4, it would have been reasonable to argue that the high school dropouts were different from other educational groups merely because they had not yet perceived that culture had assumed equal prominence with economics in shaping the American political landscape. There was a learning effect among social groups, about the vastly increased consequence of cultural values and hence about the new shape of the electoral universe, and the dropouts had not yet acquired it. Yet if this interpretation is to be sustained when the focus is joint voting relationships at Figure 8.5, it becomes necessary to argue that the postgraduates are the other group that has so far failed to learn what is patently the structure of electoral politics for society as a whole, a structure that does indeed characterize the three largest educational groups. In this light, it seems much more reasonable to argue that the high school dropouts are the one educational group in which economics trumps culture, the postgraduates the one educational group in which culture trumps economics.

Where social groups defined by education differed the most from social groups defined by income in 1984 was in their density maps (compare Figure 8.6 with Figure 6.7). Within every educational group, the disproportionate Republican vote could be distinguished from the disproportionate Democratic vote by economics, with Republicans conservative and Democrats liberal, and the same could be said of every income group. Yet when education replaced income as the basis for delineating social groups, the ongoing split *within* the parties over cultural issues was magnified—and especially so inside the Democratic Party, where high school dropouts and high school graduates at the conservative end of the cultural continuum were pitted against the some-colleges and college graduates at the liberal end.

A. High School Dropout Republican Voters

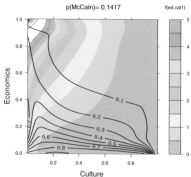

B. High School Dropout Democratic Voters

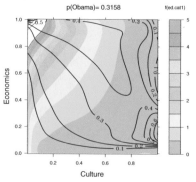

C. High School Graduate Republican Voters

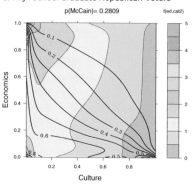

D. High School Graduate Democratic Voters

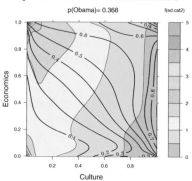

E. Some-College Republican Voters

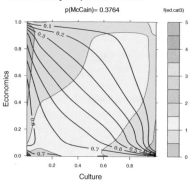

F. Some-College Democratic Voters

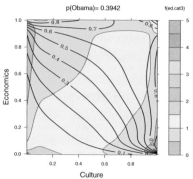

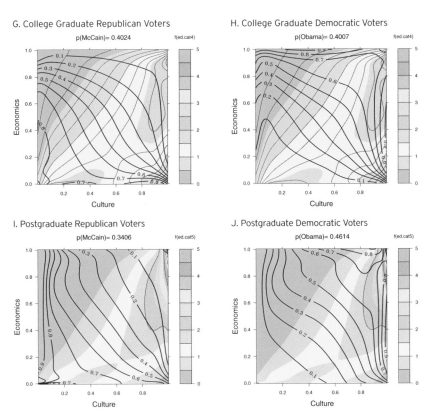

Figure 8.5   The Ideological Landscape and Voting Behavior: Contemporary Education Groups, 2008

This augmented split, in turn, makes the strategic implications of strat-ification by education more serious—more complex and with less obvious solutions—than stratification by income. Both individual and joint voting relationships have attested to the increasing complexity of the strategic landscape for electoral politics in the nation as a whole (Chapter 7). Most especially, the rise of culture as an equal influence in aligning the vote across the entire ideological spectrum immediately increased the range of alternatives potentially available to electoral strategists. Density maps for income groups have reinforced these possibilities by translating them into a specific subgroup context. Density maps for educational groups now add complexity to the picture.

Perhaps inevitably, the high school dropouts, having been least responsive to the changing relationship between political values and the vote, looked

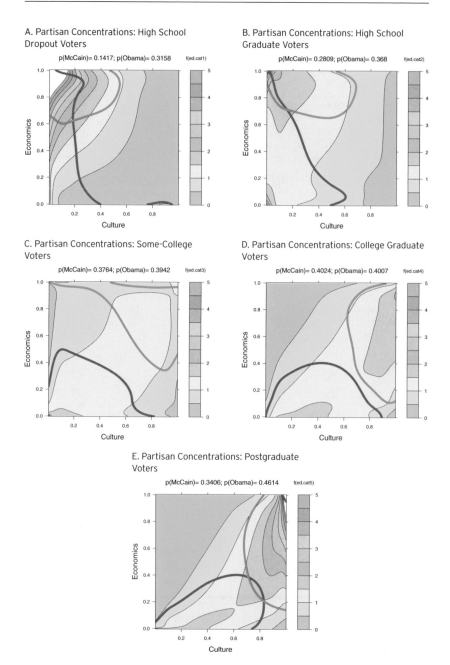

Figure 8.6 Ideological Density and Voting Behavior: Contemporary Education Groups, 2008

most in 2008 as they had in 1984. Their high ground remained culturally conservative and economically liberal among Democrats, culturally conservative across the full array of economic preferences among Republicans (compare Figure 8.6.A with Figure 6.7.A). Indeed, by 2008, these partisan profiles had become almost stereotypical. Democrats clustered where the group was clustered, among strong liberals who were culturally conservative; Republicans clustered anywhere that there were strong cultural conservatives. While this was a profile not unlike that of low-income voters (Figure 8.3.A), it lacked the improved prospects for Democrats that cultural liberalism appeared to imply when income rather than education was the organizing principle.

More surprisingly, the high school graduates of 2008 had acquired a profile increasingly similar to these high school dropouts (compare Figure 8.6.B with Figure 6.7.B). Their overrepresented Democrats were strong economic liberals who were cultural conservatives, though they reached farther over into cultural moderation. Their overrepresented Republicans were still strong cultural conservatives of any economic stripe, though they were weighted more toward economic conservatism than their dropout counterparts. In 1984, both groups, the high school dropouts and the high school graduates, had reinforced intraparty unity on economics, while reinforcing intraparty division on culture. By 2008, every Republican faction among these educational groups had moved rightward on culture, making their party less divided than it had been in 1984, while the increasing similarity of high school dropout and high school graduate Democrats made their party somewhat more divided.

Seen through these density maps, it was actually the some-colleges who had shifted the most over time. In 1984, the group had been united by culture, being moderate to strong cultural liberals, and divided by economics, with Democrats being strong liberals through true centrists, Republicans being strong to moderate conservatives (Figure 6.7.C). By 2008, the overrepresented partisan terrain for this group had instead shifted toward the joint ideological extremes (Figure 8.6.C). Democrats were now concentrated among cultural liberals who were also economic liberals. Republicans were now concentrated among economic conservatives who were also cultural conservatives. Where it was middle-income voters who had provided these stereotypical partisan factions by income

(Figure 8.3.B), it was the some-colleges—themselves the middle category on education—who provided these factions by education.

In 1984, when college graduates were the social group with a high educational attainment, their density map was easily described (Figure 6.7.D). Overrepresented Democrats and overrepresented Republicans within this college graduate group were united by strong cultural liberalism and divided, though with a surprising degree of overlap, by economics. Republicans did reach into the cultural center in a way that Democrats did not. Democrats did reach into a much wider spectrum of economic values than did the Republicans. But the point here is that all of this was destined to change.

By 2008, only the overrepresented Democrats within the group as a whole still resided on the terrain of strong cultural liberalism. The Republicans had abandoned it entirely (Figures 8.6.D and 8.6.E). For the Democrats, there was little further difference between their college graduate and their postgraduate high grounds: strongly liberal on culture, wildly varied on economics. What made the overall group picture look different was the clear shift in the Republican high ground among these college graduates and postgraduates. For the Republicans, both groups remained concentrated among strong to moderate economic conservatives. Yet both had moved clearly rightward on culture, with the modal college graduate now in the terrain of moderate conservatism to true centrism and the modal postgraduate in the terrain of true centrism to moderate liberalism.

While these postgraduate Republicans continued to lean liberal on the cultural continuum, they were now the only such group in the Republican coalition, and they themselves were more conservative than either the college graduates or the some-colleges from twenty-five years before (Figures 6.7.C and 6.7.D). On the one hand, then, the high ground among Democratic voters in what were their culturally liberal groups had shifted much less. This meant that the main ideological action had occurred within the Republican Party. On the other hand, statis within the Democratic Party meant that it continued to be deeply split on culture. Moreover, the fact that the growing groups—the college graduates and some-colleges—were also the most divided on economics meant that the Democratic electorate was arguably more split on this dimension as well.

Accordingly, the overall difference within social class between family income and educational attainment had, by 2008, become a difference of greater potential strategic consequence. Put simply, family income produced more homogeneity among relevant groups for the Democrats, while educational attainment produced more homogeneity among relevant groups for the Republicans. By extension, family income produced potentially increasing strategic stress for Republicans and potentially decreasing stress for Democrats, just as educational attainment produced potentially increasing strategic stress for Democrats and potentially decreasing stress for Republicans—although it might always be argued that with strategic stress came the potential for numeric gains, and not just losses.

There were meliorating factors in this apparent, incipient, Republican advantage. For in fact, in three of these five educational groups, the Democratic high ground contained the territory that was more popular within the group, while the Republican high ground fell on territory that was less popular. And for the other two groups, the two parties fared about equally well. For both the high school dropouts and the high school graduates, the most common opinion was liberal on economics and conservative on culture—much closer to defining Democratic than Republican overrepresented factions. Both parties were reasonably well situated with the some-colleges and college graduates, where opinion was located in a broad swath from strongly liberal to strongly conservative on both economics and culture. Yet the Democratic advantage was restored among the postgraduates, whose overrepresented opinions fell almost entirely within the Democratic high ground.

On the other hand, these were meliorating factors to any incipient Republican advantage only if Democratic strategists could capitalize on them. And the college graduates and postgraduates within the Democratic Party very clearly did not *want* the policy promises that would harvest countervailing Democratic advantages among the high school dropouts and high school graduates, especially on culture but even on economics. That was another sense in which the strategic environment for electoral conflict had become more challenging during the quarter-century from 1984 to 2008.

In any case, the strategic dilemmas inherent in these distributions were additionally altered—not necessarily meliorated for either party, just made additionally more complex—by the way that the numerical balance among educational groups had shifted over time. In 1984, that balance was roughly 60/40 for the high school dropouts plus high school graduates against the some-colleges plus college graduates. By 2008, this same balance was 60/40 in the opposite direction. On the one hand, this was a shift in favor of groups that were more likely to vote Republican than Democratic. No electoral strategist would underestimate the sheer charm of numerical advantage. At the same time, this demographic shift provided an obvious means for contesting this advantage, in the form a strategic shift emphasizing cultural values. These were more aligned with overrepresented Democratic than overrepresented Republican factions—while the Republican Party was actually moving away from just these cultural values.

Race and Ethnicity

In 1984, at the beginning of the Pew Values surveys, the social groups created by race and ethnicity—at least for the great racial minority of modern American society, Blacks, and the great immigrant population, Hispanics—had been singularly distinctive. They were not just the great examples of where group membership trumped political values when seen through their relationship to presidential voting. Group identification—social identity—actually came close to erasing the contribution of political values entirely. The same could not be said of the residual category, the Anglos (non-Black, non-Hispanic). Constituting 85 percent of the total sample, these Anglos inevitably reflected the valuational patterns characterizing the national vote. Yet the numerical predominance of the Anglos did not gainsay the fact that the three social groups showed greater intergroup differences in the patterns of their voting than did groups created by any other principle of social division.

   In terms of individual relationships between economic or cultural values and the vote, Black Americans had been distinguished in 1984 by the more or less complete lack of such relationships. Ideological values and policy preferences did not link members of this major racial minority to voting behavior, for either economics or culture (Figures 6.8.A and 6.8.D). Inevitably, this fact had major strategic implications. In the absence of any role for policy preferences, members of the group had perforce to be reached through their social identifications—that is, through group membership itself—if they were to be reached at all. This strategic fact was only reinforced by the way that the policy preferences of the numerically dominant Anglos were such as to make moves toward the joint modal preference of Black Americans, strongly liberal on economics and strongly conservative on culture, extremely unlikely.

That situation was largely unchanged in 2008, a quarter-century later. In the realm of economic values, it was entirely unchanged. Discounting for the fact that there were almost no strong economic conservatives in this population, economic values among Black Americans remained essentially unrelated—the line of relationship was still effectively flat—to the Republican vote, the Democratic vote, and the Non vote (Figures 8.7.A, 8.7.B, and 8.7.C). Note, however, that this Republican vote was so slight, at 2.7 percent of the Black total and 0.27 percent of the national total, as to make any relationship difficult to generate.

Cultural values showed just a hint of the possible coming of a policy link. The Republican vote remained derisory, and the line of relationship between cultural values and this vote was still effectively flat (Figure 8.7.D). The nascent difference, if such it was, derived from the fact that the Black Non vote was strongly associated with cultural conservatism (Figure 8.7.F). By subtraction, this meant that the Democratic vote was associated with cultural liberalism (Figure 8.7.E), though recall that this is a population with few cultural liberals, and this association still did not have anything to do with Democratic versus Republican voting.

In terms of individual relationships between economic or cultural values and the vote, Hispanic Americans had been distinguished in 1984 by the way their relationship to the vote by way of economic values more closely reflected the pattern among Anglos, while their relationship to the vote by way of cultural values more closely reflected the pattern among Blacks. This meant that economic values did link Hispanics to the Reagan, the Mondale, and the Non vote in the national manner, though the significance of these relationships was constrained by the fact that there were very few economic conservatives in this population (Figure 6.8.B). On the other hand, cultural values had linked this Hispanic group to neither the Reagan, the Mondale, nor the Non vote, especially when it is recalled that the one marginal linkage, by way of strong cultural liberals, involved a population that was essentially missing among Hispanics (Figure 6.8.E).

This latter situation, however, had undergone substantial change by 2008. Economic relationships still looked much the same: steeply negative with the McCain vote, clearly positive with the Obama vote, more weakly positive with the Non vote—recalling, as before, that these parallels to the Anglo vote were less impressive than they might otherwise appear because there were so few economic conservatives in the Hispanic population

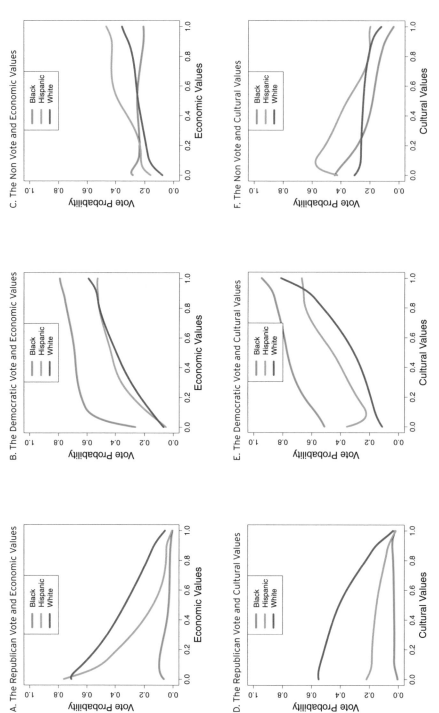

Figure 8.7 Political Values and Voting Behavior: Racial and Ethnic Groups, 2008

(Figures 8.7.A, 8.7.B, and 8.7.C). The only real element of change in the realm of economics was that the increased Non vote among strong economic liberals (where much of the group was indeed located) appeared now to be taken entirely out of the Republican tally, rather than decreasing both the Democratic and the Republican votes.

Yet a larger change had arrived in the realm of cultural values. Unaligned with the Hispanic vote in 1984, cultural preferences were now aligned with all three possible voting options, albeit differently with each:

- Hispanics continued to be the great nonvoting population among racial and ethnic groups (Figure 8.7.F). Yet by 2008, the Non vote *within* the group had become aligned with cultural preferences. Cultural conservatives, of which there were many, were far less likely to vote than cultural liberals, of which there were still few. This remained more like the Black than the Anglo nonvoting story.
- Hispanics who voted Democratic had brought their voting behavior into line with their cultural values (Figure 8.7.E). Liberals were now much more likely to vote Democratic than conservatives were, and because this was true across the entire ideological spectrum, it no longer required a reminder that there were few strong liberals in the group. So while their line of Democratic voting paralleled those of both Blacks and Anglos, it was anchored in territory much closer to the Anglos than to Blacks.
- There was now even a modest relationship among Hispanics between cultural preferences and the Republican vote, one that was weaker than among Anglos but stronger than among Blacks, while being anchored in territory midway in between (Figure 8.7.D). Accordingly, the big trade-off in this key ethnic group was still between the Non vote and the Democratic vote, but the presence of a culturally aligned Republican vote, weak as it was, constituted something new.

What had undermined even the potential for a policy relationship to presidential voting for Hispanics and not just Blacks in 1984 was the distribution of policy preferences within each group, the underlying distribution associated with Republican, Democratic, or Non voting and hence the strategic reality that lay beneath any incipient voting relationships.

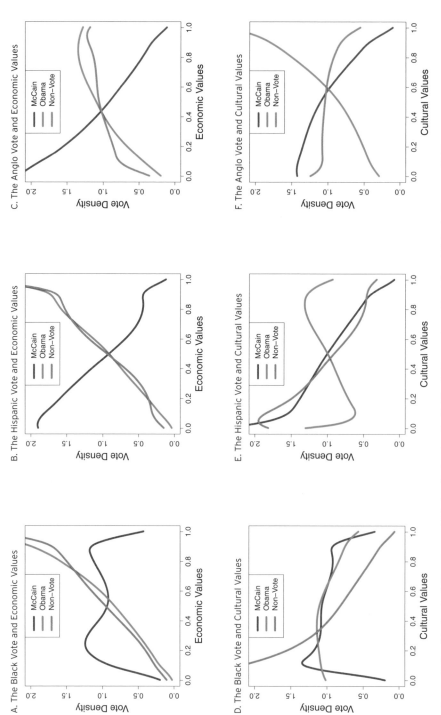

Figure 8.8 Ideological Density and Voting Behavior, Individual Dimensions: Racial and Ethnic Groups, 2008

For Black Americans, this had been especially striking: these distributions were essentially identical (Figures 6.9.A and 6.9.D). In other words, for both economic and cultural values, the policy profiles of Republican, Democratic, and Non voters were in essence an overlay. There was simply no basis for any policy-based distinction.

Much the same could be said for Hispanic voters (Figures 6.9.B and 6.9.E). As between Democratic and Non voters, policy profiles were likewise essentially overlaid, for both economics and culture. The lone exception came with their Republican vote. For economics (but not for culture), the distribution of Hispanic Republicans had not mirrored that distribution for Democratic and Non voters. This hardly guaranteed a role for economic policy preferences: Hispanic Republicans were evenly (not inversely) distributed along the economic continuum. Though as it turned out—this could not have been known at the time—the distinction between Hispanic Republicans and the two other voting categories was in fact a harbinger of larger change coming to the Hispanic population.

For by 2008, the distribution of opinions underlying this Hispanic vote looked strikingly different from the counterpart distribution in 1984. Policy preferences were now aligned with Republican, Democratic, and even Non voting in a major way. For economics, the Hispanic Republican vote was now concentrated—aligned—sharply opposite to the Hispanic Democratic and the Non vote (Figure 8.8.B). For culture, the Hispanic Republican and Non votes were now concentrated sharply opposite to the Hispanic Democratic vote (Figure 8.8.E). Both of these alignments were major changes from the Hispanic situation of 1984. Both were now parallel to those of the Anglos. Together, these two Hispanic distributions brought the group into the pattern of modern electoral politics.

Density profiles for individual voting relationships to economic and cultural values thus suggested change among Hispanics but not Blacks. With culture, there was not even a hint of change in the Black electorate: the McCain and Obama votes were essentially identical (Figure 8.8.D). With economics, there was just a hint that something might be occurring—valuational preferences might be in the process of aligning—since a minuscule Republican vote no longer resembled the Democratic and Non votes (Figure 8.8.A). Yet even this was still not an opposite alignment, so that it was, if anything, a harbinger of *prospective* development, coming to potential fruition in the longer run. In the meantime, there was no change from 1984 among Black Americans comparable to that among Hispanics by 2008.

Yet as was frequently the case elsewhere, density maps that go on to connect *both* policy dimensions actually elicit a picture of change within both groups. It is just that the new Black pattern still does not suggest any rising influence for political values. Overrepresented Black Democrats in 2008 still resided essentially where they had a quarter-century earlier, among strong economic liberals who ranged from strongly conservative to moderately liberal on culture (Figure 8.9.A). Yet the old Republican high ground, previously coterminous with its Democratic counterpart, had broken up entirely, to be replaced by three smaller and remarkably disparate populations. There were still some strong economic liberals who were strong cultural conservatives; there were now strong economic liberals who were strong cultural liberals; and there were strong cultural conservatives who were strong economic conservatives, too. On the one hand, then, the Republican vote was found disproportionately in new places, an obvious change. On the other hand, these places constituted three of the four extreme corners of the ideological landscape: they had far *less* ideological commonality than they once had.

For Hispanics in 1984, this focus on the distribution of policy preferences underneath voting relationships had actually placed the group between Blacks and Anglos in the degree of possibility for appealing to group members by way of political values (Figure 6.10.B). Like Blacks, Hispanics had been overwhelmingly concentrated in the corner of the ideological landscape that was economically liberal and culturally conservative, among both their Republicans and their Democrats. But unlike Blacks, Hispanics offered areas potentially amenable to quite different partisan appeals. Economic conservatives within the group were pulled Republican, while cultural liberals were pulled Democratic, though neither partisan population ended up very close to the dominant high ground in the rest of their respective parties.

Flash to 2008, however, and the Hispanic landscape looked very different. Hispanic Democrats had expanded their high ground into the territory of cultural liberalism and economic moderation, while Hispanic Republicans had expanded their high ground into the territory of economic

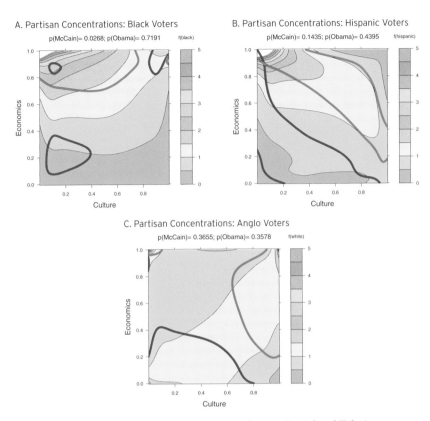

Figure 8.9 Ideological Density and Voting Behavior: Racial and Ethnic Groups, 2008

conservatism and cultural moderation (Figure 8.9.B). In effect, this gave Hispanics their own group-based version of the national pattern. What made it national was that it now featured Democrats stretching out from one joint ideological extreme, economically and culturally liberal, against Republicans stretching out from the other joint ideological extreme, economically and culturally conservative. What kept it group-based was that Hispanics were still found disproportionately in one place within these partisan high grounds, economically liberal and culturally conservative.

From one side, this meant that while Hispanics now reflected the policy contours of partisan voting in the nation as a whole, they still heavily favored the Democrats within these contours, since dominant opinion among American Hispanics fell clearly within their overrepresented Democratic terrain. Yet from the other side, if this still did not make Hispanics look like Anglos, the group as a whole was clearly in motion toward a world in which overrepresented partisan factions lived in opposite corners of the ideological terrain—the world of modern American politics nation-wide. Hispanics were in that sense now ideologically "in play," that is, amenable to contending policy promises from the two major parties. This was a major change from 1984, one that went on to help explain the over-all national shift toward a partisan vote aligned with both economics and culture across the full ideological spectrum.

The combination of voting relationships and density maps then had further strategic implications for an approach to both groups. Among Blacks, the modern world was a terrain not terribly encouraging for either party, though truly discouraging for Republicans (Figure 8.9.C). For Democrats, the major problem remained the fact that their high ground among Blacks lay far away from their high ground among Anglos. The two were effectively nonoverlapping. Democratic Blacks resided dispro-portionately on territory that was strongly liberal on economics, strongly conservative to merely centrist on culture. Democratic Anglos resided dis-proportionately on territory that was strongly liberal on culture, strongly liberal to moderately conservative on economics.

Nevertheless, if that story was discouraging, its Republican counterpart was worse, because any unified high ground among Black Republicans had more or less disappeared. As with any social group, so with Black Ameri-cans: no policy approach to any one of these three Republican clusters came with any guarantee of success. Yet now, any approach that did suc-ceed in registering with *one* might immediately alienate the other two. In earlier years, the major Republican problem was that the high ground for Black Republicanism was clear enough, but fell on turf that was unattract-ive to the rest of the party. Now, Anglo Republicans should have no trouble endorsing a policy program that appealed to the Black Republican cluster that was both economically and culturally conservative. Yet this was located in the least populated area of Black ideological terrain, where it had nothing to do with the two more-populated Black Republican clusters.[3]

Among Hispanics, on the other hand, the modern world had become not only a different but a strategically more complex place. If this key ethnic group was not yet amenable to the range of policy options that characterized electoral strategy among the Anglos, neither was it as foreboding as it had been a quarter-century ago. It was still hard to envision a circumstance in which either party would make policy promises catering to the *joint* modal preference of Hispanics: liberal on economics, conservative on culture. Yet each party did have something to offer and in that sense something with which to bid: economic liberalism for the Democrats, cultural conservatism for the Republicans. More Hispanics still appeared potentially responsive to the Democratic rather than the Republican appeal. On the other hand, the Republican coalition was much less divided over actually making the appeal that was potentially available.

Religious Background

Denominational Attachment

Four things must be said, at the start, about individual relationships among denominational attachment, political values, and voting behavior. As in 1984, so in 2008, voting relationships for the four great denominational families in American society all reflected—mimicked—those relationships for the society as a whole, with both economic and cultural values. In that sense, denominational attachment was more like social class than like race and ethnicity. Yet in 2008 as opposed to 1984, relationships between political values and the vote, as reflected by these four great families, offered a much-increased role for culture by comparison to economics. All four groups thus partook in roughly equal form of the major valuational change on the strategic landscape of American politics. In that sense, denominational groups were more like Anglos and Hispanics than like Blacks among groups delineated by race and ethnicity.

Yet here, and quite unlike the situation of either social class or race and ethnicity, the relevant social groups diverged additionally among themselves. The anchoring effect of group membership upon voting relationships thus increased more than in either alternative principle of social division. Finally, while the power of group membership by religious denomination was increasing, it was simultaneously assuming a new and different intergroup pattern. Denominational groups now stood in the same relationship to each other across both great issue domains, economics and culture, as

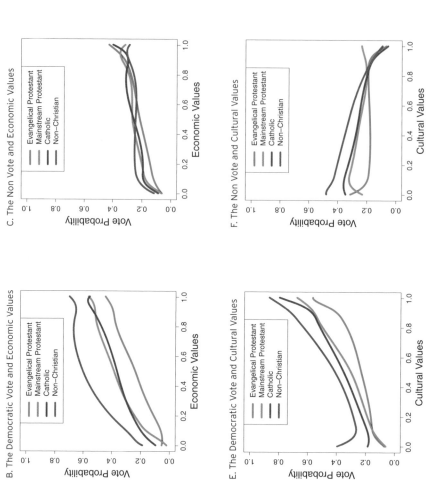

A. The Republican Vote and Economic Values

B. The Democratic Vote and Economic Values

C. The Non Vote and Economic Values

D. The Republican Vote and Cultural Values

E. The Democratic Vote and Cultural Values

F. The Non Vote and Cultural Values

Figure 8.10 Political Values and Voting Behavior: Denominational Groups, 2008

well as within all three voting categories, Republican, Democratic, and Non voting. And these relationships were not at all as they had been in 1984.

The power of denominational attachment in 1984 had been present but muted. All four great families did the dominant—the national—thing with economics: strong negative relationship to the Republican vote, clear but weaker positive relationship to the Democratic vote, even weaker positive relationship to the Non vote (Figure 6.11.A, 6.11.B, and 6.11.C). All four did the dominant national thing with culture as well: flat for most of the continuum for the Republican vote before plunging among strong liberals, flat across most of the continuum for the Democratic vote before jumping up among strong liberals, and ever so modestly negative for the Non vote (Figure 6.11.D, 6.11.E, and 6.11.F).

For economics, there had been a weak but consistent further pattern in the relationship to both the Republican and Democratic votes. Evangelicals were kindest to Ronald Reagan, followed by Mainstream Protestants, lagged by Catholics, and lagged even more by Non-Christians. This voting increment or decrement was then precisely reversed among those who chose Walter Mondale instead. Within this mix, Non-Christians stood out additionally for being less likely to vote overall. For culture, there had been more idiosyncrasy than pattern. For the Republican vote, the two Protestant families, the Evangelicals and the Mainstreams, were more supportive than the two non-Protestant families, the Catholics and the Non-Christians. For the Democratic vote, Catholics gave Walter Mondale a clear additional increment among economic conservatives. And Non-Christians, stratified by cultural values this time, stood out even more as augmented Non voters.

By 2008, these intergroup relationships, for both Republican and Democratic voters by way of both economic and cultural values, were just completely changed (Figure 8.10). Evangelical Protestants had pulled away from the other denominational groups in a Republican direction. Non-Christians had pulled away from the other denominational groups in a Democratic direction. Mainstream Protestants and Catholics had converged—they were effectively overlaid—in the middle ground between Evangelicals and Non-Christians. This was a major and altered impact from group membership, one that had further specific implications in each grand policy realm.

For economics, this meant that denominational attachment played an increased role in translating political values into voting behavior (Figures

8.10.A and 8.10.B). Ideological position still mattered more to the members of all denominational groups; that much had not changed. But group membership mattered more to these denominational groups in 2008 than it had in 1984, and more than it mattered to the members of social groups constituted from family income or educational attainment. Do not miss the further fact that this triumph of denominational attachment over social class was occurring even with regard to economic values, normally thought to be the logical register of class identities.

For culture, this same development meant not only the same increased role in translating political values into voting behavior (Figures 8.10.D and 8.10.E). It also meant a vastly expanded range for this translation process, no longer limited to the far liberal end of the ideological spectrum but now running all the way from strong liberals through strong conservatives. Yet in the process, it meant the demise of a religious divide that had characterized American politics since the latter half of the nineteenth century. This could be crudely summarized as "the Protestant nation" versus "everyone else." It had been registered in 1984 though economic values by way of the Republican division between the two Protestant families and the two others, and through cultural values by way of the propensity of Catholics to give the Democrats extra support, even when they were less in agreement with party policy. Both tendencies were simply gone by 2008.

In the modern world, a new alignment, the *same* new alignment as with economic values, could be found nearly everywhere (Figure 8.10.F). There was a tendency for denominational groups to converge among the strongest cultural liberals, but everywhere else the dominant group pattern from economics could be observed with culture as well: Evangelicals versus Mainstreams plus Catholics versus Non-Christians. Even the Non vote stratified by culture manifested this pattern (Figure 8.10.F), leaving only the Non vote stratified by economics as an exception, where the four great religious families essentially collapsed into each other (Figure 8.10.C). On the one hand, these overall group developments confirm that denominational attachments, too, partook of the grand and gross national trends between 1984 and 2008. On the other hand, specific group attachments can hardly have been impelling these national trends, since the four great religious families reflected those trends in a fashion specific—idiosyncratic—to denominational attachment.

When the focus switches to partisan gains or losses within these national trends, denominational groups have a major further explanatory role to play. Moreover, it is again the *same* explanatory role for both economic and cultural values. In this, Evangelical Protestants had become the most pro-Republican religious family; Non-Christians had become the most pro-Democratic religious family; and the two other great families, the Catholics and the Mainstream Protestants, had converged on each other while falling neatly in between the Evangelicals and the Non-Christians.

When these two sets of individual voting relationships had been put back together in 1984, they had offered two further, regularized patterns (figures not shown). Economic values were reliably more consequential among Republican voters, while cultural values were reliably more consequential among Democratic voters, just as the organizing role of cultural values rose from Evangelicals to Catholics to Mainstreams to Non-Christians among both Republican and Democratic voters, while the organizing place of economic values rose in the opposite direction. That had been a complex but reasonably straightforward set of relationships.

By looking hard enough, the analyst might still have been able to see shadows of both effects in 2008 (Figure 8.11). Yet the dominant point now, pushing these older patterns into very secondary status, was the simple fact that all of these partisan categories within denominational groups had been thoroughly infused by both economics and culture across most of their ideological spectrums. As ever, this represented an increase for both domains, but a particular increase for culture. In the case of the Catholics and Mainstream Protestants, the result was now a neat symmetry across the entire spectrum of economic and cultural values simultaneously (Figures 8.11.C and 8.11.D, 8.11.E and 8.11.F). For them, there was nothing left from earlier patterns.

In the case of the Evangelical Protestants and Non-Christians, the result was also far *more* symmetry than in the past (Figures 8.11.A and 8.11.B, 8.11.G and 8.11.F), although in producing this symmetry, these two religious families had needed to move in opposite directions. The Evangelicals needed to increase the aligning power of cultural values sharply, while the Non-Christians needed to increase the aligning power of economics, albeit more modestly. Both groups managed to do exactly that. Within their ranks, the Evangelicals retained the most economic influence among their

A. Evangelical Protestant Republican Voters

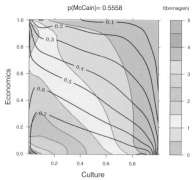

B. Evangelical Protestant Democratic Voters

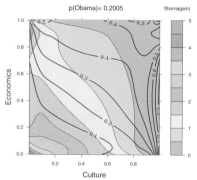

C. Catholic Republican Voters

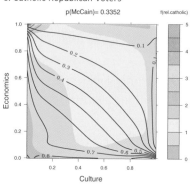

D. Catholic Democratic Voters

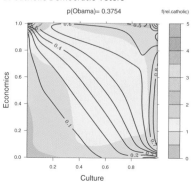

E. Mainstream Protestant Republican Voters

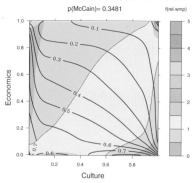

F. Mainstream Protestant Democratic Voters

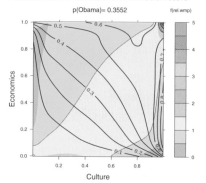

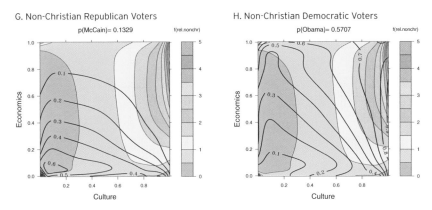

Figure 8.11 The Ideological Landscape and Voting Behavior: Denominational Groups, 2008

Republican voters, just as the Non-Christians retained the most cultural influence among their Democrats. But even for these extreme partisan factions, the story was one of substantial convergence on new national patterns, and hence substantial destruction of the old.

That said, the general convergence of these joint voting relationships did not imply—not nearly—a convergence in the ideological distributions beneath them. The relevant partisan factions, of Republican and Democratic voters by denominational group, had also shifted, and in major ways, though the Republican high ground had shifted more than its Democratic counterpart. More to the strategic point, the two parties, when viewed through the ideological territory that was disproportionately Republican or Democratic as stratified by denominational attachment, had moved farther apart. If some abstract logic had ever suggested that they should respond to the ideological map of 1984, concentrated within one party on economics and within the other on culture, by moving toward the ideological center (and hence each other), then concrete behavior demonstrated that they had in fact moved in the opposite fashion, so as to be additionally polarized on both major policy dimensions.

In 1984, this internal alignment of density maps for each party had been simply described (Figure 6.12). There was a concentration of Republican voters among all four denominational families on the territory of moderate to strong economic conservatism. Republican voters in three of these four families—Catholics, Mainstreams, and Non-Christians—were then concentrated additionally in the territory of moderate to strong cultural liberalism, though the Evangelicals were most concentrated at strong cultural conservatism instead.

These same three denominational families among Democratic voters were even more tightly concentrated in the territory of strong cultural liberalism, though the fourth, the Evangelicals, was again concentrated in the territory of strong cultural conservatism. What made the Democratic picture more heterogeneous, and less easily summarized as a result, was that all four denominational families offered substantial economic diversity among members who voted disproportionately Democratic. The modal member of each was a moderate economic liberal, yet all had overrepresented factions stretching all the way from strong liberalism to moderate conservatism on economics.

By 2008, there had been some migration of this ideological high ground within both parties, though more so for the Republicans than for the Democrats. Among Republican voters, all four of the great denominational families had shifted clearly to the right on culture. They began at different points and they shifted to differing degrees, but the rightward move was indisputable within each. For the Democrats, three of the four did not so much shift as merely add further high ground on culture, moderating the dominant cultural position within their party ever so slightly, though not nearly enough to move the parties closer together.

Instead, these ideological migrations had produced greater partisan distinction in every denominational group; that is to say, Republicans and Democrats were concentrated on increasingly distant territory within each. Yet it is important to remember that in creating this partisan polarization, and in facilitating the economic and cultural change that was necessary to produce it, different denominational groups had to do different things. Beyond that, the resulting partisan advantages differed by denominational group, where Republicans were most advantaged by the shift among Evangelicals and Democrats by the shift among Non-Christians.

Disproportionate Republican and Democratic Evangelicals were still clearly concentrated among cultural conservatives (compare Figure 8.12.A here with Figure 6.12.A). Where they differed from the earlier story, strongly, was in the way that they had pulled apart on economics. Republican Evangelicals had shed their cultural but especially their economic lib-

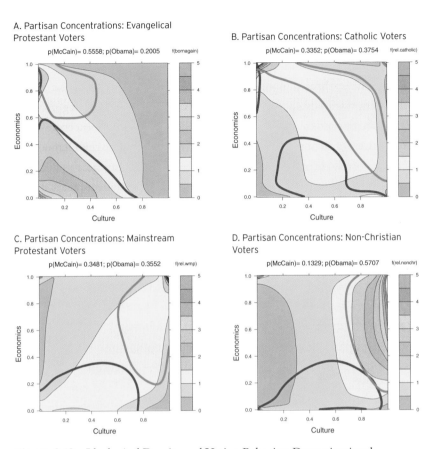

Figure 8.12   Ideological Density and Voting Behavior: Denominational Groups, 2008

erals; Democratic Evangelicals had shed their economic conservatives but gained some cultural moderates. Where once, in 1984, these two partisan factions had featured a substantial overlap—on the territory of strong cultural conservatism—their shifts in economics had obliterated this by 2008. On the one hand, partisan change among Protestant Evangelicals was thus particularly important in explaining how economics could become more consequential to the American voter over time. On the other hand, this change was not neutral in terms of partisan advantage. The Republicans, distinctively, achieved their high ground in the ideological area where Evangelicals as a whole were most concentrated.

Nevertheless, it was the Catholics, both Republican and Democratic, and not the Evangelicals, who had migrated the most when examined through their overrepresented ideological factions (compare Figure 8.12.B here with Figure 6.12.B). Two big changes had transpired, one for their Republican and one for their Democratic voters, and it was the combination of the two that made the picture of partisan voting for 1984 versus 2008 look most different within this group. Republican voters among Catholics changed little in their economic values, remaining moderate to strong conservatives on economics. Yet they changed substantially in their cultural values, moving all the way from being headquartered in the territory of moderate cultural liberalism to being headquartered in the territory of moderate cultural conservatism instead.

For the Democrats, change was equally clear but more complex. Among Catholic Democrats, 1984 had featured a deep internal split between a main ideological homeland that was tightly concentrated on strong cultural liberalism and a smaller ideological homeland that was concentrated on strong cultural conservatism instead, where the latter cluster was also more clearly liberal on economics than was the former. By 2008, this split had disappeared. In its place was instead a broad high ground centered on moderate economic liberals who were also moderate cultural liberals, while stretching away in both directions.

What these partisan ideological migrations did in combination was once more to increase the distance between Republican and Democratic high grounds, this time among American Catholics. Now, their modal partisans were clearly different on both economics and culture. Yet the situation was additionally complicated, in a way that appeared to offer greater prospects for Republican than for Democratic gains, by the fact that a substantial minority of Catholic Democrats were more in agreement with the dominant Republican than the dominant Democratic position on economics, while there was no substantial share of the Republican high ground about which the opposite could be said.

There were only echoes of the same shifts among Mainstream Protestants, though echoes there were (compare Figure 8.12.C here with Figure 6.12.C). Among Republican voters, there was no noticeable change on economics; the group remained headquartered on the terrain of strong to moderate conservatism. But the previous cultural high ground among moderate liberals had shifted to create a modern high ground among true centrists, accompanied by major gains among both moderate and strong conservatives. Among Mainstream Democrats, there was a modest expansion of the cultural high ground to include more of the moderate liberals. By itself, this might have appeared as a moderation of dominant Democratic preferences. In combination with counterpart Republican shifts, however, the result was to leave the two partisan clusters farther apart, not closer together.

The Non-Christians, finally, offered their own, slightly stronger version of the same story (compare Figure 8.12.D here with Figure 6.12.D). For Republican voters, who had been tightly concentrated among cultural liberals in 1984, the modal member moved clearly rightward. This still left Non-Christian Republicans as the most moderate denominational group within their party. Yet in absolute terms it was an impressive abandonment of past liberalism. In the process, these Non-Christian Republicans also shed their economic centrists. For Democrats, there was little to see. Nevertheless, the combination of change and adjustment among Non-Christians as a whole did result in the disappearance of any ideological overlap between overrepresented factions of Non-Christian Democrats and Republicans. In 1984, Non-Christians who were strong liberals on culture but true centrists or moderate conservatives on economics had contributed a noteworthy overlap. By 2008, they no longer did.

Yet the more electorally consequential result for these Non-Christians really involved comparison with the Protestant Evangelicals. Overrepresented Evangelicals had contributed the Republican voting cluster closest to its previous location on the ideological landscape. Overrepresented Non-Christians now contributed the Democratic cluster that was closest to its predecessor. Yet where partisan change among the Evangelicals clearly benefitted the Republican Party, partisan change among the Non-Christians just as clearly benefitted the Democrats. Among the Evangelicals, change between 1984 and 2008 kept the Republican high ground in the area where this denominational group was most numerous and moved the Democratic high ground outside that area. Among Non-Christians, change did the opposite, keeping the Democratic high ground in the area where this denominational group was most numerous and moving the Republican high ground outside that area.

Generic Religiosity

As before, generic religiosity is the degree to which individuals are involved with the regular practice of their religion, rather than their formal attachment to a specific denomination. In that sense, it captures the *intensity* rather

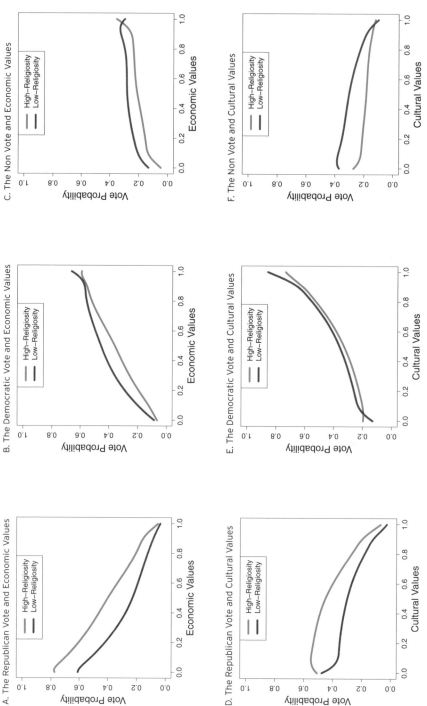

Figure 8.13 Political Values and Voting Behavior: Devotional Groups, 2008

than the *substance* of religious backgrounds. Here, three things should be said about interactions among generic religiosity, political values, and voting behavior. First, individual relationships between political values and voting behavior for social groups delineated by generic religiosity show an evolution clearly distinguishable from that of denominational attachment. Second, joint voting relationships, too, attest to differences between the two aspects of religious background, though this time generic religiosity produces less intergroup difference than denominational attachment did. Third, density maps go on to highlight a major change specific to groups defined by generic religiosity, altering what had been the most distinctive landscape for partisan conflict among any set of social groups, while leaving major challenges for campaign strategists whenever religiosity was effectively stratifying the vote.

In 1984, the strongest group-based effect on the vote for the religious, those regular church attenders, versus the irreligious, the reliable non-attenders, had been the propensity for the former to vote more at every point on both the economic and cultural continuums (Figures 6.13.C and 6.13.). As a result, the religious had contributed more than the irreligious to both the Republican and the Democratic vote, for both economic and cultural values. The difference between religious and irreligious was additionally greater among Reagan than among Mondale voters, again for both economics (Figures 8.13.A versus 6.13.B) and culture (Figures 13.D versus 13.E). Higher vote turnout among the religious was inevitably harvested by the candidate whom these regular attenders preferred, and in 1984 that candidate was Ronald Reagan.

By 2008, one noteworthy aspect of these individual relationships had changed. The religious continued to vote more than the irreligious at all points along the ideological continuum for both economic and cultural values (Figures 8.13.C and 8.13.F). Yet now, religiosity gave an explicitly partisan cast to this vote. The religious still out-performed the irreligious in their propensity to vote Republican (Figure 8.13.A). But the irreligious now outperformed the religious n their propensity to vote Democratic. Because the religious turned out more than the irreligious, the resulting edge for the Republican candidate was larger than the reverse edge for the Democrat. On the other hand, it was change within the Democratic vote that managed to create a partisan edge in the opposite direction for this electoral outcome.

The overall shape of individual economic relationships was otherwise largely as it had been a quarter-century before: strongly negative for the Republican, clearly if a trifle less strongly positive for the Democrat, very weakly positive for the Non vote. The shape of individual cultural relationships had changed hugely, however, in concert with national movements. In this, the impact of cultural values was no longer confined to strong liberals but reached across the entire ideological spectrum. Political values still massively trumped group membership in both economic and cultural relationships, although it was group membership that had opened up an explicit partisan gap in the vote aligned by either economics or culture.

In 1984, this had implied two familiar outcomes for joint relationships to the vote. First, the Republican vote had been more related to economic values and the Democratic vote to cultural values at every level of generic religiosity. Second, economic values had been more related to the vote among the religious and cultural values more related to the vote among the irreligious among both Republican and Democratic voters (Figure 6.14).[4] This was a common, though not universal, patterning to joint voting relationships in its time. By 2008, those distinctions were effectively irrelevant (Figure 8.14). Both summary relationships were essentially gone.

In their place, both economics and culture were strongly aligned with the vote among the religious and the irreligious, whether they chose the Republican or the Democratic candidate. There was a bit more economic influence among religious Republicans (Figure 8.14.A), a bit more cultural influence among irreligious Democrats (Figure 8.14.D). But the overwhelming fact about joint relationships to the vote for both economics and culture within groups delineated by generic religiosity was the neatly symmetric alignment of the two policy domains for all partisan factions in all devotional groups. This, too, was a common but not universal aspect of politics in the modern world.

That might suggest that joint voting relationships to economic and cultural values were moderating the change suggested by individual voting relationships. Yet density maps immediately restore much of the power of group membership, while helping to distinguish strategic implications that had (and had not) changed with them. Density maps for devotional groups had been among the most striking in 1984, with one partisan faction from each of the two major social groups concentrated at each corner of the ideo-

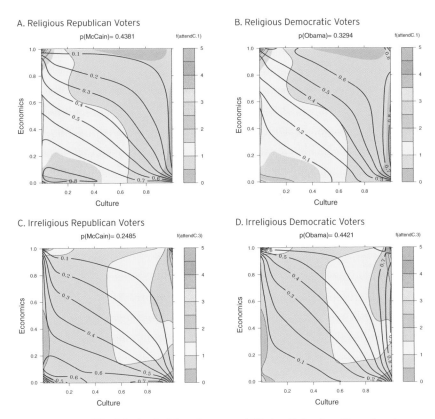

Figure 8.14 The Ideological Landscape and Voting Behavior: Devotional Groups, 2008

logical landscape (Figure 6.15). By 2008, this neat but extreme ideological dispersion had broken up. The result was a strategic environment that was easier for Republicans in some regards, still tightly contested in others (Figure 8.15 here).

In 1984, religious Republicans had been concentrated among strong economic conservatives who covered a broad range of cultural territory but leaned toward cultural conservatism. Religious Democrats had been found principally among strong economic liberals who were even more conservative on culture than their Republican counterparts. Irreligious Democrats had been concentrated among strong cultural liberals who covered a broad range of economic territory but leaned toward economic liberalism. And irreligious Republicans had been concentrated among strong cultural liberals who were strong economic conservatives. No other principle of social

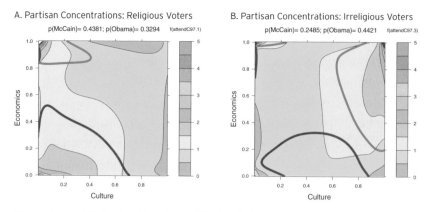

Figure 8.15 Ideological Density and Voting Behavior: Devotional Groups, 2008

division came close to putting one of the dominant partisan factions for each of its major social groups at each extreme of the ideological landscape.

By 2008, all four partisan high grounds had shifted, with cultural values providing the main axis for this shift. Along the way, the old pattern of collective ideological positioning had disappeared, and a new pattern with altered strategic consequences, neater in some ways but more complicated in others, had replaced the old:

- Once strongly conservative in their economic values but highly varied in their cultural preferences, religious Republican voters had retained their economic conservatism but moved clearly rightward on culture, gaining strong cultural conservatives and shedding moderate liberals (Figure 8.15.A).
- Once principally headquartered among strong economic liberals who were strong cultural conservatives, with a secondary population of strong cultural liberals, religious Democrats retained the first cluster as diagnostic of the partisan group but shed the second cluster entirely (Figure 8.15.A).
- Irreligious Republicans remained conservative on economics but gained moderate conservatives and true centrists on culture, while shedding the strong cultural liberals who had actually been the modal group members in 1984 (Figure 8.15.B).
- Irreligious Democrats, finally, had added strong economic liberals who were moderate cultural liberals to their previous high ground,

thereby cementing themselves into the jointly liberal corner of the ideological landscape—at the opposite extreme from the religious Republicans (Figure 8.15.B).

With overrepresented populations dispersed to the four corners of the ideological landscape, it had been hard to imagine a strategic context more demanding than the old order of 1984 among devotional groups. To put the matter most astringently: every candidate got to decide which large segment of previous party voters would be consciously driven away. Any combination of liberalism or conservatism sufficient to get the attention of internal party factions within two of these devotional groups was explicitly offensive to the other two. Only a move toward the joint center could be worse, in effect alienating all four internal party factions. Unlike so many group-based changes between 1984 and 2008, then, the breakup of the old order among these devotional groups did not ramp up the level of strategic challenge in addressing them. Still, there remained more than enough challenge to go around.

The Republican Party at the polls was hardly stress-free when examined through the lens of devotional groups in the modern world. Its voters were united by economics, but religious Republicans were strong cultural conservatives while irreligious Republicans were true cultural centrists. Yet the Democratic Party appeared to face a version of these stresses that was potentially more severe. Its voters were strikingly divided by culture, with religious Democrats still tilted toward strong cultural conservatism and irreligious Democrats concentrated among strong cultural liberals. Moreover, the party managed to feature a further division on economics, where overrepresented Democrats ranged from strong liberalism through moderate conservatism. That looked like a world of incipient Republican advantage.

Yet this advantage was rebalanced—not neutralized, just rebalanced— by the way that partisan factions within devotional groups fit (or did not fit) the underlying distribution of political values for the group as a whole. Among religious voters, the Republican Party actually had its overrepresented high ground in the territory where the group itself was concentrated, among economic *and cultural* conservatives. By comparison, the Democratic high ground lay outside the dominant opinion of the group, with the exception of that tight cluster of strong economic liberals who were also strong cultural conservatives.

Yet among irreligious voters, it was the Democratic Party that had its overrepresented high ground in the territory where the group itself was concentrated, among cultural *and economic* liberals. By contrast, the Republican high ground lay almost entirely in an area of the ideological landscape where the irreligious had comparatively few members. Said differently, the Republican Party had been more influential in driving cultural values to a powerful role in aligning the national vote, and it had secured an especial advantage among the religious in the process.[5] But it had also done so by moving away from areas of the ideological terrain where the irreligious were most numerous, leaving that area inside the Democratic high ground.

Domestic Roles

Sex

Domestic roles contributed relatively little to the benchmark relationship among social backgrounds, political values, and voting behavior in Chapter 6. As measured here, domestic roles did not approach the impact of the other great social cleavages: social class, race and ethnicity, and religious background. Moreover, the two available indicators of domestic roles, namely sex and parenthood, showed less difference between themselves than did family income and educational attainment for social class or denominational attachment and generic religiosity for religious background. Nevertheless, there were some clear, consistent, and patterned contributions to the strategic landscape for electoral politics of these groups, too. Just as there are some clear changes to these group-based contributions over time.

With individual voting relationships to both economic and cultural values in 1984, there had been only a hint of difference between men and women. For economic values, men contributed slightly more of a Republican vote at every point on the ideological continuum, and women contributed a trace more of a Democratic vote across the same range, despite the fact that men were slightly more likely to get out and vote (Figures 6.16.A, 6.16.B, and 6.16.C). For cultural values, this male edge for Republicans and female edge for Democrats was a bit larger across the broad middle of the ideological continuum, though the propensity of the male/female turnout gap to be associated with cultural conservatism did disrupt these relationships at the far conservative end (Figures 6.16.D, 6.16.E, and 6.16.F).

By 2008, the partisan *leanings* in this pattern—men more Republican, women more Democratic—had been not only confirmed but expanded, while the comparative *contributions* of men versus women had simultaneously reversed. With economic values, men were clearly if still modestly more Republican at every point on the ideological continuum. Yet women were not just more Democratic than they had been in 1984. They now featured a Democratic edge larger than its Republican counterpart among men (Figures 8.16.A, 8.16.B, and 8.16.C). Because women had also become more rather than less likely to vote, and because the Non vote among men was concentrated among strong liberals, this "sex gap" among Democratic voters increased as one moved from economic conservatism to economic liberalism.

A version of the same thing could be said with cultural values (Figures 8.16.D, 8.16.E, and 8.16.F). Men were more Republican everywhere except among strong liberals, where the gap disappeared. Women were even more Democratic everywhere except among those strong liberals. And there was a slight propensity for men who were strong conservatives to vote less than equally conservative women, with the result that the sex gap among both Republican and Democratic voters was largest among cultural conservatives. On the other hand, what looked most different between 1984 and 2008 was the transformation, among both sex-based groups, of the form of the relationship between cultural values and the vote. A quarter-century earlier, there had been little relationship at all between voting behavior and cultural values for either group, except among strong cultural liberals. A quarter-century later, there was a strong relationship along the entire cultural continuum, though it was the *same* relationship for both groups, with conservatives going Republican and liberals going Democratic.

For social groups this large—50-plus percent of American society for women, 50-minus percent for men—it would have been difficult for joint relationships between political values and the vote to deviate much from the national picture. Nevertheless, the Republican vote in 1984 had been aligned more with economics and the Democratic vote more with culture among both men and women, just as the male vote had been aligned more

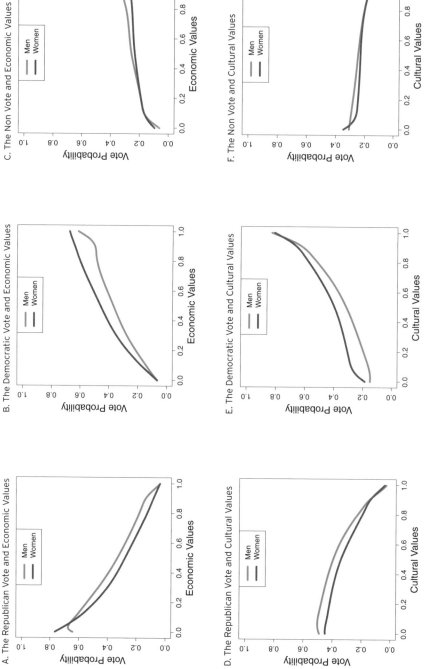

Figure 8.16 Political Values and Voting Behavior: Men and Women, 2008

with economics and the female vote more with culture among both Democratic and Republican voters.[6]

In common with the story of change in joint voting patterns for social groups delineated by religious background, these two differences among social groups delineated by domestic role had been largely eliminated by 2008 (Figure 8.17). Extreme economic conservatives contributed something extra to John McCain, the Republican. Extreme cultural liberals contributed something extra to Barack Obama, the Democrat. But everywhere else, the equivalent organizing power of economics and culture, along with the overwhelming symmetry of this link between political values and voting behavior, had become bottom-line stories for the modern world.

Underneath these joint voting relationships, however, in the density maps for men and women in 2008, there was a further, major change. This was generated principally within their Republican voting blocs, most especially

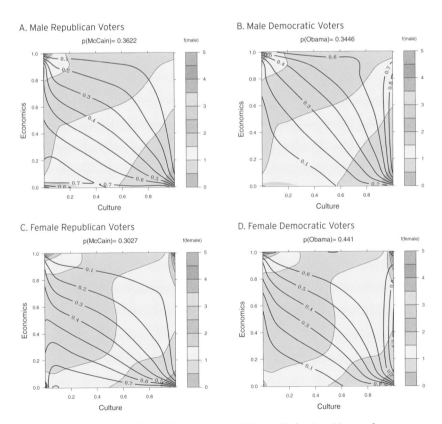

Figure 8.17 The Ideological Landscape and Voting Behavior: Men and Women, 2008

among Republican men. While it, too, represented the disappearance of an old sex-based distinction, the result represented a genuine change in the strategic landscape facing partisan strategists in modern American politics. In 1984, Democratic men and women were essentially indistinguishable in their overrepresented terrains, being strong cultural liberals who varied from strongly liberal to moderately conservative on economics (Figure 6.17 in Chapter 6). Republican men and women, however, had differed. Republican men were most commonly moderate cultural liberals, while Republican women were much more evenly distributed on culture, with a large overrepresented faction of strong cultural conservatives that Republican men lacked entirely.

By 2008, this sex-based distinction among Republicans had evaporated (Figure 8.18). Democratic men and women remained essentially indistinguishable, with both groups adding overrepresented terrain among moderate cultural liberals who were strong economic liberals as well. As with so many other group-based partisan factions, this helped cement Democratic men and women into the jointly liberal corner of the ideological landscape. Yet Republican men and women were now essentially indistinguishable, too. In converging, both Republican blocs had moved to the right on culture. Indeed, both were now most overrepresented among strong cultural conservatives, who were otherwise moderate to strong economic conservatives, too. This shift helped cement Republican men and women into the opposite, jointly conservative corner of the ideological landscape.

Yet in accomplishing this, it was Republican men who had contributed the much bigger transformation, with the modal member now found on the opposite side of the ideological center: then a moderate cultural liberal, now a strong cultural conservative. As a result, it was Republican men—not Democratic men, Democratic women, or even Republican women—who made the largest sex-based contribution to a growing national polarization between Republicans and Democrats on cultural values. Moreover, these Republican men had had farther to go in eliminating this sex-based difference, because Republican women had already been closer to the modern pattern—not exhibiting it, just closer to it—in 1984.

Among social groups delineated by denomination or religiosity, this polarization had raised additional group-based strategic possibilities, in the form of different possible mixes of economic and cultural policy. The sex-based outcome accompanying this polarization was the reverse. Men and women now manifested no further ideological distinction of the sort that could be addressed through differentiated policy promises. The two sex-based groups were effectively—ideologically—identical within their parties. To produce this result, Democratic men and women had needed to change in parallel ways, while Republican men and women had needed to change differentially, with Republican men needing to change the most of all. Obviously, all did.

Parenthood

The story of parenthood as a basis for the creation of social groups—the presence or absence of children at home—can be summarized and dispatched quickly, since it proves to be parallel with, but weaker than, the same story for sex. In 1984, there had been a slight tendency for parents to vote less than non-parents, a tendency concentrated among economic liberals and cultural conservatives (Figure 6.18). By extension, parents who were economic liberals had underperformed non-parents in their support of the Democratic candidate, Walter Mondale, while parents who were cultural conservatives had underperformed non-parents in their support of the Republican candidate, Ronald Reagan.

For individual relationships among group membership, political values, and the vote, that was really all there was, and these effects were modest. In particular, parenthood did not offer even the marginal partisan differences generated by sex. Moreover, by 2008, the modest existing effects had grown only weaker (Figure 8.19). Economic liberals and cultural conser-

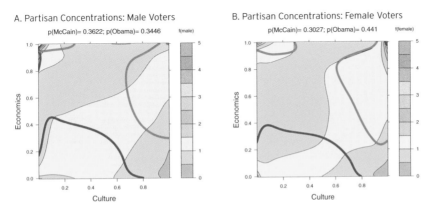

Figure 8.18 Ideological Density and Voting Behavior: Men and Women, 2008

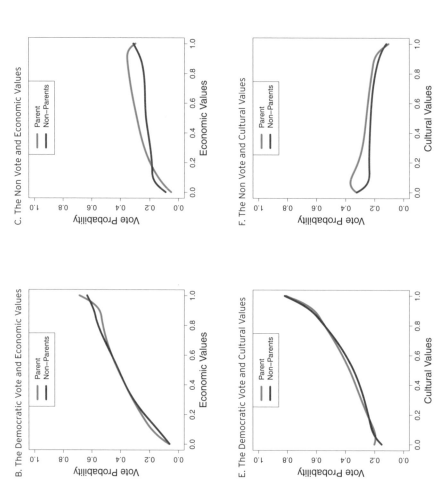

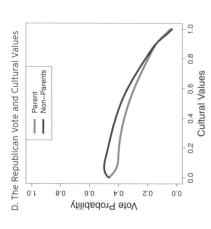

Figure 8.19 Political Values and Voting Behavior: Parents and Non-Parents, 2008

vatives in the parental group still voted a bit less than their co-ideologues among non-parents. But now, there was no difference in the Democratic vote between parents and non-parents, for either economics or culture, while the tiny underperformance of parents who were economic liberals or cultural conservatives were both concentrated within the *Republican* vote.

Even less needed to be added to the story of *joint* voting relationships for economics and culture among parents and non-parents (figures not shown). Changes among these groups were again essentially identical to, but weaker than, those among men versus women. By 1984, the group-based distinction among men and women—men more economic, women more cultural, among both Republicans and Democrats—was already missing among parents and non-parents. Accordingly, when both the parental and non-parental groups came into alignment with the expanded symmetric influence of economics and culture in the modern world, they did not have to overcome any group-based differences in order to do so.

The one group-based division between parents and non-parents that did produce an evident change with possible consequences for the strategic landscape arrived with their density maps. Here, however, the parallels between parenthood and sex were overwhelming, and the effect from sex still remained stronger. In 1984, Democratic parents and non-parents had been concentrated on essentially the same ideological high ground, among strong cultural liberals who varied from strongly liberal to moderately conservative on economics (Figure 6.19). Republican parents and Republican non-parents had modal members who shared the same general territory, too, being strong economic conservatives who were moderate cultural liberals, though parents were even more liberal than non-parents in their cultural values.

As with sex, so with parenthood: by 2008, the Democrats had added some moderate cultural liberals who were strongly liberal on economics to their ideological high ground, pulling the entire group more fully into the jointly liberal corner of the ideological landscape (Figure 8.20). The big shift, as with sex, was nevertheless among overrepresented Republican factions, both of which had now moved well to the right on culture. This required even more of a move from parents compared with non-parents,

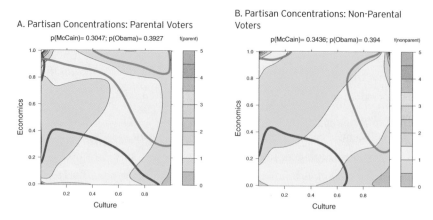

Figure 8.20 Ideological Density and Voting Behavior: Parents and Non-Parents, 2008

but the end point was once again identical, in the territory of moderate to strong economic conservatism as well as moderate to strong cultural conservatism—the opposite corners of the ideological landscape to that inhabited by overrepresented Democrats.[7]

The Group-Based Evolution of the Strategic Landscape

Individual Voting Relationships

The big change in individual relationships among social backgrounds, political values, and the vote for the quarter-century between 1984 and 2008 was the huge rise in the aligning power of cultural values. What had been irrelevant across 80 percent of the ideological continuum in 1984 was now relevant across the entire spectrum, at least when the focus was the nation as a whole (see Chapter 7). Unsurprisingly, a change of this magnitude reached into most social groups as well, though there were exceptions. Black Americans and high school dropouts showed *no* relationship between cultural values and the vote. For Black Americans, this was the continuation of a previous non-relationship, and Blacks continued to be the social group connected centrally to politics by way of group membership rather than political values. For high school dropouts, this result was new, an actual decline that made them the sole group to move opposite to the national trend on cultural values.

Yet even for the vast array of groups that did show a voting relationship, the degree to which group membership anchored this relationship in different places, along with the *change* in this anchoring effect, varied substantially from group to group. Denominational groups featured the clearest increase in the filtering effect of group membership, an increase that included a strong associated partisan impact. Evangelical Protestants now gave Republicans an extra increment at every point on the ideological continuum; Non-Christians now gave Democrats a counterpart advantage at every point. This change only gained consequence from the fact that it represented the demise of an earlier, long-standing relationship between denominational attachment and partisan politics, where Protestant groups had been more Republican, non-Protestant groups more Democratic.

Group membership likewise increased its filtering effect on the relationship between political values and the vote for social groups delineated by sex, albeit in a much weaker fashion. By 2008, men were more Republican along most of the cultural continuum, while women were even more Democratic across the same range. The two groups had thus put increased partisan distance between them over time. Though note that the other set of social groups delineated by domestic roles, parents versus non-parents, acquired no further group-based relationship to the vote even as the overall role of cultural values increased.

A different kind of linkage between group membership and political values arrived with those groups where the increased effect of group membership was conditioned by ideology. Thus for both sets of social groups delineated by social class, the anchoring effect of group membership increased sharply among cultural conservatives. Yet there was no counterpart increase among cultural liberals, so that the group-based anchoring effect found among strong conservatives declined across the ideological spectrum, disappearing entirely among strong liberals. Though recall that in the case of educational attainment, the fact that the high school dropouts showed a declining relationship between their vote and cultural values means that they are the clear exception to this ideological conditioning.

Relationships among social backgrounds, *economic* values, and voting behavior changed much less in the quarter-century from 1984 through

2008. Yet in the nation as a whole, they nevertheless managed to increase, even as relationships with cultural values were increasing simultaneously (and more substantially). This economic increase, too, was not uniform across social groups, nor was it necessarily expressed in the same way when it did occur. The most dramatic change came among Hispanics. A group that had previously been more like Black Americans, in that its vote was nearly unrelated to either economic or cultural values, came to be more like the Anglos, with a vote that was clearly related to both sets of values across the entire ideological continuum. The distribution of values within the group hardly meant that the partisan *result* looked like that of the Anglos. But Hispanics did increase the role of economic values within their group more than any other.

A very different story of a sharply changed role for economic values came among denominational groups, and the key part of this story was the way that the four great religious families both moved apart and reorganized their relationships to each other. The Evangelical Protestants generated a clear Republican increment at every point along the economic and not just the cultural continuum. The Non-Christians generated a clear Democratic increment at every point along the same continuum. And the Mainstream Protestants and Catholics converged in a roughly equidistant middle between those two outlying groups. The dramatic part of this change lay in the fact that the anchoring effect of group membership on economic values was now considerably larger for denominational groups than it was for groups delineated by social class. The overall link between economic values and voting behavior remained marginally stronger within class-based groups. But the group-based contribution to this link was clearly more important for groups delineated by denomination.

Joint Voting Relationships

The rise of cultural values as an aligning influence on the American political landscape was likewise the major contributor to a national pattern of joint voting relationships by 2008. In this, both economics and culture now stretched their organizing influence across the entire ideological spectrum, and in an essentially symmetric way. Republican support rose and Democratic support fell with both economic and cultural conservatism, in effectively equal measure. Democratic support rose and

Republican support fell, conversely, with both economic and cultural liberalism.

There remained social groups that were effectively immune to this joint national pattern. Black Americans, being aligned on neither economic nor cultural values, were certainly not aligned on their combination. Yet this was not some natural product of race and ethnicity as principles of social division, creating social groups that somehow uniformly favored group identification over political values as a means toward partisan alignment of their votes. For it was precisely the other leading group delineated by race and ethnicity, Hispanic Americans, who made the most striking leap from nonalignment to joint alignment between political values and voting behavior.

More common, however, was the situation where social groups that had previously featured group-based distinctions within their joint voting relationships saw those distinctions sharply reduced, and sometimes obliterated. Social divisions that created a small number of large groups were particularly likely to fall into this category. Thus the groups formed by generic religiosity, the religious versus the irreligious, along with the groups formed by domestic roles, men versus women and parents versus nonparents, now featured a direct embodiment of the national pattern within the confines of *all* their groups. Economic *and* cultural conservatism conduced Republican, economic *and* cultural liberalism conduced Democratic, and religiosity, sex, or parenthood did not contribute anything additional to this overall alignment.

On the other hand, both educational attainment and denominational attachment offered a hybrid pattern, whereby some social groups fully reflected the national pattern while others, though hardly resisting it, retained a group-based power to shape the application of these patterns among their members. With educational attainment, the three largest groups—high school graduates, some-colleges, and college graduates—conformed overwhelmingly to the national pattern. Republican voting blocs within each retained a small additional role for economic values in aligning their vote. Democratic voting blocs within each retained a small additional role for cultural values. But intergroup convergence and simultaneous conformity to national patterns was the overwhelming story. The two other educational groups, however, the high school dropouts and the

postgraduates, were different. Neither was immune to national developments. Yet the high school dropouts retained a larger role for economic
values than the other educational groups, while the postgraduates featured
a larger role for cultural values than direct application of the national pattern would have entailed.

With denominational attachment, a different version of this group-based
story appeared. Two of these groups, the Mainstream Protestants and the
Catholics, featured clear and direct conformity to national patterns, converging on those patterns within their own confines and converging on
each other in the process. Both Mainstream Protestantism and Catholicism
had once contributed group-specific twists to joint voting relationships. By
2008, they no longer did. Said the other way around, adherence to Mainstream Protestantism or Catholicism no longer distinguished group members from the nation as a whole, something that would not have been said
of them a quarter-century before and something that could definitely not
be said of the other two main denominational groups, the Evangelical
Protestants and the Non-Christians.

These latter were, in fact, the growing denominational families in American society, and they retained the power to shape joint voting relationships
among their members. On the one hand, both were closer to national patterns in 2008 than they had been in 1984. Their members had not rejected
these patterns; they had merely integrated them differently from Mainstream Protestants and Catholics. Yet the Evangelical Protestants retained
more internal influence for economic values than the other three denominational groups, just as the Non-Christians manifested even more internal
influence for cultural values than the other three. The combination meant
that the Evangelical Protestants had moved farther on culture than the
other groups—they had much farther to move, after all—while the Non-
Christians had up-weighted economics more than the others.

Density Maps and Strategic Implications

None of these joint voting relationships, however much or little they approximated national patterns, implied that the various social groups had
somehow converged on the same political values—and hence on the same
ideological locations—within these overall relationships. Indeed, for many
groups, the very reason that joint voting relationships had gained power

and scope was that sharply divergent group values had become activated in politics. And the strategic implications of this fact had very much not changed. If a group was concentrated in a particular place on the ideological landscape, and if one party had an inherent advantage in appealing to its members as a result, then the worst possible strategic advice with regard to this particular group was that party candidates should move somewhere else!

Once again, there were important idiosyncratic shifts among partisan voting blocs—the Republican and Democratic high grounds—within groups created by social class, race and ethnicity, religious background, or domestic roles. Republican prospects among Black Americans, for example, received what was in effect a further setback because the previous Republican high ground in this group, small and challenged as it had been, had by 2008 shattered into three lesser concentrations that could not conceivably be attracted by the same policy program. In a very different effect with a similar partisan upshot, Hispanic Americans remained disproportionately headquartered in Democratic territory. Although the coming of national voting patterns to the Hispanic population did open fresh opportunities for Republicans—unlike the Black world, the Hispanic world was kinder to them in 2008—the actual distribution of the Hispanic electorate still sharply constrained potential Republican gains.

Yet two overall developments characterized the density maps for most social groups in the modern era. The extent of their reach still varied, and individual groups still did different things within these two overarching tendencies. Yet two general developments did characterize partisan change as captured by density maps. The first was a generalized propensity for Republican voting blocs within most groups to move to the right on culture. This was in fact the single largest factor impelling the rise of cultural values as a co-equal principle for aligning partisan votes. The second, partly a result of the first, was a generalized tendency for Republican and Democratic voting blocs within those groups to move farther apart rather than closer together. This constituted a growing and general partisan polarization, and in most cases, it implied a move toward jointly conservative or jointly liberal territory.

Both main indicators of social class, for example, saw the Republican voting blocs within their social groups move to the right on culture.

Republican voters were thus the engine of change, and increased partisan distance was an inevitable product. What had been areas of ideological overlap in 1984, where both parties could reasonably compete, disappeared by 2008, while disproportionately Republican and Democratic groups moved toward the ideological extremes, either jointly conservative or jointly liberal on both economics and culture. Yet the two main indicators of class, namely income and education, still generated a distinguishable strategic environment. Groups delineated by family income made Democratic voting blocs more homogeneous and thus less stressed, while groups delineated by educational attainment rebalanced these effects in a manner more potentially charitable to Republicans.

Both main indicators of religious background partook of the same general developments, while differing even more among themselves. All four denominational groups saw their Republican voting blocs shift to the right on culture, three of them substantially. (The Evangelicals began with little space to move farther right.) The same three denominational groups saw their Democratic voting blocs add moderate liberals to their disproportionate concentrations of strong liberals on culture. Yet rather than reduce the gap between Democrats and Republicans, this Democratic move painted the party even more neatly into the territory—the corner—of joint economic and cultural liberalism.

The same general effect among groups delineated by generic religiosity then worked somewhat differently. Again, Republican voting blocs among both the religious and the irreligious moved culturally rightward from 1984 through 2008. Yet what this did was unify the Republican Party on culture, while leaving the Democratic Party divided in ways that had once characterized them both. This effect was further exaggerated by the fact that Democratic voting blocs within these groups were additionally diverse in their economic values. The result was a factional structure that made the process of defining a party program easier among Republicans, while simultaneously exposing less of their party to countervailing appeals by the Democrats.

Finally, the same situation among social groups delineated by domestic roles was in some sense at its most stereotypical. It was Republican voting blocs among men *and* women, or parents *and* non-parents, that moved noticeably during this period, shifting rightward on culture. Yet within them, it was Republican men and Republican parents who moved additionally, making them the lead vehicle for the increased power of cultural values when observed through the lens of social groups delineated by domestic roles. In completing a picture of changing partisan factions within social groups, they in effect completed an even larger picture of the group-based evolution of the strategic landscape for electoral politics.

Conclusion

The Landscape of Modern American Politics Ideological Evolution and Strategic Incentives

Partisan patterns on the ideological landscape of American politics changed substantially in the quarter-century between 1984 and 2008. Voting behavior that was principally aligned by economic values at the beginning of this period saw the aligning power of those values increase within society as a whole. Yet the grand change lay not with economics but with culture. Voting behavior came to be powerfully—indeed, equally—aligned by cultural values. In the process, the aligning power of these latter values needed to increase much, much more. It did, to the point where a national picture of economic and cultural values jointly with the vote featured roughly equivalent and nearly symmetric relationships, relationships ranging from the far economic and cultural right to the far economic and cultural left.

The Evolution of Voting Relationships

The Nation as a Whole

Achieving an accurate version of this national picture was greatly facilitated by conceiving of the vote as a tripartite (and sometimes a quadripartite) phenomenon, always composed of Republican voting, Democratic voting, and Non voting, along with the occasional Independent tally. In 1984, Republican voting had been powerfully aligned by economic values. Economic conservatives were attracted, economic liberals repelled. By contrast, Republican voting had been effectively unrelated to cultural values across the vast bulk of society, before falling dramatically among strong cultural liberals. In 1984, Democratic voting had been clearly if less powerfully aligned with economic values, albeit in the opposite direction. Economic liberals were attracted, economic conservatives repelled. Democratic voting, too, had been effectively unrelated to cultural values across the vast bulk of society before rising dramatically among strong cultural liberals.

These same patterns were again present and easily elicited in the subsequent election of 1988, a contest with different presidential nominees and a closer ultimate outcome. Together, the two elections constitute the old world of electoral politics and campaign strategy when approached through the Pew Values surveys. Their patterns were disrupted subsequently by the elections of 1992 and 1996. The main vehicle for this disruption was—or appeared in its time to be—H. Ross Perot, the independent candidate for president. Voting relationships in national politics were in additional disarray because the Perot vote of 1992 looked so different from the Perot vote of 1996, not just in the aggregate but, more critically, in its internal composition.

When voting patterns in 2000 looked different yet again, contemporary observers could not easily interpret their evolution. With 2008 added to the account, however, 2000 looks very much like the earliest crystallized version of the modern world. In passing, note that this raises a very different possibility for interpreting the Perot interlude. The usual view is that Perot was a quixotic candidate who elicited idiosyncratic voting patterns. Yet if there is both an old order and a new world in this election series, it may as easily have been the case that voters were already in motion in 1992, having come loose from older voting patterns, and that Perot served more as a parking place, a kind of holding pen, while these voters attempted to find their proper modern alignment.

In either case, Republican voting for 2008 remained powerfully aligned with economic values, still attracting conservatives and repelling liberals. Yet now, Republican voting was also powerfully aligned with cultural values, likewise attracting conservatives and repelling liberals—and attracting or repelling them proportionately across the entire ideological spectrum. For 2008, Democratic voting remained aligned with economic values, attracting liberals and repelling conservatives, a relationship that had actually strengthened more than its Republican counterpart. Yet the big change in Democratic voting, too, featured a new and powerful alignment with cultural values, attracting liberals and repelling conservatives, likewise across the entire ideological spectrum.

Where voting behavior was largely unchanged was among those who failed to turn out. In 1984, this Non vote had risen principally with economic liberalism and secondarily with cultural conservatism, achieving its joint high point among those who were strong economic liberals *and* strong cultural conservatives. For 2008, there was a bit more culture and a bit less economics, so that the Non vote was rising principally with cultural conservatism and secondarily with economic liberalism. Yet its continuing high point among strong economic liberals and strong cultural conservatives remained its distinguishing characteristic. Methodologically, the ability to see this proved to be an extra advantage of the tripartite voting variable. Strategically, a lack of ultimate change had multiple (and discouraging) implications for reaching these Non voters and converting them into voting partisans.

Key Social Groups

In the meantime, recall that a national picture, however distinctively changed and impressively symmetric, nevertheless contained a plethora of group pictures for social groups with their own (group-based) contributions. No major groups actually featured voting patterns opposite to the national composite. There was no group where economic conservatives voted clearly more Democratic than economic liberals, no group where cultural liberals voted clearly more Republican than cultural conservatives. Though there *were* groups whose members were less aligned by political values in 2008 than they had been in 1984. The high school dropouts were the poster children here. Just as there were groups whose members remained unaligned by political values in 2008 as in 1984. Black Americans were the outstanding example of this.

For most principles of social division, however, the group story was more one of adjusting to national trends by integrating them into group-based behavior, sometimes while shifting that behavior additionally and in important ways. The outstanding example of this latter were the denominational groups, where old intergroup relationships—a coalition of the two great Protestant families against all others on economics, an extra Democratic increment from Catholics who were conservative on culture—were entirely displaced. By 2008, it was just Evangelicals tilting reliably Republican, Non-Christians tilting reliably Democratic, and Mainstreams plus Catholics converging in the partisan middle, regardless of whether the focus was economics or culture. This did not gainsay the national pattern in voting relationships within each group, but it actually reordered the denominational groups in their partisan reflections of that pattern.

A different version of the normal blend of national trends with group-based developments was exemplified by social groups divided by sex, men versus women. In purely group-based terms, the partisan division between these two huge groups increased for both economic and cultural values between 1984 and 2008. While modest, this increase was sufficient to create clear Republican majorities among men and clearer Democratic majorities among women, again for both valuational realms. On the other hand, the dominant story remained the power of a rising cultural alignment to pull both groups into the national pattern, a pull that was sufficient to eradicate older joint relationships between political values and the vote. In 1984, Republican voters were more economic and Democratic voters more cultural among both men and women, while men were more economic and women more cultural among both Republican and Democratic voters. By 2008, both relationships were effectively gone.

A third mega-story came with social groups delineated by educational attainment. Here, the biggest driver of change was demographic in a different and more mechanical sense. Education was the great principle of social division whose groups had grown and shrunk most disproportionately between 1984 and 2008. The low end of the educational continuum, the high school dropouts, was in precipitous numerical decline. The high end of the continuum had expanded so much that it made sense to create a whole new educational category, the postgraduates. This mattered additionally because high school dropouts provided the great example of a vote that was responsive to economics but nearly impervious to culture, even in an era of generally expanding cultural power. Just as postgraduates provided the great example of a vote that was responsive to culture but nearly impervious to economics.

That is the evolution of voting relationships for the nation as a whole, along with key instances where social groups adjusted differentially to them. These relationships—to political values individually and jointly, for the composite nation and within major social groups—were recurrent and patterned, but they were hardly static. The old world of the 1980s, not all that long ago, managed to look considerably different from the new world of the 2000s, a mere quarter-century later. Political values in general had increased their ability to align the vote in the modern era, for the nation as a whole and among most (but not all) social groups within it. Cultural values in particular, previously confined in their voting relationships to the sharply different partisan choices of strong cultural liberals, now reached across the entire ideological spectrum, with an impact sufficient to rival that of economic values.

An Evolving Political Landscape

Density Maps and Voting Behavior

Yet voting relationships were not nearly all that there was to the strategic landscape for electoral politics. Often they were not even the dominant aspect of that landscape. Sometimes they were even actively misleading as a guide to the ideological terrain to which candidates could be expected to respond—and which would affect the success of their campaigns whether they responded appropriately or not. Two points are important:

- In the first, the ideological distribution of voters beneath similar voting relationships could vary widely, and these distributions often trumped those relationships as a strategic consideration. This is the essential reason to have—and check—what we have here called density maps.
- In the second, partisan choice was capable of varying in a partially autonomous fashion, that is, over and above changes in these under-

lying distributions. There was real valuational change in the nation and its groups. Yet there was more change in partisan voting blocs than these valuational shifts would have required.

For the first of these points, it is essential to remember that similar voting relationships could mask sharply dissimilar preference patterns, where the latter could be the critical consideration for any given target population. Cultural values might have increased their aligning potential across the full ideological spectrum, but if this relationship characterized a target population that was fundamentally conservative or fundamentally liberal, then that ideological location—the density map for this target population—was likely to be the dominant strategic concern. This is what campaign strategists learn from experience and what social scientists so frequently forget. Conceptually, it is the reason for distinguishing between relationships and distributions. Methodologically, it is the justification for emphasizing density maps: they are what unite the experiential lore of practitioners with the self-conscious measurement of scholars.

The second major point emerging from these density maps is that partisan choice, within targeted social groups and indeed for the nation as a whole, was capable of changing more than the underlying distribution of economic or cultural preferences. For the nation as a whole, there had in fact been a modest but clear shift in the underlying distribution of political values between 1984 and 2008. Economic and cultural values became more closely aligned, which had to mean that by 2008 there were more strong economic liberals who were also strong cultural liberals and especially more strong economic conservatives who were also strong cultural conservatives.

There remained an obvious unaligned exception, the cluster of strong economic liberals who were strong cultural conservatives. This cluster was smaller in 2008 than it had been in 1984, yet its members were even more of an outlying group in the modern era than they had been in the old world. A different testimony to the power of partisan change was the near-disappearance of the other off-diagonal concentration, of strong economic conservatives who were strong cultural liberals. There had been many groups in 1984 whose overrepresented ideological factions among Republican voters leaned this way: upper-middle and upper-incomes, some-college and college graduates, Mainstream Protestants and Non-Christians, the irreligious, even men and parents. All that remained in 2008 was the Republican voting bloc among the postgraduates.

There were echoes of these national effects within most individual groups, though group values were still impressively stable. When the focus is the comparative ideological location of social groups, few among them, whether delineated by social class, race and ethnicity, religious background, or domestic roles, changed ordinal positions with any other group delineated by the same principle across this entire period, and the few such shifts that did occur involved groups with close to the same mean scores on economic or cultural values. As a result, political values served as an important anchor in adjusting group members to national trends.

On the other hand, for most groups as for the nation as a whole, partisan change among group members could be considerably larger than valuational shifts. That is, groups could change the ideological factions that were overrepresented among their Republican and Democratic voters without requiring a comparable change in the distribution of ideologies for the group as a whole. Constant values could thus acquire new partisan connections, in the process changing the strategic nature of the political landscape. The critical embodiment of this distinction—even more critical to campaign practitioners than to social scientists—thus involved partisan voting blocs *inside of* social groups.

Disproportionate concentrations of Republican and Democratic voters within social groups did indeed evolve differently over this quarter-century. Note, however, that such change did not require that any given individual within the group, nor even the modal individual, be making the change that came to characterize ascendant Republican or Democratic voting blocs. All it required was that individuals at a given ideological position begin to vote disproportionately Republican or disproportionately Democratic. No doubt some specific individuals changed their political values and subsequently their partisan choice. No doubt some individuals kept their political values but found it necessary to change their partisan choice, because party links to political values were changing around them. All that was required for a noteworthy change in partisan voting blocs, however—and hence in the incentive structure of the political landscape—is that ideological areas began (or ceased) to vote disproportionately Republican or Democratic.

The Evolving Place of Partisan Factions

The great generalized example of this movement among overrepresented voting blocs was the rightward shift on cultural values that characterized most group-based concentrations of Republican voters. On the one hand, this was consistent with the increase in American society as a whole of voters who were strong economic *and cultural* conservatives. On the other hand, the associated partisan shift was bigger than that underlying increase would by itself have demanded. This specific change came to characterize every group delineated by educational attainment, for example. Both high school graduates and college graduates moved impressively rightward, though the power of this effect in the case of the college graduates was easy to underestimate because their modal member began and ended at a more culturally liberal place than their high school counterparts. Such change looked even more dramatic in the case of the some-colleges: their modal member actually went from being a moderate liberal to a strong conservative on culture.

Nevertheless, the most dramatic incarnation of this effect, whereby overrepresented voting blocs within social groups could move impressively on the political landscape *without* pressure from changing values, came with those partisan blocs where clusters of disproportionate Republican or Democratic voters were no longer found even within the modal opinion for their group as a whole, but instead turned up outside that opinion. The largest concentration of Democratic voters among Protestant Evangelicals, for example, went from being inside to outside of dominant Evangelical opinion, just as the largest concentration of Republican voters among Non-Christians went from being inside to outside of dominant Non-Christian opinion.

Yet where a focus on density maps rather than voting relationships came most strikingly into its own as an analytic device, because the resulting picture looked so different from conventional portraits, was with the ideological factions that were most overrepresented in one party versus the other when observed for the nation as a whole. The 1984 portraits had already been striking in this regard. In that year, the high ground of overrepresentation within the Republican Party had been located among strong economic conservatives who otherwise varied across nearly the entire spectrum on culture, with a modest edge to moderate cultural liberals. Yet the high ground of overrepresentation within the Democratic Party had been located among strong cultural liberals who otherwise varied from strongly liberal to moderately conservative on economics.

The backbone constituencies of the two parties—their so-called bases—were thus not opposite to each other on either great ideological dimension. Republicans were disproportionately conservative on economics, while Democrats could be found nearly anywhere. Democrats were disproportionately liberal on culture, while Republicans could be found nearly anywhere. What distinguished the two backbone constituencies—these two partisan high grounds—was the fact that they were organized by different fundamental concerns. One ideological dimension belonged to one party, and one belonged to the other. Republican voters could be isolated by their economic values. Democratic voters could be isolated by their cultural values. As a result, moving away from mainstream Republican economics did not bring you to core Democrats, just as moving away from mainstream Democratic culture did not bring you to core Republicans.

The great advantage of the Pew Values surveys in pursuit of these underlying distributions is that they offer unchanging survey items year after year, thereby offering protection against the possibility that apparent change was nothing more than an artifact of a changed polling instrument. Because these surveys do not begin until 1984, it is not possible to know whether this curious initial picture, with the parties organized around two fundamentally different principles rather than at opposite ends of one, was a long-established feature of the great party coalitions. Perhaps it was just that the Democrats had moved first toward what would be the decisive change in the coalitional bases of *both* parties, the up-weighting of cultural values. Much impressionistic literature would suggest that the two parties were indeed once organized around a single ideological dimension, of economic values, and that this unidimensional pattern of ideological alignment merely came apart first within the Democratic Party, in the 1960s and 1970s.[1]

In any case, the Pew Values surveys were sufficient to isolate the big subsequent change. This shifted the strategic landscape for partisan conflict in a major way, one that was, in passing, powerfully inconsistent with major efforts at theorizing about such change. The more dramatic part of the shift was concentrated within one of these parties, the Republicans.

The Republican high ground moved sharply to the right on cultural values. Strong cultural liberals as an overrepresented part of the Republican coalition disappeared; moderate cultural liberals became an endangered species; strong cultural conservatives actually became the modal Republican voter. In the process, the party additionally up-weighted the territory of moderate (rather than just strong) economic conservatism. Apparently, strong cultural conservatives did not need to be as rigorously conservative on economics in order to be staunch Republicans. Accordingly, a party that had previously been concentrated along only one ideological dimension was now concentrated at the intersection of two, in the territory of strong economic *and* cultural conservatism.

The Democratic version of this development was less dramatic in its contours, though mostly just because it had less ground to cover in order to achieve the same result. The important point is simply that a weaker echo of Republican developments did take the Democratic Party to its version of the same—albeit ideologically opposite—territory. There was no dramatic movement off in some other direction among the strong cultural liberals who had previously characterized the disproportionately Democratic terrain. Instead, where the Republican high ground had moved sharply to the right on culture, this Democratic high ground moved more modestly to the left on economics. Yet in expanding the Democratic high ground to include moderate rather than just strong cultural liberals, the party simultaneously up-weighted the territory of strong *economic* liberalism, thereby digging itself further into the ideological combination opposite that of the Republicans. A party that had previously been concentrated along only one ideological dimension likewise ended up concentrated at the intersection of two, among strong economic and cultural liberals.

Theoretical Understandings

Social Scientists and Campaign Strategists

To say the same thing differently, party coalitions diverged, and as they did, electoral strategists came to understand the necessity of moving with them, not thereby deliberately abandoning some hypothetical median voter but most definitely moving away from the ideological center. Much analytical mischief has been sown by failing to attend to this elementary conceptual difference. For most social groups, the median voter was reliably left or reliably right of the ideological center, sometimes strongly so. For most principles of social stratification, there was no resulting social group with its median member at the ideological center of society. Even then, in years when group identifications—or, especially, the combination of values associated with group membership—were an important electoral influence, members who converged on the group median were in all likelihood moving away from the ideological center of the nation as a whole.

It might still be argued abstractly that for society as a whole, the median voter remained in the center, by definition. Yet this is precisely the point in the argument where social scientists with a theoretical framework and campaign strategists with experiential lore diverged most sharply. The latter knew from experience that on policy concerns that maximized any given group-based effect, it was often the case that the largest number of voters was already not in the ideological center of the nation as a whole. Yet their job was to extend an electoral appeal to one or more additional groups, and this often meant moving, not back toward the ideological center, but across toward the ideological extremes on the alternative policy dimension. Below, we shall make some theoretical points about why this might regularly be so. Here, the point is just that when likely Republican or Democratic blocs within these social groups were added to this strategic picture, such behavioral considerations were only intensified.

Seen differently, of course, this divergence of the party coalitions is a familiar phenomenon, perhaps even the defining phenomenon of the modern political era. A veritable cottage industry has developed among those studying (their version of) *partisan polarization*. Yet two-dimensional pictures of this development still manage to look striking and distinctive. The Republican vote now rises regularly and symmetrically toward the combination of economic and cultural conservatism. The Democratic vote now rises regularly and symmetrically toward the combination of economic and cultural liberalism. Density maps underlying (and underpinning) this development then look additionally different, featuring three-dimensional partisan coalitions that are not mirror images but that are united by the apparent inconsequentiality of the ideological middle.

What makes these pictures look so distinctive? We think that there are a number of related answers. One basic answer is that arraying opinion data in this way—as dispersions of opinion for each individual, cumulated to obtain national or group-based portraits—facilitates simultaneous consideration of voting relationships and the density maps beneath them. Another answer is that breaking out the electorate into Republican voters, Democratic voters, and Non voters allows the full ideological nature of the electoral landscape to appear, and thus to look inherently different from approaches that effectively suppress these distinctions by forcing Republicans to be the reciprocal of Democrats. A third answer is that fostering the simultaneous consideration of voting relationships and their density maps implicitly pits social scientists against campaign strategists—the theorists versus the practitioners—in a particularly astringent way.

Because our goal is actually the opposite, to do a serious analysis of political values and voting behavior that might satisfy social scientists while addressing a world more recognizable to campaign strategists, it is probably worth a short digression into what may be a fourth reason that these partisan portraits look unconventional. This involves the interpretive difference that implicitly follows from choosing voting relationships rather than density maps as the key methodological tool to understand voting behavior and partisan change.

Voting relationships are the great intellectual means of studying politics for those who prefer to think in terms of abstract median voters, since these relationships implicitly but reliably counsel a move left by the more conservative party, a move right by the more liberal party. If, as is indeed the case, people with a higher family income vote more Republican while people with a lower family income vote more Democratic, then a strategy based on relationships to income is neatly consistent with this argument. A Republican moving left or a Democrat moving right will expand the party coalition. This is true more or less by definition. It remains true so long as voting relationships are the evidentiary base for the analysis.

Density maps add not just complexity but also an implicit challenge to this argument. They are the great intellectual means of studying politics for those who prefer to think in terms of "where the ducks are"; that is, how to appeal to actual concentrations of existing voters and how to mobilize relevant Non voters as compensation if these initial appeals fail. Seen through this lens, the same phenomena look crucially different. For the devoted student of density maps, the fact that higher-income and lower-income groups are likely to be found disproportionately among Republicans and Democrats means that both parties will ordinarily feature a constituent base that is not attracted by a median argument, as well as a base that is likely to have both motive and means for resisting the strategic implications that follow from it.

Admittedly, these elaborations on the strategic advice implicit in the choice of analytical tools are overdrawn as presented above. Sophisticated students of voting relationships do acknowledge the complexity that comes with more than one principle of social division or more than one ideological dimension, moving quickly on to *joint* relationships. Honest employers of density maps do acknowledge—albeit privately, not publicly, if they are hired campaign operatives—that democratic politics might function better, the world might even be a better place, if a search for the ideological center was indeed the key to their work. Yet there is a theoretical warning about the logic of campaign strategy inherent in even this more-sophisticated version of the same comparison.

Or at least, the argument from voting relationships has a further empirical premise that the argument from density maps—voter distributions—denies, and in two senses. This underlying premise is that votes in the ideological center can be gained without shedding votes at the ideological extremes. Otherwise, this is the classic opportunity to trade a bird in the hand for *one* in the bush:

- The argument from voting relationships is true if those in the ideological center are turning out less because no political party is presenting candidates whose programs are pitched toward them. In this view, those near the center are both numerous and potentially supportive *if candidates cater to them.* The argument becomes much weaker if those in the ideological center reside there because they have less interest in public policies or even less intrinsic interest in politics. If lack of interest is a key component of moderation, then fresh political gambits—especially nuanced centrist gambits—should have very limited prospects.

- Likewise, the argument from voting relationships is true if those at the ideological extremes really do have nowhere else to go when initiatives aimed at mobilizing the center are implemented. In this view, those farther from this center are always stuck: they can accept a weaker version of their preferred program, or they can see the opposition get elected. Yet this argument, too, becomes much weaker if those at the ideological extremes are not just more attentive to new initiatives but more likely to defect from centrist variants, moving toward options that are even more economically or culturally extreme. If they are indeed happier with a policy program closer to their own preferences, win or lose, they quickly become unstuck.

Normative Concerns

Resolutions for these further theoretical questions are not directly within reach of this analysis. Neither are the grand normative questions that are only barely implicit in the structure of American politics elicited by adding density maps to voting relationships. Yet the theoretical conflict between two related but separate ways of thinking about social backgrounds, political values, and voting behavior does have a normative analog in a grand and long-standing debate about democracy itself. To wit: Does democratic politics work better if electoral campaigns seek moderation or if they seek instead to sharpen differences? If the current structure of American politics is more consistent with the latter, the sharpening of options, but if most Americans would be better served by the former, the seeking of consensus, then the picture elicited here, with the strategic incentives that it brings to the fore, is indeed the basis of a democratic dilemma.

What can be said in closing is that there *are* major aspects of the empirical analysis here—our version of thick description—that appear highly relevant in formulating answers to either set of questions, the theoretical or the normative, because they powerfully constrain the possibilities for each. The first of these further implications involves the bedrock strategic question: Do campaign strategists actually possess in practice both of the two great options that they appear to possess in theory: (1) cater to the base or (2) reach out to the middle? Or does the landscape of American politics effectively foreclose one of these options and thus predetermine the outcome?

The density maps presented here are, after all, developed from the general election vote. This suggests that pictures of a disproportionate presence within the two party coalitions at the nominating stage would likely be more, not less, sharply drawn. If they were, then the alternative strategy of moving to the ideological center might be effectively unavailable—foreclosed by the structure of the ideological landscape—by the time of the general election. At the very least, candidates committed to overrepresented terrains should ordinarily begin the nominating quest with an edge over candidates who have abandoned this terrain in favor of a move toward the center. The triumph of centrist candidates would then require either convincing or circumventing the actual (and not hypothetical) overrepresented voters who constitute potential constituents for the ideologues.

A dispute in theory between seeking the centrist voter and hunting where the ducks are could thus be irrelevant in practice. Yet there is more. For the preceding analysis also contains elements that speak to the potential behavior of fresh voters who might be newly motivated in cases where the existing partisan base does not reliably veto such an effort. These implications are, however, immediately perverse, since they involve the true location of disproportionate Non voters. We already know the empirics. These individuals reside disproportionately on the turf of strong economic liberalism coupled with strong cultural conservatism. *They do not reside at the center.* Nothing in this prevents a Republican candidate from emphasizing cultural conservatism or a Democratic candidate from emphasizing economic liberalism. Both ordinarily do.

Yet the disproportionate cluster of Non voters remains so far from the Republican *or* Democratic high ground that modest further steps to close the Republican distance on economics or the Democratic distance on culture risk being invisible to the stereotypical Non voter. At the same time, larger moves in these same directions seem profoundly unlikely. Such a strategy implicitly asks the far economic right among Republicans to move into territory acceptable to the far economic left, or the far cultural left among Democrats to move into territory acceptable to the far cultural right. In such an environment, it should probably not be surprising that the overrepresented terrain among Non voters remains the least changed from 1984 through 2008.

At the same time, the preceding analysis speaks to the behavior of those who obviously *are* prepared to move away from their usual party in response to the policy alternatives on offer. These are the individuals who have been willing to turn to major independent candidates for president, as with Ross Perot in 1992 and 1996, or to minor versions of the same, as with Ralph Nader or Pat Buchanan in 2000. On the one hand, these individuals have occupied wildly disparate locations on the political landscape. The Perot vote of 1992 compared with 1996 varied hugely just on its own. On the other hand, not one of these third-candidate votes featured a concentration of aspiringly independent voters at the ideological center.

Instead, it is the far economic right or the far cultural left—sequentially in the case of Perot, simultaneously in the case of Nader and Buchanan— that have been the ideological landing places for those who are most easily moved by fresh electoral options. Or, to say the same thing the other way around, evolutionary movement by the two major parties toward the joint ideological extremes has not generated a single independent candidate who has prospered disproportionately by claiming abandoned territory at the ideological center. A vast and increasingly alienated middle has not been the seedbed of major independent alternatives. Rather, non-major-party candidates have found real support by pitching their programs even farther from that center, thereby augmenting the risks of—and reducing the incentives for—major-party candidates to make a centrist move.

Many social scientists, raised on the abstract logic appropriate to strategic pursuit of a median voter, have responded to these all-too-concrete developments in the evolution of American politics by adding complexity and exceptions to a simple model in which candidates move to the center to pick up votes. "The model is accurate, but partisan activists countervail it." "The model is powerful, but partisan voters are easily misled as to its application." Most campaign strategists, and certainly most survivors in the campaign consultancy business, have given these adumbrations short shrift. They have focused instead on particular gambits and concrete techniques for mobilizing existing concentrations of overrepresented partisans.

The Territory Ahead

In the end, then, the story of the evolution of the two parties has been clear and striking, not just on its own terms but in its implications for both theoretical and practical debates. At a minimum, that story suggests that movements away from the ideological center have been carrying the day. More of the recent impetus for this story has belonged to the Republican than to the Democratic Party. The Republican coalition has remained strongly conservative on economics. At the same time, it has not only become much more conservative on culture, it has actually moved across the ideological center of American society, moving toward the ideological center from the cultural left merely as a route away from the center and toward the cultural right. Yet the Democratic part of this story, if less intense during this time period, has been fully reinforcing. The Democratic coalition has remained strongly liberal on culture, while becoming more liberal on economics as well.

Both parties thus end up more or less naturally at opposite corners of the ideological landscape, the Republicans jointly conservative, the Democrats jointly liberal. On the one hand, there is presumably some inherent limit to this evolution. An individual party that moved far enough away from effective majority opinion should ultimately start losing elections. On the other hand, the differential preferences of numerous social groups within the nation as a whole have not been sufficient to prevent this overarching evolution to date. Indeed, some groups underlined the power of contrary national trends by seeing one or the other of the partisan voting blocs within their membership actually move outside of dominant group opinion. Apparently, the practical limits on partisan polarization have not been reached.

If there is a further, final subtext to all of this, it is that study of the evolution of the American political landscape has not been facilitated by theoretical propositions about what *should* have happened historically or what *should* happen now. Here, that study has instead been facilitated by updating a classic focus for political analysis, utilizing the interaction of social backgrounds, political values, and voting behavior. This focus has provided a theoretical framework that can be carried from election to election and group to group, eliciting pictures of the electoral landscape that serve as the practical context for decisions by campaign strategists, re-gardless of whether they ultimately get those decisions right or wrong.

In the process, this study has affirmed the power of social backgrounds, in their own right and as they shape political values. It has affirmed the power—a growing power—of political values to shape voting behavior. It has affirmed the power of implicitly political intermediaries, the major so-cial groups, as well as of explicitly political intermediaries, the major politi-cal parties, to move voters additionally. And it has affirmed the structuring power of the interaction of these basic influences to shape the ideological evolution of the American political landscape. To quote Durkheim at the end of this volume and not just at the beginning: "The strongest wills can-not elicit non-existent forces from nothingness."

Notes

1. The Strategic Landscape How to Find It, How to Read It, What It Reveals

1. The extent of this disconnect between social scientists and campaign strategists is embodied in the fact that the two camps rarely even describe themselves with reference to each other. An exception is Petrocik and Steeper 2010, which also quotes Cohen 1999 approvingly. The best way for social scientists to follow the world of campaign strategists is probably by way of the trade journal for the latter, *Campaigns & Elections*. A grab bag of occasional efforts to work across this divide might include Luntz 1988, Thurber & Nelson 2000, Johnson 2001, and Dulio 2004.

2. Mapping the Political Landscape The Nexus of Demographics and Preferences

1. The classic roots of item response theory are usually traced to Rasch 1960 and Lord and Novick 1968. Their migration to, and evolution within, the study of politics is summarized in Poole 2005.

2. The psychometric applications used in the study of politics are most commonly those known as *ideal point models*. Best known is probably Poole and Rosenthal 1985 on congressional voting behavior, producing the much-used DW-NOMINATE scores, though ideal point models have been employed to investigate such diverse phenomena as political knowledge in the general public (Delli Carpini and Keeter 1996), legal decisions in the Supreme Court (Martin and Quinn 2002), or the democratic nature of nation-states (Treier and Jackman 2008).

3. There are other ways to enforce monotonicity. One that is probably even more general but also more complex would be based on the ideas of Ramsay 1988 and more specifically Ramsay 1998.

4. Further examples of the methodological considerations in constructing item response curves and the resulting implications can be found in Shafer and Spady 2002, Spady 2006, and Spady 2007.

5. Carmines and Wagner 2006 summarizes the overall evolution of this conceptual approach. Lipset and Rokkan 1967 is often cited as the fountainhead for this way of thinking. Shafer and Claggett 1995 applied such thinking to the specifically American context. Miller and Schofield 2003 and Schofield, Miller, and Martin 2003 adapted it to questions of change over time. Inglehart 1977 and 1990 used it centrally in making international comparisons.

6. This item referred to drug dealers before 9/11, to terrorists after 9/11.

7. The 2009 Pew survey does not ask all items of all respondents, but the design is still easily sufficient to estimate the same underlying model as in other years.

8. The exception is culture item # 2, where they are instead asked to choose between the two alternatives and then asked if they feel strongly about their choice.

9. In all the estimates presented here, we use only the first two terms of the polynomial basis. The software that we developed permits the use of an arbitrary number of terms, but going beyond the second term does not substantially affect any inferences of attitudes or behavior (though it can affect the shape of some individual item response curves). The problem with employing more terms is that some surveys have sample sizes that can support this, while others do not. We have opted for simplicity and consistency in this regard.

10. It might be thought that the inclusion of the item "improve black position" accounts for the distinctive liberality of African Americans while skewing results for the nation as a whole. In fact, this is not the case: the differential is virtually unchanged when this item is dropped from the model.

11. The step from one to multiple dimensions is likewise important to classical item response theory (Reckase 1985 and 1997), as well as to other applications in the study of politics, including those most directly related to our own (as with Ansolabehere, Rodden, and Snyder 2006, or Treier and Hillygus 2009).

12. There appears to be a limitless supply of alternatives: Waitress Moms and Office-Park Dads come immediately to mind.

13. An analyst who thought that these categories required further specificity— that Soccer Moms should be defined additionally as Mainstream Protestants or that NASCAR Dads should be defined additionally as Evangelical Protestants— could add those categories to the definition. For this exposition, we rest content with the stripped-down version.

14. There is no authoritative definition of the concept of Soccer Mom, and its inherent ambiguity can be seen in early attempts to define it (Safire 1996). While the term itself can be traced at least as far back as 1982, it achieved widespread usage in conjunction with the 1996 presidential contest. There, its resurrection is

often credited to Alex Castellanos, Republican campaign consultant, as memorialized by E. J. Dionne, columnist and commentator (Dionne 1996). It achieved immortality by being dubbed "Word of the Year" for 1996 by the American Dialect Society (Worland 1998).

15. NASCAR Dads appear to be the most successful of a number of efforts, following the spread of the notion of Soccer Moms, to isolate a fresh, critical, swing group in each election after 1996. NASCAR Dads achieved their moment in conjunction with the 2004 presidential contest (Drehs 2004). They did not subsequently become a "word of the year," but they did make the *New Oxford American Dictionary*—and in precisely the form used here (Stephenson and Lindberg 2010).

16. With only two sets of survey results displayed, one or the other of these years might be just deviant, an outlier. But in fact, examination of the intervening surveys suggests that this is indeed a true evolution of preferences.

3. Structure and Substance Demographic Cleavages and the Roots of Political Values

1. This kind of analysis can be rooted at least as far back as the work of Emile Durkheim. It was reinvigorated in the behavioral revolution of postwar social science, in such works as Lipset 1960. A modern incarnation is Manza and Brooks 1999, which uses the same demographic categories that we use and sets out the argument for their continuing priority.

2. For the record, $1990 + 1992 = 1988$; $1993 + 1994 = 1992$; $1997 + 1999 = 1996$; and 2002, 2007, and 2009 are the only surveys tapping 2000, 2004, and 2008, respectively.

3. Recall that this is not an implicit income effect, whereby postgraduates move toward the center because they make less than college graduates. Income is, as ever, already in the model in its own right.

4. With an average of 8–9 percent of the total sample, Black Americans are more prone to generate idiosyncratic outlier scores, a tendency that becomes even more serious with a Black subpopulation, the Black Evangelicals, below. Thus our presentational rule for Chapter 3 of suppressing the main outlier does create a missing year for economics as well as for culture among Blacks in Table 3.4.

5. Hence, to sustain this basic denominational distinction in the tables and analyses that follow, it must be recalled that "Protestant Evangelicals" are not Black, while "Black Evangelicals" are. When we mean all Evangelicals without regard to race, we need some further modifier such as "White and Black."

6. Indeed, the metrics that makes the rich and the poor seem easily explainable in their economic values—namely family income and educational attainment—run the wrong way around in the case of Evangelical versus Mainstream Protestants, where the latter are clearly better-off than the former. Differences in biblical literalism do exist among the five great religious families, and they may well be performing this function, but they also remain amorphous, especially away from the extremes, so that they offer nothing like the sort of interval ranking that comes with income or education.

4. Structure and Substance Social Groups and the Incarnation of Political Values

1. Merton with Rossi 1968, among others, notes that the translation from demographic categories to social groups can be additionally enriched by knowing whether group members interact with other members and whether they conceive of themselves in terms of groups in which they are objectively members. The Pew data confine our analysis to the narrower—but more transparent—issue of what being classified by demographic categories as a member of a social group contributes to political values (in Chapter 4) and to voting behavior (in Chapters 6 and 8).

2. Similarly, low-income groups are more likely to be Black Evangelicals and high-income groups to be Non-Christians, another reinforcing effect, though this one is moderated by the fact that low-income Anglos are most likely to be White Evangelicals, a denominational attachment that pulls them to the right on economics.

3. Thus low-income group members are pulled rightward on culture by the fact that they have lower educational attainments, are more likely to be Black or Hispanic, and—cumulatively with cultural values, where it was partially countervailing with economics—are more likely to be Evangelical Protestants, White or Black. At the other end of the income continuum, the upper-income group likewise experiences social reinforcement from associated characteristics that drive its cultural values farther to the left. These include greater educational attainment, a greater likelihood of being Anglo, and a greater tendency to be Non-Christian.

4. Tiny upticks exist at the other extreme corners of the landscape, but there appear to be almost no individuals actually residing there.

5. Mapping the Political Landscape Three Routes across Ideological Terrain

1. This assumption can easily be relaxed for specific effects—if, for example, Blacks answer affirmative action questions differently than others even after conditioning on their attitudes toward other issues—though we have found no compelling evidence for doing so in this work.

2. Throughout, "Vote" is to be understood as including the alternative "No Vote" or "Non Vote."

3. "Normal-esque" because, while we can arbitrarily assign a defined subpopulation a distribution of $N(0,1)$, the very act of doing this renders the total population to have, in general, some other distribution. This will be so even if all other subpopulations are themselves normal, for then the whole population is a *mixture* of normals, which is not normal. However, as an empirical fact, the population is indeed roughly normal on this scale.

4. The method we use is very much in the spirit of Wu 2010, although the operational details do not necessarily coincide.

5. This is, of course, a different picture of exactly the same presentation as Figure 4 of Chapter 2.

6. After the addition of three numbers representing the proportion in each voting group, as above.

7. Landmark works in this tradition would include Hotelling 1929, Black 1948, and Downs 1957a and 1957b. See Congleton 2004 for an overview. Landmark authors should, of course, not be held responsible for frequently unnuanced applications by their acolytes.

6. Political Values and Presidential Votes A Benchmark Year

1. Readers who remain curious about the status of 1984 as a benchmark should jump ahead to the sections of Chapter 7 involving the presidential contest of 1988, which make it clear that the relationships presented in Chapter 6 are, at a minimum, essentially invariant to the passage of time between 1984 and 1988 or to the change in candidates from Ronald Reagan to George H. W. Bush and from Walter Mondale to Michael Dukakis.

2. At first glance, it may seem that the high-income group does something additionally distinctive vis-à-vis all three others when it comes to voter turnout: extreme cultural conservatives within the high-income group are disproportionately likely *not* to vote (Figure 6.4.F). Yet as we shall see, this impression is misleading, practically, because there are nearly no individuals within the high-income vote who actually hold extremely conservative cultural values.

Where the high-income group does merit a short note is in the power of its cultural values within the two (Reagan and Mondale) voting electorates (Figures 6.4.D and E). The high-income group makes its standard contribution across the vast bulk of the cultural continuum, providing the greatest Reagan support and the least Mondale support. But its Reagan support then drops the most of all income groups and its Mondale support rises the most among its extreme cultural *liberals*—and this time, as we shall also see, there are many individuals within the high-income group who actually hold these extremely liberal values.

3. Modest exceptions are contributed by the upper-middle group for economics and the upper-income group for culture.

4. The vote stratified by culture does show bigger *intergroup* effects for education than it did for income, and this constitutes the largest difference between individual relationships for the two measures of social class, though it is still quite modest.

5. This time, the most obvious difference between income and education is that the lowest educational category, the high school dropouts, shows more of a role for cultural values than did the lowest income category, the bottom tercile.

6. Because the Pew Values surveys do not attempt to distinguish between group members who are and are not in the United States legally, this particular Non vote distinction might well be exaggerated by the disproportionate number of undocumented immigrants there. We simply cannot know.

7. Reagan 46.7%, Mondale 26.4%, and Non 26.9%.

8. Black Evangelicals, while a comparatively tiny denominational family, did show distinctive political values in Chapters 3 and 4. But when the focus is

economic or cultural values *and the vote*, what matters among Black Evangelicals as a social group is race and not religion. That is to say: like non-Evangelical Blacks, they show almost no policy relationship to the vote. Such voting relationships as they do exhibit are effectively covered by a focus on race and ethnicity.

9. There is a middle group (more than once a month and less than once a week), but they comprise only 14% of the sample, so that graphical display is facilitated by suppressing this group in the figures presented here. Be assured that in no case does this group fail to fall between the two main categories, which otherwise divide in roughly equal proportion.

10. Recall that neither of these "obvious implications" is graven in stone, such that it is the same at every point in time. There were periods in American history when the Republican Party was more committed to economic intervention, even to social welfare, just as there were periods in American history when the Democratic Party was more committed to cultural traditionalism, in its many guises.

11. Unlike sex, this principle for creating social groups does not capture precisely what the underlying concept implies, since there are, most especially, households which previously had children at home but no longer do. If the fact of raising (that is, nurturing and protecting) children has an effect on political values and/or on voting behavior, then contemporary parent versus non-parent is not quite as accurate a conceptual distinction as male versus female. But in the aggregate, it should be enough to test for voting relationships.

12. Had Reagan not been thumping Mondale everywhere else on the cultural continuum, the latter would obviously have become president.

13. Though even this shifts a bit for education as opposed to income when the category of postgraduates can be added to the story. Indeed, it had already begun to change in 1984 when religiosity rather than denominational attachment was the key indicator of religious background, as Chapter 8 will confirm.

7. The Evolution of the Strategic Landscape 1984-2008

1. Of books and articles about specific presidential elections there appears to be no end. A simple refresher for their specifics can, however, be drawn from the elections series assembled by Pomper (1976 onward, published 1977), Abramson, Aldrich, and Rohde (1980 onward, published 1982), Nelson (1984 onward, published 1985), and Ceaser and Busch (1996 onward, published 1997).

2. Because his vote was consequential in 2000 in the decisive state of Florida, though trivial overall, we shall pay some attention to Ralph Nader, the Green Party candidate for president, in a later section of this chapter. His vote was so small nationwide, however, that it had little potential impact on the relationships considered in this section.

3. A third alternative, hypothetically possible, was to switch the *entire* analysis into the General Social Survey or even the American National Election Study. Both surveys had the advantage of even greater temporal reach. Neither, however, could offer the same stability of policy items and item wording. The superior size of the Pew Values surveys weighed additionally in favor of staying with them, though obviously at the cost of losing presidential 2004.

4. For the linkages among these three measures—individual relationships, joint relationships, and their associated density maps—see Chapter 5, especially the section on "Graphical Strategies for Understanding the Vote." While it is much more effective in exposition to proceed from individual relationships to joint relationships to density maps, that section of Chapter 5 serves as a reminder that all three are ultimately derived not just from the same datasets but from the same underlying analyses. In that sense, individual relationships are in effect extracted from joint relationships and density maps, rather than vice versa.

5. For one such comprehensive platform analysis, see Layman 2001, pages 111–123. Layman is also a forceful—and in our view, convincing—exponent of the argument that subsequent Republican moves on cultural issues follow from an earlier set of Democratic moves toward the opposite extreme, occurring in the period 1972–1984. In that sense, the Pew Values surveys can capture the product but not the evolution of these Democratic shifts.

6. Figure 7.7.A (like Figure 6.2.A) might suggest that the Republicans, too, had a small secondary high ground on the electoral landscape. Subsequent figures will suggest, however, that this looks more like one of a number of very tiny shares of the American public that pop up occasionally on density maps. If they are real at all, they are small indeed—hardly the stuff of serious strategic adjustment. But because this analytic framework is also least reliable at the far margins of economic or cultural values, these intermittent occurrences of tiny valuational extremes may be completely artifactual. We ignore them in the analysis that follows.

8. Social Groups and Electoral Evolution 1984-2008

1. Extreme economic liberals within the highest-income group appear to give Barack Obama an extra contribution. Yet there are so few extreme liberals in this social group that any increment is not worth much—and may not reliably exist.

2. Though the three will, as below, have these parallel relationships anchored in very different group densities of political values.

3. It might seem that 2008 overstates these problems, since Black Americans had the first-ever major-party Black candidate for president. Yet if comparable figures for the year 2000 were substituted for 2008, the aggregate Republican result would be better, but the density map would not look appreciatively different. The underlying strategic dilemma would thus not be altered.

4. In both time periods, the small slice of the sample (13–15%) that was marginally religious, falling in between the religious and irreligious in their generic religiosity, fell in between them on these joint voting relationships as well.

5. Though recall that, because the Pew Values surveys do not begin until 1984, it was possible that the Democratic Party actually moved first in bringing cultural divisions into national politics, so that what one sees between 1984 and 2008 is, in effect, a Republican response.

6. Though note that while the first of these links—Republican vote more economic, Democratic vote more cultural—was shared with most other social groups, the second link was much more of an open-ended, group-based result. The fact

that the male vote was more economic and the female vote more cultural was an empirical finding in the sense that it did not follow from any innate ordinal characteristics associated with sex.

7. Journalistic accounts often have men and parents more conservative on economics, women and non-parents more liberal on culture. Among Republicans in 1984, that was clearly not accurate, while by 2008, any such distinctions had been more or less completely wiped out within both parties.

Conclusion The Landscape of Modern American Politics

1. The argument about this movement within the Democratic Party as it happened can be found, inter alia, in Sundquist 1973, Ladd with Hadley 1975, and Ladd 1976. A comprehensive review after the fact is in Layman 2001.

Bibliography

Paul R. Abramson, John H. Aldrich, and David W. Rohde, *Change and Continuity in the 1980 Elections* (Washington, DC: Congressional Quarterly Press, 1982).

Stephen Ansolabehere, Jonathan Rodden, and James M. Snyder, Jr., "Purple America," *Journal of Economic Perspectives* 20(2006), 97–118.

Andrew R. Barron and Chyong-Hwa Sheu, "Approximation of Density Functions by Sequences of Exponential Families," *Annals of Statistics* 19(1991), 1347–1369.

Larry M. Bartels, *Unequal Democracy: The Political Economy of the New Gilded Age* (New York: Russell Sage Foundation, 2008).

Duncan Black, "On the Rationale of Group Decision-Making," *Journal of Political Economy* 56(1948), 135–150.

Campaigns & Elections: The Magazine for People in Politics.

Edward G. Carmines and Michael W. Wagner, "Political Issues and Party Alignments: Assessing the Issue Evolution Perspective," *Annual Review of Political Science* 9(2006), 67–81.

James W. Ceaser and Andrew E. Busch, *Losing to Win: The 1996 Elections and American Politics* (Lanham, MD: Rowman & Littlefield, 1997).

Jonathan Cohen, "Irrational Exuberance: When Did Political Science Forget about Politics?" *The New Republic*, October 25, 1999, 25–31.

Roger Congleton, "The Median Voter Model," in Charles K. Rowley and Friedrich Schneider, eds., *The Encyclopedia of Public Choice* (New York: Kluwer Academic, 2004).

Michael Delli Carpini and Scott Keeter, *What Americans Know About Politics and Why It Matters* (New Haven: Yale University Press, 1996).

E. J. Dionne, Jr., "Clinton Swipes the GOP's Lyrics; The Democrat as Liberal Republican,", *The Washington Post,* July 21, 1996, C1.

Anthony Downs, *An Economic Theory of Democracy* (New York: Harper & Row, 1957.)

Anthony Downs, "An Economic Theory of Political Action in a Democracy," *Journal of Political Economy* 65(1957), 135–150.

Wayne Drehs, "NASCAR Dads Could Provide Swing Vote," ESPN.com, February 15, 2004.

David Dulio, *For Better or Worse? How Political Consultants are Changing Elections in America* (Albany: SUNY Press, 2004).

Emile Durkheim, *Suicide: A Study in Sociology* (Paris: Felix Alcan, 1897); trans. John A. Spaulding and George Simpson (New York: The Free Press, 1979).

Emile Durkheim, *The Elementary Forms of the Religious Life* (Paris: Felix Alcan, 1923); trans. Karen E. Fields (New York: The Free Press, 1995).

Hugh Davis Graham, *The Civil Rights Era: Origins and Development of National Policy, 1960–1972* (New York: Oxford University Press, 1990).

Harold Hotelling, "Stability in Competition," *Economic Journal* 39(1929), 41–57.

Ronald Inglehart, *The Silent Revolution: Changing Values and Political Styles among Western Publics* (Princeton: Princeton University Press, 1977).

Ronald Inglehart, *Culture Shift in Advanced Industrial Society* (Princeton: Princeton University Press, 1990).

Ronald Inglehart and Pippa Norris, *Rising Tide: Gender Equality and Cultural Change around the World* (Cambridge: Cambridge University Press, 2003).

Dennis W. Johnson, *No Place for Amateurs: How Political Consultants are Reshaping American Democracy* (New York: Routledge, 2001).

Desmond King, *Making Americans: Immigration, Race, and the Origins of the Diverse Democracy* (Cambridge: Harvard University Press, 2000).

Ethel Klein, *Gender Politics: From Consciousness to Mass Politics* (Cambridge: Harvard University Press, 1984).

Andrew Kohut, John C. Green, Scott Keeter, and Robert C. Toth, *The Diminishing Divide: Religion's Changing Role in American Politics* (Washington, DC: Brookings, 2000).

Everett Carll Ladd, Jr., "Liberalism Upside Down: The Inversion of the New Deal Order," *Political Science Quarterly* 91(1976), 577–600.

Everett Carll Ladd, Jr., with Charles D. Hadley, *Transformations of the American Party System: Political Coalitions from the New Deal to the 1970s* (New York: Norton, 1975).

Geoffrey C. Layman, *The Great Divide: Religious and Cultural Conflict in American Party Politics* (New York: Columbia University Press, 2001).

Seymour Martin Lipset, *Political Man: The Social Bases of Politics* (New York: Doubleday, 1960).

Seymour Martin Lipset and Stein Rokkan, "Cleavage Structures, Party Systems, and Voter Alignments: An Introduction," in Lipset and Rokkan, eds., *Party*

Systems and Voter Alignments: Cross-National Perspectives (New York: Free Press, 1967).

Frederic N. Lord and Melvin R. Novick, with contributions from Allan Birnbaum, *Statistical Theories of Mental Test Scores* (Reading, MA: Addison-Wesley, 1968).

Frank I. Luntz, *Candidates, Consultants, and Campaigns: The Style and Substance of American Electioneering* (Oxford: Basil Blackwell, 1988).

Jeff Manza and Clem Brooks, *Social Cleavages and Political Change: Voter Alignment and U.S. Party Coalitions* (Oxford: Oxford University Press, 1999).

Andrew D. Martin and Kevin M. Quinn, "Dynamic Ideal Point Estimation via Markov Chain Monte Carlo for the US Supreme Court, 1953–1999," *Political Analysis* 10(2002), 134–153.

Robert K. Merton with Alice S. Rossi, "Contributions to the Theory of Reference Group Behavior," chapter 10 in Merton, *Social Theory and Social Structure*, enl.ed. (New York: The Free Press, 1968).

Gary Miller and Norman Schofield, "Activism and Partisan Realignment in the United States," *American Political Science Review* 97(2003), 245–260.

Michael Nelson, ed., *The Elections of 1984* (Washington, DC: CQ Press, 1985).

John R. Petrocik and Frederick T. Steeper, "The Politics Missed by Political Science," *The Forum: A Journal of Applied Research in Contemporary Politics* 8(Issue 3, 2010), 1–17.

Gerald M. Pomper, ed., *The Election of 1976: Reports and Interpretations* (New York: D. McKay, 1977).

Keith T. Poole, "The Evolving Influence of Psychometrics in Political Science," working paper, December 1, 2005.

Keith T. Poole and Howard Rosenthal, "A Spatial Model for Legislative Roll Call Analysis," *American Journal of Political Science* 29(1985), 357–384.

Alejandro Portes and Ruben G. Rumbaut, *Immigrant America: A Portrait* (Berkeley: University of California Press, 1990).

R Development Core Team, *R: A Language and Environment for Statistical Computing* (Vienna, Austria: R Foundation for Statistical Computing ISBN 3-900051-07-0, http://www.R-project.org/, 2012).

J. O. Ramsay, "Monotone Regression Splines in Action," *Statistical Science* 3(1988), 425–461.

J. O. Ramsay, "Estimating Smooth Monotone Functions," *Journal of the Royal Statistical Society, Series B* 60(1998), 365–375.

Georg Rasch, *Probabilistic Models for Some Intelligence and Attainment Tests* (Oxford: Nielsen & Lydiche, 1960).

Mark D. Reckase, "The Difficulty of Test Items That Measure More Than One Ability," *Applied Psychological Measurement* 9(1985), 401–412.

Mark D. Reckase, "A Linear Logistic Multidimensional Model for Dichotomous Item Response Data," in Wim J. van der Linden and Ronald K. Hambleton, eds., *Handbook of Modern Item Response Theory* (New York: Springer-Verlag, 1997), 271–296.

William Safire, "On Language: Soccer Moms," *The New York Times Magazine*, October 27, 1996, p. 30.

Norman Schofield, Gary Miller, and Andrew Martin, "Critical Elections and Partisan Realignment in the United States," *Political Studies* 51(2003), 217–240.

Byron E. Shafer and William J. M. Claggett, *The Two Majorities: The Issue Context of Modern American Politics* (Baltimore: Johns Hopkins University Press, 1995).

Byron E. Shafer and Richard H. Spady, "The Issue Context of Modern American Politics: Semiparametric Identification of Latent Factors from Discrete Data," Working Paper CWP 16/02, Centre for Microdata Methods and Practice, Institute for Fiscal Studies, London, August 2002.

Harvard Sitkoff, *The Struggle for Black Equality, 1954–1980* (Englewood Cliffs, NJ: Prentice-Hall, 1974).

Richard H. Spady, "Identification and Estimation of Latent Attitudes and Their Behavioral Implications," Working Paper CWP 12/06, Centre for Microdata Methods and Practice, Institute for Fiscal Studies, London, June 2006.

Richard H. Spady, "Semiparametric Methods for the Measurement of Latent Attitudes and the Estimation of Their Behavioral Consequences," Working Paper CWP 26/07, Centre for Microdata Methods and Practice, Institute for Fiscal Studies, London, November 2007.

Angus Stephenson and Christine A. Lindberg, eds., *New Oxford American Dictionary* (Oxford: Oxford University Press, 2010).

Jeffrey M. Stonecash, *Class and Party in American Politics* (Boulder, CO: Westview, 2000).

James L. Sundquist, *Dynamics of the Party System: Alignment and Realignment of Political Parties in the United States* (Washington, DC: The Brookings Institution, 1973).

James A. Thurber and Candice J. Nelson, eds., *Campaigns Warriors: Political Consultants in Elections* (Washington, DC: Brookings, 2000).

Shawn Treier and Simon Jackman, "Democracy as a Latent Variable," *American Journal of Political Science* 52(2008), 201–217.

Shawn Treier and Sunshine Hillygus, "The Nature of Political Ideology in the Contemporary Electorate," *Public Opinion Quarterly* 73(2009), 679–703.

Gayle Worland, "Coming to Terms with 1997: Linguists Pick the Words Minted for the Year," *The Washington Post*, January 12, 1998, B1.

Ximing Wu, "Exponential Series Estimator of Multivariate Densities," *Journal of Econometrics* 156(2010), 354–366.

Index